Easily
ENTREATED

JOYCE DIXON HIGHTOWER

Copyright © 2022 Joyce Dixon Hightower.

All rights reserved. No part of this book may be reproduced, stored, or transmitted by any means—whether auditory, graphic, mechanical, or electronic—without written permission of both publisher and author, except in the case of brief excerpts used in critical articles and reviews. Unauthorized reproduction of any part of this work is illegal and is punishable by law.

ISBN: 979-8-88640-022-9 (sc)
ISBN: 979-8-88640-023-6 (hc)
ISBN: 979-8-88640-024-3 (e)

Because of the dynamic nature of the Internet, any web addresses or links contained in this book may have changed since publication and may no longer be valid. The views expressed in this work are solely those of the author and do not necessarily reflect the views of the publisher, and the publisher hereby disclaims any responsibility for them.

One Galleria Blvd., Suite 1900, Metairie, LA 70001
1-888-421-2397

This book is dedicated to the loving memory of

Evelyn Dixon,

my mother, her wisdom and love made our lives rich.

Chapter

1

THE PAIN HAD FOUND her hiding in the depths of sleep and was dragging her back to consciousness. Joy desperately struggled to escape from the looming shadow of pain threatening to overtake her and hurl her into an abyss of discomfort. Sharp stabs began piercing inside her head. As she reached up in reflex to shield her head, her fingers touched soft gauze bandages taped in place. Confused, she squinted her eyes open in the bright daylight and found herself in a hospital bed with an IV in her left arm leading to a blue box on a shiny pole with an empty bag suspended from it. On the front of the blue box, a red light silently flashed in alarm.

The sunlight was shining through the open window blinds, around her she noticed the stark furnishing of a hospital room. She groaned as the pain increased, and memories slowly returned of the events over the last two months leading up to the surgery. The bothersome tumor was removed from her head and declared noncancerous five days ago.

The red alarm light continued to flash from the blue box beside her. The nurse had explained that the IV in her left arm carried pain-relieving medication. The alarm light meant the medication vial was empty and, hence, the reason for her pain. As she tried to change her position, hoping for some relief, her right hand brushed across the drawing tablet lying on the bed beside her with a pencil. She automatically picked them up. Placing the tablet across her knees, she touched pencil to paper. Then there was nothing. It was as if she were riding on a train that entered a dark tunnel. Her hand was poised intent on doing something without follow-through. An indistinct hollowness and expectation of soon leaving the darkness of the tunnel and reentering light and clarity engulfed the moment. She waited for what seemed like too long and then, in frustration, slid the tablet back onto the bed beside her.

What is the problem? She thought. I am an artist for goodness' sake! I have done this a thousand times without a problem. A feeling of dread came over her. What am I going to do if I can't draw anymore? What if, I have lost my gift? She looked around to make sure the room was empty as tears threatened to spill over. Confirming no one was there, she quickly wiped her eyes dry with the sheet. One thing is for sure, I cannot tell Dad. Imagine all of the money and time invested in art school and degrees, not to mention the fact that my present job and livelihood depends on my ability to draw. He would be devastated.

The door opened quietly, and her father slipped into the room. When he saw that her eyes were open, he sighed. "I knew you were going to wake up as soon as I stepped out for a coffee. I've been here for hours, watching you sleep."

"Hi! Why didn't you wake me up? There's not that much more time to spend together before you head back to Kenya. Sleeping is something I can do anytime. It's what I've been doing more than anything else over the last week."

"That must mean you need it. You'll be going back to your little house on the hill this weekend, so you need to be rested."

"I'll be okay!"

"I know you will and I wouldn't be leaving otherwise. Now that you're on the mend, I can think about getting back to work. Your mom stayed as long as she could to make sure you were okay.

You know she wouldn't have gone unless she had to. This is high season for people in education, what with the school year ending, and graduation ceremony preparation. Even with all that waiting on her, she wasn't going to be pried away until you were out of surgery, and she was sure everything had gone well. You know she warned me as she was leaving. She said 'Now Marshall, I'm leaving you in charge. You're good at details and technical stuff, so make sure our little girl gets back on her feet.' She is so funny."

"She was so sweet to stay such a long time. I was sure glad that she was with me these last two months. I don't know what I would have done to make all of those tests and doctors' appointments if she hadn't been here. I mean, I was in shock at first, when they gave me the results of the CT scan, then there was the MRI. I almost believed the tumor was the end of me."

"No. No, little one, God still has a lot lined up for you to do."

"You both are so sure of that. Mom showed me she believed that everywhere we went. Every time we went into a doctor's office or a clinic or department for a test—at every office, at every step she would ask, 'What do we have to do next?' It was like we were on our way to a certain destination. She was sure we would get there if we just had the right directions. I'll tell you honestly, Dad that two-centimeter tumor in my head became the biggest thing in the world."

"Now it's gone and you can get on with your life."

"Yes, it's true, but there's only one problem. Now that it's gone, it's left a whole lot of pain in its place."

"Is that why you're frowning and your eyes are red?" Marshall stood up and turned toward the door. "Let me call the nurse. I'll be back in a second."

As Marshall slipped back out the door, Joy had a glimpse of the noisy and activity-filled hallway. The distinct sound of clanging dishes and flatware signaled that the serving of lunch had begun. The door swished closed, and all was quiet again. Joy leaned back and closed her eyes to wait, but the door opened again almost immediately. She squinted through one eye as her father entered with the nurse right behind him.

"Miss Anderson, the doctor changed your medicine to pills because you'll be going home in a few days. You have to be steady on your feet, though. He ordered the therapist to come and work with you for the next two days to make sure you're ready. I came in a few minutes ago to tell you about the medication and the therapist, but you were sleeping. Here you are; the medicine and a little water to wash it down."

"Thank you, Nurse Cindy." Joy took the medicine.

"Good. I'll just remove this IV now. You'll have one less thing to worry about. But you must keep up with drinking and eating." The nurse slipped on a pair of gloves, deftly removed the needle and tape, and placed a bandage over the entry spot. "There! If you have any questions or need anything, remember you can always use your buzzer. You don't have to send your father."

"Yes, ma'am. I forgot about the buzzer."

"That's okay. The therapist will be coming this afternoon to get you up and walking the halls." She smiled at them both and left.

"Thanks, Dad. By the time I get used to the buzzer, I'll be going home."

"Which is exactly why, I am so glad that Peter is going to be helping you out for the next two weeks."

"I don't know if this is supposed to be something to be glad about. He drives me crazy."

"Now, Joy, you know we couldn't just let you go home up there on top of the hill all alone, without someone to help you out. Your brother has volunteered to spend his *vacation* at your place to help you out."

"Wait a minute! I thought he was going to be coming up every day after work. Why does he have to be there all day?"

"First of all, you'll need him most during the day. Second, even though it's only forty miles from his work to your house, the times he would be driving are heavy traffic hours. He tried it out two days ago, and it took him two hours to get to work in the morning. He decided to put in the request for his two-week leave that day. Fortunately, it was approved this morning. I think that's pretty big of him, considering his other choices for spending his vacation time."

"You have a point... It is a little surprising."

"The fact that Peter will be there to help you at home for two weeks is not only a great comfort to us, but the only way I would accept going back to Nairobi on schedule."

"Okay, okay. I just hope we both live through it."

"You will; I'm sure of it. It will also be a good thing for both of you to spend some time together."

"Okay, if you say so."

"I do say so. Say, young lady, what's wrong? You would usually have filled your sketchbook by now."

"Oh, Dad, I wasn't going to say anything to you."

"I'm not trying to hurry you."

"No, I don't mean that you're pressuring me. I mean... I can't! I cannot draw—at all."

"What?"

"I've tried... there's like a block... or something between my brain and my hand. The message won't go through."

"That's almost unbelievable. The human brain is amazing."

"But it *is* true. I can't draw anything ... What am I going to do? I know you spent all that money and I've spent all my life, every day trying to get better at drawing and now, I can't draw at all. I'm almost afraid."

"Now, now, Joy. Don't start 'working yourself up into a tizzy', as the old folks used to say. I wouldn't worry about it. It's only been five days since the surgery. The doctor warned you there might be a temporary loss of memory or motor skills. Remember? Just give yourself a little while. In the meantime, why don't you focus on something else?"

"What do you mean focus on something else? I'm an artist!"

"I know who you are, but do you? For example, you used to write poetry. Maybe you can try that again. You know Peter and I went into your studio the night he drove up. You have a lot – maybe hundreds — of paintings and sketches that are just sitting around. It started me thinking. You could make greeting cards out of some of them if you had verses to go with them. You know you could even use your work to illustrate a book of poetry. I don't think you've come to the end of your drawing career by any means, but you have already done so much."

"That would be horrible if I was never able to draw again."

"Even if you never sketched again, there is a lifetime of things you could do with the ones you have already done."

"I guess you're right about there being so many already. I once thought about a coffee table book, but never seemed to have the time to let it get beyond a thought, what with classes and other projects. The main hassle would be getting someone to take photos of the sketches so that they could be arranged and formatted."

"Peter is pretty good at photography. I was amazed at some of the photos he was showing me the other night. He was explaining the change in lighting and the angle that makes things look completely different. It was like talking to a professional. You two have more in common than you know."

"Really?"

"Yes. I'll tell him to bring his camera Friday when he comes up. He's going to spend the night to make it easy to take me to the airport and get you home. I've enjoyed driving your little 'bobsled', but we can't have two cars at the hospital. We'll come Saturday morning with my things loaded in his car. We can pick you up first, then head over to take me to the airport across town. Afterward, he'll take you home."

"Oh. It seems like you're leaving so soon."

"As I said, it's only because Peter will be there."

"That's fine. Just don't let him arrange anything."

"I'm sure you two will work things out...what would you call the book?"

"The book? Oh, I don't know I've had an idea rolling around in the back of my mind."

"Okay, good. What's the idea?"

"Now this may sound kind of silly."

"Has that ever stopped me from listening to you, before?"

"True! Okay then, every day in my back yard, I hear this little bird first thing in the morning, right after the sun rises. Everything else is quiet. It's always only him that sings, or at least he has for the last two years. It was kind of a natural wake-up alarm. Then last month with all the running around and worries, I noticed the song wasn't there in the morning. I would wake up for some reason at the very time, but when I listened to hear the song, there was only silence. On a few occasions, I must have imagined I heard him. I ran out to the backyard to welcome him back and to hear him more clearly, only to find silence. You see, it wasn't him. The song was only in my head, my memory. It started me thinking about all of the other things that we continue to hear and see through our memories. Some of which can fill us with joy or longing, even though they are no longer physically there."

"The Silent Songs."

"Yes, that's it, *exactly.*" She excitedly sat up suddenly and pain stabbed through her head again. "Ouch!" She cried falling back against the pillow.

"Careful! Don't move so quickly. They told you to take it easy." Marshall stood to his feet beside the bed and patted her shoulder.

"I will have to remember that one way or another," she sighed with her eyes closed.

"*Pole-Pole* (Slowly), Little Sister."

"*Ndiyo Baba.* (Yes, Dad.)"

"You never have been good at doing things at normal speeds." He chuckled as he sat down again.

Joy heard this last comment from a seeming distance, as her mind was flooded with a mixture of ideas and drowsiness. The pain medication was carrying her away to sleep again.

"Silent Songs, that's it," she mumbled to herself as she drifted off.

⁕

Two days later, Joy sighed impatiently as the nurse pushed her wheelchair down the hallway toward the exit. Marshall walked beside her, carrying the small overnight bag with one hand and a large envelope with the discharge papers and medication in the other.

"Peter went to bring the car around to the exit curb so that the transfer would be easier for you, Joy. He should be here any minute."

"The therapist said that I can walk without a problem, you know. I could have walked out to the car, without all of this hassle."

"It's the hospital rules Ma'am," Nurse Cindy assured her.

"Joy, just let the lady do her job. You'll have to excuse her impatience, Nurse Cindy. She's always found it hard to sit down. She'd rather be dancing or running or …"

"You get the point, Nurse Cindy, right? Thank you for understanding. I mean, not just for now, but for the entire stay. You have been wonderful."

"It has been a pleasure."

The automatic sliding door swished open and the last few steps brought them outside. It had only been a week inside for her, but Joy's senses thirstily drank in every detail—the brightly colored landscape flowers, bobbing in the gentle breeze, the chilled morning air, and bright sunshine—and she relaxed.

"There he is already," Marshall said as Peter pulled his car next to them at the curb.

"I think Joy should sit in front, in case she needs to recline the seat," Peter said as he jumped out to open the passenger side door.

"Sounds like a plan."

"Okay." Joy stood up too quickly and felt dizzy enough to pause and hold on to the wheelchair arm."

"Take it easy, Miss Anderson." Nurse Cindy was quickly at her side with her hand under Joy's elbow, to steady her.

"Pole-pole (slowly), little one, there is plenty of time."

"Yeah. You don't want to fall and break something and have to go back into the hospital," Peter said.

"Oh, Peter! You always think of the worst things," Joy snapped.

The transfer was completed and they were off to the airport. Joy slept on the way, having taken a dose of pain medication before discharge. She woke up as Marshall stepped out of the car onto the airport curb. He opened the car door, bent down next to her, and hugged her goodbye.

"Thanks, Dad, for everything. Even though I told her this morning on the phone, please tell Mom thanks and I love her, again. Call, when you get home."

"I will and you take care of yourself. Let Peter help as much as he can." He warned carefully closing the car door.

Joy watched through the side view mirror as Peter unloaded the single bag from the trunk and hugged Marshall goodbye. He said something she was unable to hear, which made them both laugh. Marshall walked toward the terminal door, stopped and turned to wave to his two children, and then walked through the automatic door. Joy watched his figure disappear inside as Peter returned to the driver's seat.

"Let's try to beat the lunchtime traffic, through the valley pass. If you're not too tired, we can eat lunch in Newhall do some grocery shopping and then head up to your place. By grocery shopping, I mean you tell me what you want and I'll go in and get it, while you rest in the car."

"I am not an invalid."

"But you are still recovering and I want you to feel like you can take your time, at least for the next two weeks."

"Fine."

"Good!" Peter said. Looking over his shoulder, he pulled away from the airport curb and into traffic.

Joy settled back in her seat.

"I am excited about the system I developed for your studio. I've got everything organized so that you can find each piece immediately."

"Peter, I asked you not to touch my things."

"Yeah, but you also asked me to take photos of all of the sketches. I had to be able to keep track of what I had already done, what was left, and how I could find any of them again. Keep your mind open for a few hours. When you see what I have done, I know even you will be pleased."

"Can we just stop and get something on the way at a drive-thru, then. I want to get home."

"Okay. I can always go back into town and do the shopping. No problem."

Joy slept as the freeway led from the airport through the crowded sky-scraper lined Los Angeles downtown and the spacious San Fernando Valley. Forty minutes later, as they entered Canyon Country, she stirred slightly.

"What do you feel like eating? There is a bit of everything here at the Lyons Avenue off-ramp. Of course, with your school staring down at us, you may prefer another place that I am unaware of, being a stranger in this area."

"Maybe we should go in and sit down someplace. Let's keep going to the café before we turn off for the connection to Highway 126 to my house."

"Junction Café it is."

⁂

Peter parked his car right behind Joy's car in her driveway, turned off the ignition, and turned to Joy. "Do you need help walking in?"

"No, I'm fine. I didn't have any problems at the café, did I?"

"Okay then. I will get all of your things unloaded and bring them in."

"That's fine."

Once inside, Joy headed straight for her studio. Opening the door, which was usually never closed, she was immediately struck by the mechanically arranged tight rows of paintings occupying the center of the room. The easels and pallets were pushed to the back wall along with the blank blocked canvas. All of the artful disarray was gone!

"Peter!"

"Now Joy, take it easy. Let me explain what I did and why, before you get upset. Here, sit down, and let me show you these."

She sat and glared at him. She kept her arms crossed as he tried to hand her a digital camera.

"Will you just look?" he pleaded.

His tone was one she remembered from childhood. He is frustrated she thought. He has been trying to help. What do I have to lose? Uncrossing her arms, she reached for the camera.

"Okay, okay. So, what am I looking at?" She looked at the unfamiliar camera with a frown.

"These are photos of your sketches taken in different lighting and angles. Push this button to see the next one. I took four pictures of each sketch to have a different effect. See how the blue looks different in a darker light?"

"Huh! That's very interesting."

"Yeah, and that's just four of the possibilities. I also made it easy to find a certain sketch by arranging them in rows by the dominant color and the type of object in the sketch. Say you write a poem about a sad girl. You would go to this blue color row and look under the object/topic section labeled 'girl' to see if you have a blue girl. Doesn't that make sense?"

"Yes, but this place looks like a commercial art shop instead of a studio."

"You can always put it back the way you like it, once the book is done. This system in the meantime is guaranteed to save you a lot of time before you're finished."

"You have a point."

"Thank you."

"No, I'm sorry. I really should be thanking you for all your hard work. You must have spent most of the night arranging all of this and taking the photos. I mean it. Thank you, Peter." She smiled, and handed him the camera. "I was just so shocked to see everything moved. I feel like I'm already losing control over so much in my life.... I just wanted home to be the same."

"I can understand that, Little Sister, but you're doing something you have never done before. Sometimes you need a new environment to allow that to happen in the best way. Right now, you need to go rest... and I will go back into Newhall to do some shopping. Tomorrow we can start arranging things for how you see the book layout. The rest is up to you. I can assure you that writing poetry is out of my domain of contribution or interference."

"I think I will lie down for a while. We can talk later."

"Good. I have a couple of other ideas I would like to pass by you. Just to make things easier for you. You are heading into a faster-moving world with this book and there are some little, even tiny changes that would make it easier. Speaking of shopping, are there any favorites you want me to be sure to buy, while I'm at the store?"

"No. You can buy whatever you enjoy eating or think you can cook."

"Okay, I'll see you soon. Don't try to do anything while I'm gone. Oh yeah, I'll put a glass of water by your bed and all your medicine. Anything else you think you'll need before I get back."

"No. I'll be fine."

"Oh, I forgot to tell you. Joe called to talk to Dad last night. He and Faith are thinking about coming down here after they visit Faith's Grandparents in Vancouver."

"Oh, I hope they do. That would be great. You know I hardly know Faith and I, of course, have never seen the new baby."

"Well, he's supposed to let us know for sure next week or so."

"I hope they come."

"I do, too. It's been almost two years since they got married, huh? I miss him."

Chapter

2

"Hello, Visions of Joy Studio. How may I help you?"
"Oh, I'm sorry. I must have dialed the wrong number … Wait, did you say Joy's studio?"

"Yes, Visions of Joy. Who's calling please?"

"I'm looking for Joy Anderson This is Joseph Anderson."

"Joe? Joe, this is Joy. How are you?"

"Hi, Joy. You had me confused for a minute. What is this with the Visions of Joy Studio?"

"You can thank Peter for that. He's the one that put me up to it. He's got my world turned upside down."

"How is that going—you two under the same roof, again?"

"Well, it's been almost two weeks and both of us are still alive. Not that I haven't thought of violence."

"It's saying a lot that you both are still talking to each other."

"Yes, a pleasant surprise. He has helped me a lot in getting things organized for the book. You'll see. He went into town about an hour ago for the weekly grocery shopping. So, when are you arriving?"

"That's why I'm calling. We're supposed to arrive in two days at noon and I wanted to ask Peter to pick us up at the airport."

"Let's see. That will be Saturday. I'm sure he'll be able and happily willing. He's chomping at the bit to get out of here. This way he can be back in LA on Sunday and ready for work Monday morning. I'll let him know. Do you have a telephone number so that I can reach you to confirm?"

"Yes. We're at Faith's grandparents' house, so don't call too early in the morning or too late at night."

"Okay, I have that number already, then. I'll call as soon as Peter gets back from the supermarket, in about another hour. How is it there in Vancouver?"

"It's colder than I expected for summer, but beautiful countryside. Her grandparents are wonderful. You know they used to be missionaries in Kenya. It's like their family is one generation ahead of ours. They have no idea where their ancestors came from, just like Dad, but they wanted to do church work in Kenya. Their church sponsored their work for years. That's why Faith's dad was born in Meru."

"Oh, I get it, now. I thought her dad was Mumeru, they have so many ties and so much history."

"When he grew up, he wanted to do something like his father had done. So, he campaigned to get support for starting the theology college. When he arrived back in Kenya, he found one of his former classmates was the church secretary. They soon fell in love and married."

"So, her mom *is* Mumeru?"

"Yes, but from up in the colder part where they grow tea."

"Remember we went to the tea factory in Nkobo once? We all laughed when they told us that they sent the lowest quality tea to the US?"

"Yeah, they said it was because Americans mostly drink coffee and don't know good tea from bad."

"Well, I've found out that it's true. There is no real sense of good or bad tea, here."

"Well, you better have some good tea when we come, because Miss Kenya Tea will appear in person."

"Thanks for the warning."

"I think the first theology college campus was built not far from that tea factory."

"Really?"

"Anyway, while the college was developing, Faith was born and grew up. She eventually went to the academy, which is where I first saw and heard a little bit about her. But you know me, I was so determined to qualify for the university that I didn't spend much time away from my books. Plus, she was a year behind me in school.

"After graduation, I went off to University in Liverpool for Business Management, with the idea of coming back to Nairobi with ideas and skills that would change how business is done in Kenya. I came back to Nairobi and dived right into my job. Shortly afterward, I saw her again for the first time in six years at church one day, singing on the worship team. I didn't recognize her at first, and I had no idea that she had gone off to Vancouver to University with a plan to somehow find a way to improve the capacity of pastors by coming back and offering management classes at the theology college. She had stayed with her grandparents for four years and became almost a native, she knows the area so well. We're having a great time."

"Well, that's good. Just don't let all of that make you decide to stay any longer in Vancouver. I'm anxious to see my very first niece, the first member of the next generation."

"Okay, Joy. Don't start getting too excited. The baby sleeps most of the time."

"That's all the better. Kids are usually hard to draw because they don't stand still. This should be relatively easy to get some good sketches. I can just sit and stare at her and talk to you guys. I want to hear the whole story of how you two met. I'm talking about all the details."

"It's just amazing how God has all of these separate lines going like threads on a weaver's loom. When my friend, sometime later, told me about what Faith was trying to do, I thought it was interesting but saw no connection to me. One day she came looking for me after church, to ask me to help her write a syllabus for a pilot class proposal. The rest is, as they say, history."

"It may be history to you, but I haven't heard the story yet."

"Oh boy, I can tell we're going to be keeping late hours. But I want to warn you, we can't make up for six years in one week, Joy. It is a shame that we didn't have more time to talk at the wedding, seeing as how you had not been home for the four years before that."

"I know. I promise I won't make you miss too much sleep. This is so nice of you to come, Joe."

"We are so close, it's not a lot of trouble. I'll wait to hear from you in a little while about the airport pick up."

"Okay, bye."

This is going to be so much fun! Hanging up the phone, Joy did a happy dance. How fortunate that Joe and Faith had decided to take an extra week of vacation and swing down to California. The timing could not have been more perfect.

Peter had been such a great help over since her discharge from the hospital. His meal fixing and running errands allowed her the leisure to gradually regain her physical strength and the mental ease of starting to get ready for some of the rigors of getting back to work and projects. Now his annual vacation was over and he was scheduled to return to work. Joe and Faith's visit is a welcome reprieve from a house that would seem emptier than ever with Peter's departure.

Even more important she would get to see Joe and his new family. This was a rare treat since they lived 13,000 miles away. Having only seen Faith during the week of their wedding, it was a welcome opportunity to be able to see and get to know her. To have their new baby within arm's reach for a week was nothing short of a miracle. It's very fortunate, I have no work or school obligations because of my surgery.

"It's the cherry on the top of the hot fudge sundae!" she declared out loud.

Long before the car pulled into the yard, the sound of the engine's efforts to mount the hillside, announced Peter's return. Joy waited to open the door as Peter gathered the bags of groceries from the trunk.

"Well, you got back in record time."

"I did? It seems so inconvenient to have to drive fourteen miles to reach a decent store to buy everyday things."

"I know, but it's just the way it is. If I'm going to have the wonderful space and mountains around me, I have to be willing to give up some conveniences. There is a small store further into the canyon, before the park."

"That place! There's no variety, and everything there is stale. Besides, the prices are double what they should be."

"See there! You just sealed your choice to go fourteen miles into town. You know, this canyon has historically been a summer vacation area for the rich Black professional. It's not until recently that many people have been living here year-round. It won't be long before the demand for services like gas stations and grocery stores brings about a change. There's already a clinic down by the church."

"Sure. Anyway, for now, you have everything you'll need for a week."

"Thanks, Brother. Oh! I almost forgot. Joe called. He wants to know if you can pick them up on Saturday."

"Sure, no problem."

"I want to go with you."

"I don't think there is enough room for the two of them, the luggage, the car seat for the baby *and* you."

"You just want to see the baby first."

"Baby? I want to see Joe again. It's been almost two years. This will be the only time I've seen Faith, except for the week of the wedding. The baby can't even see clearly, much less talk. No, it's not the baby I'm trying to see."

"You always try to take all of the fun out of everything. The baby will be very different the next time you see her, you know. Even her name speaks of all the potential, all the surprising possibilities neatly wrapped up in that tiny new being."

"Poets! I'll wait to see some of that surprising potential realized."

"I guess when she can count and stack blocks, you'll be interested."

"Yeah, like that for example."

"You are so crazy. I'm glad you will have your twenty-four hours with Joe and Faith before you move back home and start back to work. You'll take them back to the airport, of course, at the end of the week. So, you'll get to see them again at least for a couple of hours. You can't come up on Friday?"

"You're right, I should come up the night before. Aren't you fortunate to have such a big house that you can house a large family?"

"Yes! Yes, I am."

"She is just wonderful. You must be so happy." Joy said watching little Hope lying asleep on the sofa.

"Yeah, most of the time, but there are also nights around two or three am when she wakes up and will not stop crying. That's when I question why we did this to ourselves, voluntarily."

"What?"

"Seriously? That question only lasts a short time and I find myself in awe of God's power all over again."

"I should say so."

"What about you? Have you had any further thoughts about marriage and having kids?"

"I've had thoughts, but no actions."

"Oh, come on, Joy."

"No, I'm serious. I am active at church. My cell group has nice people, we fellowship, we have an occasional cell group night out.

They are my brothers and sisters, and I love them dearly but would never marry any of the young men. They're too lightweight."

"What do you mean lightweight... not as smart or as rich as you are?"

"No, that wouldn't be a problem. What I mean is, they are caught in a current that sweeps them toward doing trivial things and not thinking of anything ... bold or different or world standard. I don't mean doing something crazy. I mean doing something inspiring or meaningful to them. They talk about goals that stop with getting a job that will allow them to have a certain kind of car and live in a certain kind of neighborhood. What are they going to do for the rest of their lives, Joe? They know nothing about the world or events happening outside of what they can hear on the local television evening news. At least, when you talk to older people, they know of Nkrumah, Nyerere, and Kenyatta. They've read books like Things Fall Apart or Negritude. They know what a Bible concordance is. The young guys I know think they have to have a study book to be able to find related verses. They think Africa is one country. Outside of the USA, the majority of them could probably not name two countries other than Mexico and Canada. The advanced ones could maybe go as far as England, Spain, and France."

"These are young people, Joy. They don't often think about impacting the world or growing old."

"That's the problem, Joe. I do. I believe they should be thinking outrageously about learning and doing things. I don't think they should wake up one day and find they are limited and have to think about not doing things because of their back condition or their hypertension or bad eyesight. They don't have any sense of value for their lives or their work. Some of these guys don't even know what their talents or strengths are. They are given almost everything immediately and abundantly by their parents. When are they supposed to find out who they are? What have their parents been doing for the last 25 years?"

"Everyone can't have Marshall and Kathombi for parents. Sounds like you should be teaching a class on discovering your calling or something."

"Somebody should, but not me. I don't have the patience. I would probably end up yelling at them. Don't get me wrong, I do try to encourage them during our Bible studies. Let's leave it at that point. I would not marry someone who I would have to lead. I would like to be with someone I could walk alongside through life and share learning and teaching."

"That makes sense to me. If that's your heart's desire, then God will help this guy find you. Even if he has to climb this hill and search in the back of your studio hideout, he will find you."

"I don't hide in the back of my studio. Don't make it sound like I'm a recluse. I'm in church every Sunday and in cell group every Thursday. I work with a big staff on the campus with hundreds of students, every day of the week. I volunteer at the community art outreach on Saturday mornings at the park. I am not hiding out in my studio."

"Even better then, he could find you anywhere."

"Yes, but he hasn't."

"He hasn't, **yet.**"

"Yes, he hasn't yet. So, I will keep waiting. I'll wait until it is God's time for him to find me. I just hope it is soon."

"You hope what's soon?" Faith asked as she entered the room.

"Joy is waiting for a husband to find her."

"You are?" Faith asked as she sat down next to her husband.

"Why is that so hard to believe, Faith?"

"You seem so busy."

"Yeah, Joy. You could be hiding in being busy. I know some men are discouraged by a woman who is busy or who does not seem to have time for him or to give him any clear sign that he is important"

"But God is there. They can't ask Him to show them? I'm not going to stop doing things so that I can sit and wait for some scaredy-cat to come along."

"Hear! Hear! At the same time, though, you can't use your busy activities as a barrier," Faith added.

"Well, it seems like you got some rest, dear. Hope has been on her best behavior in here with Joy or else she would have changed the request from 'soon' to 'maybe later', Lord."

"Oh Joe, you stop trying to put words in my mouth. Faith will think I am awful."

"Not at all, Joy. You, Joe, my love, are such a comedian. Yes, I am fully rested, thank you, and …. ready to cook our hostess a good Kenyan meal," Faith declared.

"Did I dare dream of such a treat on top of everything? Joe, you have baby care duty, but just temporarily, while I help Faith. Come on, I'll show you the layout of the kitchen and where I keep the special things, like the Ugali pot and wooden spoon."

"Your sister is seriously homesick, Joseph."

"I know. She doesn't realize it though. One of my missions is to get her to come home for a while."

"What? You didn't mention this at all."

"Joy, just think about it. All you can remember is the way people were seven years ago and the food. The place had changed in six years, for the better I might add. Things are more convenient in every way. Meru will have its mall soon."

"You're kidding?"

"This sounds like a good dinner conversation, don't you think? Let's work on the dinner, and we can discuss more while we eat."

"Good idea. I like you more and more every minute. The kitchen is right through here."

"Don't think she's always so nice, Faith; the woman is seriously home food hungry."

"Now Joe, while it is true, I am seriously longing for home cooking, I am also very nice. Come on Faith, you can be the judge."

Joy looked over her shoulder and scrunched her face up at Joe as the two women left the room. He winked at her in return.

Chapter

3

"Joy, is that you?"

"Hello, Yes I'm Joy Anderson," she looked up at the man next in line. "Kyle Bundi? My goodness! What are you doing here?" Joy stood up from the book signing table to greet her old high school classmate.

"I could ask you the same thing. Last I heard, you were on your way to art school in America. Here I am walking through the mall when I see this book being advertised by an author with a very familiar name. I had to come and see if fame and fortune had come to my friend so soon."

"I wouldn't say fortune, but maybe a little fame. My goodness! Look at you."

"I bought a book and got in the line to have you sign it so that I could stare at you to make sure you were the Joy of Kenya, without being arrested," he chuckled.

"You're still quite the character. That hasn't changed after all of this time. My goodness! I haven't seen you in… it must be seven years!"

"Yes exactly. I went on to university in Nairobi and became a business and finance manager. When I heard about an internship in Los Angeles, I decided that it would be a very good move for my career. I applied and was one of six chosen."

"Wow."

"Yeah, I arrived here last month, at the beginning of September. It's an internship with Dixon, Cruz and Wyatt."

"They must be very big because even I have heard of that company."

"They're not that big compared to some others, but they do all right for themselves."

"Maybe I heard Peter mention them. You know Peter, my brother, is in finance and accounting. I'll have to tell him that I saw you. So, what have you been doing the last month?"

"I have been running for my life. This place is so different. I'm learning a lot and have a good handle on things at work. Once I step outside the office, I feel like I'm from a different planet."

"I know that feeling quite well. Look, let me sign your book. Thanks for buying it, by the way." She sat back down to autograph the title page. "Here you are."

"Thanks."

"I'll be finished in about forty minutes. If you'll still be around, we can talk for a bit and I'll give you some survival strategies."

"Sounds great! I'll be back in forty minutes."

"Okay."

Just as she finished talking with the book signing manager, she spied Kyle walking toward her.

"So, there you are."

"Yeah, did a little shopping," he said holding up two small plastic bags.

"Good, I was hoping I wasn't causing you to waste time."

"Hey, window shopping is one of my favorite hobbies. I always learn so much. You want to get something to drink? I passed by this little café place, back this way."

"Okay, I'll follow your lead."

"You must be thirsty after all of that talking."

"The talking is not so bad, the worst part is trying to think of different things to write in their books, one after the other."

"I took a look through your book and I must say I'm impressed. I remember you sketching some cute things in school, but the drawings in the book and the poems that I glanced at are nothing less than striking and eloquent."

"Thank you, Kyle."

"Here we are. Is this table, okay?"

"Yeah, this is fine."

"So, tell me, how do you come up with something like this?"

"I have to be honest and say that the idea came together when I found myself in a situation where I could not continue my normal life. There I was lying in a hospital bed and my father had this bright idea. It was an option for something to do, which would tie up all of my loose ends and extra time."

"You did this in your spare time?"

"I only wrote the poems, recently. The drawings I had done long before. My brother took the photos of the drawings and voila!"

"It's just sounding more amazing by the second."

"What's amazing is that so many people are buying the book."

The waiter came over and asked, "Good afternoon. Would you like menus?"

"No. I think we'll just have something to drink. Joy, what would you like?"

"I'll take a tea with milk."

"Would you like a flavored tea, herbal tea, or black tea?"

"I would like just plain black tea, please."

"And would you like soy milk, 2% milk, or regular whole milk?"

"Regular whole milk."

"And what will you have, sir?"

"I'll take the same."

"That will be two black teas with whole milk, right away." The waiter hurried off.

"Why are you so surprised that people are buying the book?"

"Oh, I don't know. I guess it seems so magical that God could put a thought in your head and allow you to draw a picture that gives that thought color and form. Then He allows you to write words in a poem, put them beside the picture, and suddenly people have the same thought that you started with, without ever seeing or talking to you or you even being there when you had the original thought."

"I guess, when you put it that way, it does seem sort of magical. I know it must have taken some hard work and a lot of time, but that's not the only thing. Hundreds maybe thousands of people could have sat down with the same materials and spent the same amount of time and would not have produced such a lovely and extraordinary thing."

"That is very nice of you to say so."

"You have an amazing talent. Anyone would say so."

"Here you are. Two black teas with whole milk. Sugar is on the table. Will there be anything else?" Brad placed the teas in front of them and paused for further instructions.

"Joy, do you want something else?"

"No, thank you."

"That will be all, thank you."

"You're welcome. I'll be your cashier today. Let me know if there is anything else." Brad nodded, placed the leather bill holder near Kyle, and hurried on to another table.

"I have been drinking coffee a lot these days. Doesn't this remind you of home? I mean it is simple tea with milk, without all of those complicating choices to make," Joy said.

"You'd be surprised. It's kind of the same choices nowadays at home. Soy milk may not be available everywhere, but the array of teas is even greater with all of the influx from India. When was the last time you were home?"

"It's been a good while. I went back the summer after my first year here. Then I went to Nairobi two years ago in what felt like a whirlwind, when my brother Joe got married. It was only for a week, and I couldn't make myself go back to the village. My great-grandma had died … it was just after we graduated. She must have been well over a hundred years old, but nobody kept birth records back then. I had gone to see her before the graduation ceremony. She was too frail to make the trip upcountry. She was making me this beautiful basket as a graduation present, and she made me promise to come back and get it when she finished. My grandmother called with the news that she had died; I just could not believe it. When we went for the burial, my grandmother told me that JoJo had come with the finished basket to show her and asked that she send a message that I should come and get it. She said JoJo was very proud of how it had turned out and was happy that she could give me such a nice gift. She went to sleep that night and never woke up again. They found her the next morning still lying peacefully in her bed."

"So, you were the last thing on her mind."

"I wouldn't go so far as to say that, but that basket is beautiful and of course very special to me. It seemed like her death closed a chapter in my life. I came here a few months later to attend the art institute. I brought the basket with me; and when I bought a house, I put it in the living room so that I see it each day as I leave and when I return. It reminds me of the fact that love is always active and giving."

"You are truly a poet. That was very lovely said."

"Thank you."

"So, do you have someone here in the US who is lovingly giving to you?"

"There are many people. I am virtually surrounded."

"I mean is there anybody special, a boyfriend or something?"

"Kyle, this conversation has taken a sharp turn that I am not willing to follow. So, I'm putting it back on track, if you don't mind. It's been six years since I've been home. I finished the institute and while working on my graduate degree, did some teaching and found that I liked it. I was offered a position this last year and I have been enjoying getting things in place. I'm thinking about going back home around Christmas time. Now, what have you been doing the last seven years?"

"Well, I also started the university at the end of the year we graduated. I worked for a year before starting a master's degree; and during my last year, I decided that I wanted an international experience. I applied for this internship with Dixon, Cruz and Wyatt and was accepted. It was a stiff competition, I might add, to spend six months with this very high-ranking company here and I arrived a month ago. It has been quite something to get situated."

"Fortunately for you, I have some handy tips that will help you get settled and have a good five or six remaining months."

"Great! I need all the help I can get. Tell me everything."

"I will tell you as much as I can think of, right now. If I come up with something else that might be helpful, I will call you and let you know."

The phone rang in the studio and Joy ran to get it before it went to the answering machine.

"Hello?"

"Hi. What's wrong, Joy? You sound like you're out of breath?"

"I had to run to get the phone; nothing's wrong. How are you, Peter?"

"I'm still trying to keep up. How are things going for you?"

"I'm doing well. No problems at work. The book is doing well. I started on another one but decided to take a break. What are you up to this weekend?"

"Natalie and I are going to the observatory at Griffith Park."

"I have never been there. Is it any good?"

"Yeah, I always enjoy it. They change the constellations show there pretty often and I try to go when they do. You remember how Dad used to point out constellations from the swing on the front porch?"

"That was always exciting with us sitting out in the dark, all huddled together."

"This beats that by a ten thousand awe factor. Why don't you come with us? Wait, before you answer, I have to let you know that we always go over to the park and ride the carousel afterward."

"You ride the carousel? This is a real carousel?"

"Yes, with a brass ring and everything, like in an old movie - a ride back to the past."

"Sounds like a new book title, Brother."

"Be my guest. I certainly won't be writing any book soon to be using it for. You don't have to ride. You can sketch it while you wait. Maybe you would like that better. It's quaint, with all of the trappings. They have cotton candy, caramel apples, and fresh popcorn. You won't be bored."

"Okay, I'll take you up on that invitation to the observatory for sure. I'll have to see the carousel to decide about riding it."

"Great! Natalie is always saying that you don't like her because you never want to do anything together with us."

"Really? That's not true," Joy said. "You have to admit that most times I'm a fifth wheel for dinner or a movie."

"Anyway, I'm glad you're coming. We leave at 9:00. Hey, you want to come down Friday night and have dinner with us? That way you'll already be here for the morning. We can even go out to breakfast. Natalie will think she's in heaven, seeing you so much."

"I'll see how early I finish up Friday afternoon."

"Wow, Joy, this is the most available you've been in years. What's going on?"

"There's nothing special. I want to get away from the place for a while."

"You wanting to spend a weekend away from your studio is something special."

"I'll call you Friday afternoon."

"Make it before 3:30, so we can plan, okay? Natalie lives and works near the Crenshaw Shopping Center. It's usually easier to meet somewhere near her place than trying to have her negotiate the rush-hour traffic downtown. If you're coming, maybe we could all meet downtown. It would be equally disadvantageous traffic-wise for both of you. Plus, there are some great restaurants."

"Okay, I will call early. Tell Natalie I'm looking forward to spending time with her."

"Wow, Joy. I don't care what you say; this is quite a change from your usual attitude. I will have to do an investigation to see what's at the bottom of all this. Are you sure they only took out the tumor?"

"That's funny, Peter. I think your time would be better spent investigating Natalie. This is getting pretty serious between you two, by all of the outward signs."

"Oh, I see. Little Sister's protective instincts are coming out."

"You've got to be careful. People aren't always what they seem to be."

"I know; I have personal experience to give as evidence. Believe me, Natalie had to pass through a rigorous checklist of testing before I even considered asking her out on the first. Then I started the detailed interrogation. You know what? I was very pleasantly surprised time after time."

"Really? Well, she's even more interesting then. I'll just come with my magnifying glasses on."

"Now, Joy, don't give her a hard time."

"I wouldn't give her a hard time. I'm sure you have already done that. And another thing Brother, my advice is that don't you dare take up all of Natalie's weekends unless you're seriously thinking of taking up all the rest of her life. Do you hear me?"

"I hear you."

"Did you already meet her parents?"

"Yeah, they're nice: Michael and Margaret. Her dad is a pilot retired from the Air Force and her mom is a school teacher."

"That's funny!"

"Why is that funny?"

"It is funny because your dad is in the business of the force of air and your mother runs a school of teachers."

"That is interesting, I never thought of that."

"Leave it to you to miss the small amusements in life."

"Well, at least I didn't miss the big delight of Natalie."

"That's true. You had better clinch the deal or you just might."

"Hey, Joy, I was wondering when I would run into you."

"Kyle? What are you doing here on campus? Don't tell me you have decided to go into a new field?"

"No, it's nothing as dramatic as that. It seems your school is planning a multi-million-dollar project and called on Dixon, Cruz, and Wyatt to do the financial impact and planning study. I'm part of the project team. I volunteered so that I could at least see where you work. You've never invited me."

"Wow, I'm impressed."

"Impressed enough to go to lunch with me later?"

"Oh sorry, I have a lot of work to catch up on. Maybe we can try for next time."

"How about going tomorrow for coffee, before you start your classes?"

"It would have to be early."

"What time?"

"My first class is at 8 am."

"I can meet you here at 7:30 and you can show me the coffee place."

"Okay then, 7:30."

When Joy arrived at 7:30 the next day, he was standing right in the same spot, hands in his pockets and shoulders hunched against the cold.

"Sorry, I should have told you to wait inside. It's getting a bit chilly in the mornings these days."

"No problem. I didn't wait long. So, where's this place that is inside and has coffee?"

"Right this way."

Joy hurried across the quad to the café. She was a little distracted as she reflected on what she had been thinking about all evening concerning her meeting with Kyle. She had decided the meeting might work out to be mutually beneficial if she could find a way to ask him for a big favor. The problem was she had not quite figured out how to introduce the subject. As they sat down with their muffins and coffee Kyle provided the perfect opening.

"I want to thank you for your survival strategy points. This last month has been so much easier."

"Good I'm glad they helped."

"It's amazing what a big difference such little things can make. Like telling me about the weekly supermarket sales. I have saved so much money. Let me know if there is any way that I can help you out and return the favor."

"Kyle, there is something I was thinking you could help me out with."

"Great! What is it?"

"Well, I was wondering if you would volunteer to be the Santa Claus for the kids at the Val Verde Park Community Outreach Project Christmas Party. Now before you answer, hear me out. This is the first year I have been involved with the Saturday Arts project and I learned that they have always had a white Santa for these black kids. Now I know that there are pros and cons for both sides of the argument, but I thought that, for once, it would be nice if they had a Santa that looks like them giving out the presents."

"So, you want me to play Santa Claus for some kids?"

Chapter

4

"Yes, Kyle. That is exactly what I'm asking," Joy said.

"Can I ask why you are asking me? Be honest, now. Is it because I am so jolly or because I am so plump?"

A frown crossed Joy's face. *What should I say? He was outgoing and even entertaining at times, but if he was not a little plump perhaps I would not have thought to ask him …*

"Your hesitation is answer enough. Okay, I'll do it, for the kids and because you asked me. What exactly do I have to do?"

"Great! Thank you. We give you the costume and buy the gifts. All you have to do is show up, call them to the front by name, act as Santa and hand them the presents. You can leave after that. I know this is a bit more effort than it took me to provide you with survival tips. So, although we don't have a lot of money, we can give you a token payment for your services."

"Okay, I'll do it! What day and time? Val Verde Park? Isn't that's where they had the big Thanksgiving party that I saw advertised everywhere?"

"Yes. It's the big clubhouse in the middle of the park. The kids will be delighted."

"No problem. It's a wonderful thing you are doing. I'm glad I could help a little. So, I just show up right? I don't have to bring anything?"

"No. You just show up. Everything will be there. I'll have everything ready. Come to the side door and let me know you're there. I'll let you in the back, so you can change into the Santa suit, at 7:00 the evening of the twenty-second."

"Okay. See you then."

"Thanks again, Kyle."

∞

Surprised by the full house that turned out for the Art program Christmas party, Joy and the two other art instructors, Janice and Debra, surveyed the room. Every art student had shown up with at least one parent. The snacks and punch prepared were disappearing a lot faster than anticipated. Janice and Debra had a discussion between the two of them and then crossed the room to where Joy was standing by the door with an uneasy expression.

"Maybe we should give out the gifts a little early," Janice suggested.

"Otherwise, the food might run out, before the end of the activities," Debra added.

It was a good idea. It wasn't early, actually, by her agenda. It was 7:30 and there was only one problem, Santa had not arrived.

"I agree that it's time, but let's wait another few minutes for Santa."

Her annoyance rose as she consulted her wristwatch a few minutes later. There was no sign or word from Kyle. He was not answering his phone. *I should have known better than to depend totally on him. He used to always be late back in high school,* she chided herself.

At 7:45, she decided with Janice and Debra to look for any male in the park outside who would be willing to dress up in the suit and hand out the gifts. She decided she would never talk to Kyle again! How can he disappoint all these kids?

Just as she walked out the back door, she saw him. He was running up the sidewalk from the parking lot.

"Hi, Joy. Look, I'm sorry I'm late, but my car had a flat tire. I changed it as fast as I could to get here. I didn't hear your calls because my phone was on the seat inside. I didn't want to take the time to call you and make myself even later. I am so—"

"Okay, Kyle. We can talk later. Come on, you need to change as quickly as possible and get in there to give out the presents." Joy held the door open for him to enter.

"Okay. Show me where everything is!"

"Here's the suit. There's the bathroom to change. Now, hurry!"

Once he had the suit on and came out of the bathroom, Joy realized that she should have brought some pillows or something to make him look plumper. He was a pretty slim Santa, but there was no time. She hurriedly led the way through the hall toward the entry door to the main auditorium, then turned suddenly and cautioned him.

"We have to go through that door, to stand in front of the kids. Are you ready?"

"Hey! Ho! Ho! Ho! How does that sound?"

"Great, just great. Now listen. The gifts are in the big red bag behind the tree. You're supposed to stand between the tree and the fireplace."

"Okay, so how are we doing this?"

"Here is the list with kids' names. I will be your helper and hand you the right gift for each kid. They're mostly the same thing for the girls and another thing for the boys."

"You don't have individual gifts? What kind of Santa do you think I am?"

Joy pursed her lips and stared at him in disbelief.

"Okay. Okay. Then we will have to do something else to make them feel special."

"We have to do something else to make them feel special? Like what?"

"Let me think."

"There's no time for you to think, now!" She started toward the entry door again.

"Wait, I know what we can do. Do you know the kids?"

"Yes, at least by sight."

"Okay, then you stand right beside me and feed me information."

"What? What kind of information?" She turned around to face him again. They now stood in front of the auditorium entry door.

"Come on. You'll see. Go ahead. What are you waiting for? Go introduce me."

"Since when does Santa need an introduction?"

'Think of something and I will come out on cue. Now, go."

"You are insane," she said as she took a deep breath and shook her head. She put a smile on her face, opened the door, and quickly walked through to the center front of the room.

What in the world am I going to say? This is ridiculous. Why does Santa need an introduction? The answer came to her: For the same reason, you have to prime the canvas before you start painting. This whole night was a painting of a Christmas celebration. Yes, Kyle as Santa was a major part but would have to be put in context, she thought. *I will just place it in context.*

"Can everyone please take your seats? We have a special guest who sent a message that he will be coming by very soon."

People scurried to find seats and sat expectantly.

"Can we all say Merry Christmas?"

Hesitating initially, there was a half-hearted response, "Merry Christmas."

"Oh, it doesn't sound like you mean it. Do you think anyone can hear you outside?"

At a slightly louder volume, they chorused, "Merry Christmas!"

"Can you say it any louder?"

"Merry Chris mas!" This time they yelled very loudly,

"Ho! Ho! Ho! Merry Christmas!" Kyle called out as he burst through the door. "I have seen you, children, trying to be very good and working hard. I am so proud of you all. I have a little something for you."

He turned toward her in the manner he would repeat before each child on the list. He pretended to look for something but whispered an information exchange to Joy.

"You stay right here and answer my questions like nothing is happening. Which kid is your favorite?"

"It's Christie, the little girl in the yellow blouse, sitting near the back, with her mother," Joy said smiling and holding her mouth like she had seen a ventriloquist do for some unexplainable reason.

"Okay, she will be last."

"Last? Why last?"

"You'll see. Who's this Carey, eight-year-old?"

"He's a little trouble maker, but a smart kid with talent."

"Carey, come on up here!" Kyle called. "You have got to stop causing trouble, little brother. You know you are smarter than that. Here's a gift for you. Merry Christmas." he said as he handed the gift to Carey.

"Thank you, Santa."

"Now, next year, if you don't start helping the teacher, I don't know if you'll be getting a gift from me. Are you going to do better?"

The wide-eyed Carey promised, "Yes. I am going to do better."

"Good. Mom, did you hear that? Okay, now." He patted Carey on the back and the boy ran back to sit beside his mom, Kyle turned to Joy again.

"Next is Timmy nine-year-old."

"Timmy is a bit quiet, not a natural talent, but he tries."

"Hey, Timmy! You may be quiet, but your hard work speaks loudly. I want you to keep doing a good job. Mom, you keep encouraging him. You should be very proud."

"Thank you, Santa." Timmy's mom was moved to tears, as Timmy returned proudly to her side.

Joy watched in awe as something miraculous unfolded until every child but one, had been called in front of Santa.

"Christie, come on down. You didn't think that I had forgotten you because you're the last one, did you? I am so proud of you."

Grinning from ear to ear, Christie came down the aisle. Seeing her so happy made Joy's eyes misty. When she arrived in front of Santa, she shyly looked over at Joy.

"I want you to know something," Kyle said, drawing her attention back to him, as he paused for emphasis. "I'll be watching you and smiling for years to come because I am sure that you will do astonishing things."

Christie's eyes were wide in delighted surprise, as she accepted the gift being handed to her.

"Thank you, Santa," she said and ran back to her mom's side. "Mom, you're the best and you have someone very special by your side," Kyle called to Christie's mom.

She nodded back and wiped a tear from her cheek.

Joy turned to Kyle to smile her gratitude, but he was looking over the room and waving good-bye.

"Merry Christmas!" Kyle called out again.

"Merry Christmas!" the room replied wholeheartedly,

He waved again and then walked back through the door. For a few seconds, the room remained quiet under the effect of Kyle's performance. Suddenly, as if everyone woke up, the room was full of conversation. Parents and children gathered their things, said goodbyes, and drifted out to their parked cars or along the road to nearby homes.

With the last guest gone from the clubhouse, Joy was approached by the other two instructors.

"Who was that guy? He was fantastic!" Debra exclaimed.

"He almost had me believing in Santa Claus again," Janice added.

"I know! Wasn't he great? He's a friend from high school I asked to help out. I never imagined he had such a talent."

"Good job. Tell him, thanks a lot, Joy!" Debra smiled.

"Where did he go, anyway?" Janice asked as she looked over the room.

"My goodness, I forgot about him when everyone started leaving. He's probably gone, although he should have at least said goodbye. Maybe he's still in the back. Let me see."

She walked into the hall and was surprised to find Kyle casually leaning against the wall, with the Santa suit folded under his arm.

"I thought you would at least come and get your suit, sooner or later."

"I'm sorry, Kyle. I got all caught up with seeing people off. I do want to thank you for such a wonderful job. You surprised and impressed me. You impressed everyone; even the other two instructors wanted me to express their thanks. Everyone was touched. It was so beautiful. I don't know how we can ever repay you."

"I do."

"You do what?"

"I know how you can repay me."

"Now, Kyle as much as I'd love to be able to pay you for the wonderful performance, I told you from the beginning that we did not have more than a small token to pay you …"

"No, I don't mean money. I will even donate this small token back to the program.

"What do you mean?" She was suddenly a little wary.

"Look, you have refused to take me seriously when I have invited you out. You don't even know who I am anymore. You just said that I 'surprised and impressed' you tonight. Let me take you out to dinner."

Joy sighed. "I told you before—"

"I know what you told me and I have accepted and respected that, but now I am asking if you can just go out with me once?"

"Kyle, I …"

"I'm just asking you to eat with me," Kyle threw his hands up, "at my expense. What is wrong with that? Plus, I would consider the Santa debt paid in full."

Joy sighed again.

"Joy what is the problem with going out to dinner? Two hours of your time ... I didn't give you a hard time when you asked me to be Santa." He handed her the suit.

"Okay! Okay! Two hours."

"My goodness. Was that so hard? Thank you." Glancing at his watch, he offered, "By the time we drive into town tonight, most of the places will be closed. How about if I pick you up Saturday around six and we drive to a nice restaurant in the valley? There won't be much traffic, but you can't count the time to get there and back as part of my two-hour dinner time. Okay?"

"Okay. Travel time is not to be counted. Wait a minute! You don't know where I live."

"I'm good at following directions, just write them down."

"It's easy. I live at the top of the road to the first hill in the canyon."

"Good enough. I'll see you Saturday, then." He nodded and walked out the back door into the darkness.

Joy watched as he disappeared into the night. This was not the same Kyle she had known just seven years ago. He had changed a lot in interesting ways.

"What am I getting myself into?" she wondered out loud. The door from the auditorium opened.

"Oh, did he already go? I forgot to give you the check for him." Janice approached, holding an envelope in her hand.

"Yes, he just left, but he said he wanted to donate the check back to the program."

"Wow, a wonderful talent and a big heart. He seems like a great guy, Joy," Debra sighed.

"Yeah, he does."

"We should at least give him the thank you card. Do you have an address for him?" Janice asked, as she removed the check and placed the card back in the envelope. She began rummaging through her bag to find a pen.

"It would be better if you could give it to him the next time you see him. You said he was a friend, right?" Usually the logical one, Debra pointed this out as she handed Joy her purse and papers.

"That's a great idea, Deb," Joy said.

"So, you'll be seeing him again, huh?" Debra asked as they looked at Joy expectantly.

"Yes. Yes, I'll be seeing him, and I can give it to him. Thanks." She accepted the envelope along with her purse and papers.

"Good, that saves us a stamp. Well then, it looks like we're done for the night." Janice placed the check carefully in her bag and closed it.

"We already turned the lights out, except the one at the center top, and made sure the doors were firmly closed as instructed. We just need to exit through the back door," Debra confirmed to Joy and led the way to the door and made sure it was securely closed. The three women walked silently to the parking lot, each with their thoughts of the night.

"Let's be sure everyone has started their cars before we take off," Debra called to the others as she unlocked her car.

"Good idea."

Headlight on and motors started, they turned their cars toward the exit.

"Thanks, ladies. See you next week!" Joy called out.

"Good night! Merry Christmas! Thanks," they called to each other as they drove out.

Chapter 5

"So, did you think it over?"

"I know. You have been gently pushing from all sides, first from Joseph and then you. I have this feeling, though, that something ominous is waiting for me there."

"That's the artistic drama side of you poking out. No, I just think folks want you to come home. You know, it has been a long time. You don't want the neighbors to think you came over here and got lost, do you?"

"Lost?"

"Yeah, you know, forgetting where you came from and wandering around the world?"

"It has been a long time, but I'm not going just to show some neighbor that I can still find my way back. I have a much more serious reason for going. I was daydreaming the other day and I could not, for the life of me, remember whether it was the second or first road after the town that we turn down to go to the village. I could see that red dirt road, but it was fuzzy when it came to the short distance from the monument to the road. I started trying to piece some other details together and it was a little disconcerting that there were several fuzzy places. I want to go back and sketch everything so that I can just look at the pictures and be reminded."

"That's going to be a bit difficult at times. So much has changed and a lot of those red dirt roads you remember are black asphalt paved roads, now. Maybe you are lost."

"All of those big things can change. It doesn't mean anything. I want to draw the details of personal memory places and some open country that I haven't seen before it's all gone. I want to sit in the sunshine in front of JoJo's hut until my bones are warm and—it's still there right?"

"Yes, even though it has been falling for the whole of my lifetime. It was still standing last year, at least."

"I need to go home. And I need to go see the compound again. And I need to visit Grandma Nkatha. The more I think about it, the more I miss home in the general sense. Of course, the house in Nairobi will be very different without you and Joseph, there."

"Joseph will be around, I'm sure. I'll be here checking on your house and getting the wedding planned."

"So, you finally made the big decision. I was kind of expecting it and at the same time surprised that you made the move."

"Believe me, it was no small decision and I spent a lot of time talking with Mom and Dad. They're amazing."

"They always are."

"I admit, I did think things would calm down after I asked her. Instead, they got more complicated, and every day there are new decisions to make. We finally decided to get a wedding planner to work out the calendar for all of those things that have to be done. Before we hired her, it was really kind of hard to answer the questions and at the same time figure out what the other and next questions should be. The planner was such a good idea."

"Well, I want you to know, I feel honored that Natalie asked me to be one of the bridesmaids. And I love her colors."

"Very good! Now, you go home and soak up all that good energy and come back and help her. Time seems like it is flying."

"She already had me go in for measurements for my dress. You've got several months. Knowing you, the date was chosen for perfect timing purposes."

"I had to choose a time when people would be free and it would be pretty good weather. Not planting or rainy season, not school exam time on either continent. So, April it is. We're 'bringing two worlds together as Uncle John says. It's really good that Savannah is helping her, too. Did you know that Savannah is the reason that we met?"

"No. How funny."

"Yeah. I think that Mom and Dad and Uncle John and Aunt Sylvia kind of thought that it would be nice if maybe Joseph or I married Savannah, you know, to have a real tie between the families."

"Really?"

"I think so, even though they have never actually said it. Well, anyway Uncle John was always having a barbeque or some kind of event that they invited me to come to. He and Aunt Sylvia were always really nice. You know how lively Uncle John is?"

"He is such a comedian."

"One day, Savannah had this friend over, and it was Natalie. I wasn't paying much attention to them. You know, Savannah is a lot like you are in the realm of 'artistically ordered' and all."

"Nicely put."

"It's Natalie's term. Savannah mentioned she'd misplaced something. I can't remember what it was."

"It doesn't matter. Go on."

"Natalie suddenly said to her: 'Savannah, you are going to have to get more organized or you are going to lose something very important.' I couldn't believe it."

"I'm sure that caught your attention."

"Yes, it did because it was something that I always thought when I was around Savannah but never had the courage to say."

"Why do you say you didn't have the courage? What were you afraid of?"

"I didn't want her to be permanently mad at me, like you."

"Oh, Peter!"

"No, it's true! Anyway, here was a person who thought like me and dared to speak her mind. I admired that. The more I saw and listened to her, the more I admired her. I found out that she was also in finance and then, lo and behold, we ended up at the same finance conference one day. We had lunch together, and I invited her out for a movie on Thursday. You'll never guess what she said."

"I would have said she said yes because obviously, you ended up together. However, because you are acting like you were surprised by her answer, I'll say she said no."

"Well, not in so many words. She told me she couldn't because she had church small group on Thursdays."

"Even deeper she pulled you into her web." Joy said.

"Yeah, I guess so. I had made plans that weekend, and I have cell group on Wednesdays, so we arranged to go on the next Tuesday, and then we didn't see each other for a couple of months until we were both at Uncle John's again. There was an unexpected call from Tana using this new thing where you can talk to people over the internet. You know Tana is a computer specialist, right?"

"It has been a couple of years since I have seen Tana. He's making a lot of money, I hear. I bet Uncle John and Aunt Sylvia are proud of their son."

"I would say so. I think they expected big things from him. He's the only one I've ever met named Tana River." Peter said.

"Uncle John had an interesting story around that. Something about an idea he had on the way home from Mom and Dad's wedding at the spot where a bridge crosses the Tana River."

"Maybe if he wasn't always flying around the world, you could see if he was marrying material. You should keep closer ties with Savannah. She could let you know when he'll be back in town. He used to have a crush on you, you know."

"Thanks, Peter, but we are talking about you and Natalie at Savannah's house."

"Yes. So, the three of them go into the house for a family conference, and that left Natalie and me alone for about forty minutes. She made me laugh so much, and I felt relaxed with her. Then she asked that catalyzing question: 'Peter have you ever been to the Griffith Observatory? It would be fun to go there and see the new program, sometimes.' I could not believe it."

"You were hooked, I know. Anything with stars and you're in."

"I was still careful. It just seemed too good to be true. I didn't trust that Savannah wasn't setting me up. That was three years ago; and as you know by now, I am convinced."

"What a sweet story. I am happy for you," Joy said.

"Thanks."

"So, I will be back in time to be of some use to Natalie. I promise."

"Hey, I forgot to tell you that I've been hearing some good things about the art school in Nairobi. You may want to pass by and see what they are up to."

"That sounds like a good idea."

"I had forgotten about it. Natalie keeps up with their newsletter, and she told me one of the graduates just had an art show in London."

"Wow, that is doing well. I'll be sure to pass by."

"I'll remind Natalie to get some more information about it for you. I think she went to school with a professor there who was an international student at her university."

"That would be great."

"What made you decide to go now?" Kyle complained.

"It worked out at work with the school's winter break and then for my parents, too."

"But I'll only be here for two more months I leave in February."

"I'll be back before you go."

"How long will you be gone?"

"I get to spend thirty glorious days, maybe more. I want to have a chance to visit everyone and every place. I'll sketch some of my favorite places. They are a bit blurry in my memory, so I want to go to the spots and sit and let them soak into my memory again in detail. This time I'll take the precaution of drawing them in detail so that I can refresh my memory from time to time."

"When was the last time you were home?"

"It was almost seven years ago since I was out to the village, remember? Why?"

"So much has changed everywhere, new highways and roads, new hotels new houses, new ..."

"I get the point."

"I don't want you to be disappointed if things aren't the way you expect them to be."

"Don't worry about that, Kyle. The most important things for me are the people, and I expect them to have aged over seven years."

"I just want you to have a good time and come back soon."

"And why should you care if I come back soon?" Joy said coyly. She immediately checked herself. What was she doing?

If this had been anyone else, I would have tried to quickly clarify that it shouldn't matter to him when I returned because our relationship was not personal and any other artist, instructor, poet, or whatever was needed could provide the service.

"Joy, you're special to me. I'm going to miss you, even if it's for thirty hours. I like being in your company. I wish I could always be, but you're always running away from me."

"That's not true. I have a lot of things going on, right now. I see you more than anyone else. So, you must be important to me."

"Is that true?" He smiled brightly. "Then I have hope. Anyway, we'll talk more when you come back, okay?"

Joy smiled back. It was very okay for some reason.

"The new road through Embu is supposed to be better for travel." Joseph took another sip of tea and then relaxed, leaning back on the sofa in the familiar living room of his parents' home.

"Really? I've never been to Embu to go around Mount Kenya. The road was always so bad that we went through Naro Moru and Nanyuki."

"They put a big project for rice fields in Mwea, right before Embu. To provide for transporting the rice, they built beautiful roads. The government however forgot to pay any attention to the old road on the other side of the mountain, and it is now in terrible condition."

"You know, that might work out to be a good thing if you don't mind letting me stop and visit for a short while at Kyle's parents' home. He's from Embu. It's funny, though. He didn't mention anything about the new road to Meru, passing through Embu. I would have offered to carry a gift from him to his parents. Anyway, I can stop and pay my respects."

"That could turn into an all-day affair, you know?"

"We'll have to insist that we have to get home before dark or something. I know! We'll say we have to leave because of the baby."

"I see you are determined to visit them, so we will make a stop, but a very short visit."

"I understand, completely. Thank you, Joe!"

"So, what is all of this about Kyle? What's going on Little Sister?"

"He's become a good friend, again. That's all."

"He's a good friend, huh?"

"Yes, a good friend. Joe, is there something wrong with that?"

"Okay, okay. Just asking."

"I'll try to call and ask him if he wants me to take anything special to them for him. I think I put his number in my address book. It should be in my purse. I'll be right back." She hurried down the hall to her old room, looking for the phone number.

"Okay. I found the number." A few minutes later, she came back down the hall holding the number in question. Finding no one there, she tried to call the number. The phone rang at the other end without an answer. By the end of the evening, she had called Kyle's number at least thirty times and left numerous messages to have him call her back. There was no reply. Initially thinking that she would certainly reach him for advice on what to take his parents, she was now faced with having to take something generic and in her name. She had no message to take them or even the support of Kyle being aware she was going. Knowing she would talk to Kyle about the trip when she got back, she felt she could not just pass by without greeting them. It would simply be unexplainable to Kyle.

At the same time, without a mandate from him, I have no logical motive to give them a visit. There is no declared relationship between us and it looks like I'm not going to be able to contact him, beforehand. I will say I'm coming to pay my respects to the parents of a friend who I saw recently in America. His parents could draw whatever conclusions they wanted to draw.

The one catch is I have never been to the house, so it might take a little effort to find it. Both of his parents had begun as teachers and his father had been the headmaster at the teachers' training college for years. The fact that they lived on campus, makes me certain it will be relatively easy to find.

Joe is right. Why am I so determined to visit them? What am I expecting? Without a clear answer, she made up her mind to follow through on the plan. She dashed out to the market for three kilograms of sugar, and then returned to pack her bag for the trip early the next morning.

As expected, Joe was on time. Joy was at the kitchen window watching the driveway when the car arrived. She hurried quietly to the front room, grabbed her suitcase, and locked the door behind her. She hoped that the sounds of her movement had not awakened her parents, a full hour before the usual time. Joe opened the trunk and Joy threw her bag in. He motioned her to settle into the front passenger seat. Pointing out that Faith and baby Hope were sleeping peacefully in the back seat.

"You have everything?" he asked before he started the engine again.

"Yes. I hope so."

"Life is so simple without a baby. We have to have a checklist, now. You can't adlib on things like diapers or formula or clean bottles. Anyway, let's get on the road. Next planned stop, is Embu. Let's see, it's 5:30. We should arrive around 8:00—a decent hour for working people to receive guests on a Saturday."

"Yes Sir, full speed ahead."

There were a few times that she asked Joseph to stop for her to sketch a scene that she found delightful—small wooded areas, streams, and rivers, distant hills backed by clear perfect skies. Faith and Hope stirred only slightly at each stop.

"They can sleep through a lot. They barely sigh when we hit the largest potholes, and the car jolts my entire spine."

"It's not usually like this. Faith was up all night with Hope. She just would not go to sleep. No fever, no sign of illness, just cranky. Every time it seemed that she was going to sleep, she'd wake up crying for no apparent reason. She was inconsolable. The usual songs, rocking, walking, nothing made any difference. Faith finally stayed in the baby's room, so that I could get some sleep to be able to drive this morning. She is worn out. I should say both of them are worn out."

"Poor things! I hope I'm not disturbing their rest with the stops. I could just wait and do the sketches on the way back."

"I don't think anything could disturb them. Just do what you need to do. They'll be well-rested by the time we reach Embu. I forgot to tell you. Karimi, one of Faith's old school friends, called yesterday morning. She is from Embu, but now works and lives in South Africa. She happens to be home this week and Faith is eager to see her. I'm sorry we won't be there for your visit to Kyle's family. If we plan to arrive in Meru before dark, we are going to have to do the visits simultaneously."

"No. No, this is a good thing. I was beginning to feel bad about delaying the journey, so it works out well. You can drop me off, and

I can use the fact that you are going to be back to pick me up as an excuse to keep the visit short. I love it when everyone's happy."

As she expected, locating Kyle's parents' home was a mere matter of asking someone at the schoolyard. Agreeing to return for her in one hour, Joseph drove away from the front gate, leaving her cradling the sack of sugar. Rehearsing the story once again, she walked up the path to the front door and knocked lightly.

The door was opened instantly by a young woman. "Yes, can I help you?"

"I'm sorry. I may have the wrong house. I was looking for the headmaster, Mr. Kinoti."

"This is the right house, but Mr. and Mrs. Kinoti left early this morning for Nairobi. Please come in. I'm Leah Mutua."

"It's nice to meet you, Leah. I'm Joy Anderson. I just came from California, but my mom is from Meru. My brother and I were on our way to visit my grandparents, and I thought I'd come by to show my respect to Kyle's parents."

"You know Kyle? Have you seen him?" Leah asked smiling widely.

"Why yes, actually, I have." Joy smiled back offering the bag of sugar. "I brought this for the house."

"How nice of you! Thank you. Let me call Grace to come and take that. I'm not supposed to lift heavy things. Grace! Grace! Come here." She pointed to the small table in the entry hall. "Why don't you put it there? She'll be here any minute. You will of course stay for tea. Come in and have a seat."

Joy was just about to ask her the reason that she was not supposed to lift heavy things. When Leah turned to go into the next room. Her silhouette revealed a pregnant abdomen.

"Joy placed the sugar on the table as instructed and followed Leah into the sitting room.

"Please have a seat. So, when did you see Kyle last? How is he adjusting to the climate? He is such a poor writer. Do you know him from work?'

"I saw him last week. I know him from school years ago." Joy sat on the sofa facing Leah.

"I can't wait until he comes back," Leah sighed.

"Leah, I'm sorry. Perhaps I didn't listen well enough to Kyle when he was speaking about his family. I don't remember hearing him mention anyone staying with his parents. Are you a relative?"

"Not actually or not yet." Leah smiled shyly. "I came to stay here after Kyle left. I didn't find a job as I had planned and I couldn't pay the rent on our little house in Nairobi. Then I was so sick because of the baby, I couldn't work. When I told my mom, she told Kyle's mom. Kyle's parents insisted I stay with them until he returns. When he returns, we'll get a house in the city where he'll be working."

"I don't think I understand," Joy heard her voice echoing in her head from a deep hole of confusion she had fallen into.

"Well, my mom is an old school friend of Kyle's mom. When I finished school, I needed a place to stay in Nairobi, so that I could look for a job. Somehow, they figured that Kyle's little townhouse was a logical short-term solution. I went to stay at his house and as you can see; instead of finding a job I found a husband," she said patting her abdomen. "Baby Kyle arrives soon but we'll have to wait until Kyle returns to have the wedding. This internship is very important to his career."

Joy's head had begun to spin slowly. Now the spin was in full force. *Kyle had never mentioned Leah or baby Kyle. But then again, why would he if he was trying to give the impression that he had intentions ... of what? Had it all been her imagination?*

"Yes Madam," Grace had finally appeared.

"Please take the gift on the table to the kitchen, and prepare tea for our guest."

"Thank you, but I won't be able to stay for tea." Joy stood up as calmly as she could. "This was supposed to be a short pass by. My brother with his family and I are on our way to Meru. Thank you very much for your hospitality. I wish you all the best." Joy headed for the door.

Leah rose to her feet as well and frowning, hurried to open the door where Joy stood waiting to exit.

"Thank you for the visit and the sugar. I will let them know you came by. Joy Anderson, did you say? Oh my, yes! You are one of the Andersons who have the school in Nairobi, A New Song, right?"

"Yes, my mother founded that school."

"It is such a pleasure to meet you," Leah said as she extended her hand.

"Yes, thank you. Good-bye, then." Joy shook Leah's hand and stepped onto the stairway.

Leah, who had stepped outside as well, looked along the road in both directions and turned questioningly to Joy.

"Where's your car?"

"I'll meet him down at the main road," Joy quickly explained. She quickened her pace down the stairway and path as the pressure was building inside her. *I have to get out of here or risk either breaking down in tears or ranting angrily about the deceptions of men. Neither of which would be a good thing in front of a pregnant woman.* Arriving at the gate, her sweaty hands managed to open and close it behind her before tears stung her eyes. She hurried down the dirt road leading out of the school compound, glad that it was a Saturday morning when students were not present. Tears ran down her face as she now marched in the direction of the main road. She didn't care that she had no idea in which direction Faith's friend lived. She only knew she needed to get as far away from that house as possible. She decided to walk along the main road in the opposite direction they had come. She made the assumption she should head toward Meru since no indication was given that they had passed the house of Faith's friend on the road from Nairobi.

She had left Kyle's parents' house, feeling raw and numb at the same crying until there were no more tears, thoughtlessly adrift on a raging sea of emotion. By the time Joe came flying back down the road toward the school, her tears had dried, and her demeanor had calmed. She had decided that Kyle neither merited her anger for being such a liar, nor her accusations of being an unfaithful, insensitive husband. She would not even waste her time speaking to him again. As soon as he was able to slow down after passing her, Joseph made a U-turn and pulled up beside her.

"What happened? I'm not late."

"No, you are not late. They were not home, so I decided to try to save time by walking, That's all," she said getting in the car. She pretended to look out the window to avoid Joseph's scrutiny. She could only imagine what the tears had done to her makeup.

"So, Joy your eyes are all red. Why have you been crying? What happened?"

"Joe, it doesn't matter. Where are Faith and little Hope?"

"Faith wanted to spend a little more time together with Karimi, so I came to get you since we have to pass by there. We'll stop and pick her up and continue to Meru. Are you sure you're okay, Little Sister?"

"I'm here to collect memories. Everything else is secondary. If I can do that, I will be okay, Joe. Let's go get Faith and Hope. Meru is our next destination," Joy said and took a deep breath.

"All right then, Meru it is."

Chapter 6

"So, how was the visit to the village, Joy?" Kathombi asked.

"You know, Mom, it was okay, but kind of sad and empty without JoJo. I was glad to see Grandma Nkatha, though. You know she still walks that hillside pathway back and forth to the shamba every day?"

"She's amazing, but then she always has been."

"You're all amazing. There's hardly anything left in the world to do that one of my relatives hasn't already done amazingly."

"Now, you're sounding like a young man named Alexander from Macedon. He complained there would soon be nothing for him to conquer, no glory to gain if his father didn't stop campaigning."

"Really? This is the one who went on to become Alexander the Great?"

"Yes, the very one. What he didn't realize earlier on was there will always be room for new efforts, innovations, new technologies, new medicines, and new discoverable worlds."

"Your point is well taken. I guess there's hope for future generations after all."

"How's the drawing project going?"

"I did get some really good sketches of the countryside on the way and then around the village. It's like I was so thirsty to see all of the little old familiar places, like the road from town, the path to the compound bordered by the thick juniper hedges, JoJo's hut in the corner still threatening to fall with its lean to the left, the well-worn footpath down to the recently rebuilt footbridge over the river and finally around the bend to the shamba field. I filled pads and pads with sketches, even things I'd forgotten. I will now have them to refresh my memory if I ever forget the details again. I'm so glad I came *and* that I can draw again. There is nothing like having to draw each line to make the details stick. Treasures I did not know I had."

"It's a blessing to be wealthy with love-filled memories."

"Yes, I do feel so blessed," Joy said.

"You look blessed, rested, not worried or stressed like you were before the surgery. Your hair has grown back nicely. You can't even tell you had surgery on your head."

"Yes, the secret is safe with a tight inner circle … and my work colleagues … and my church congregation. I guess it's not a secret anymore."

"So, how are you doing? How are work and church?"

"Good. No complaints there."

"So where are your complaints, Joy?"

"What?"

"What's *not* going well with you? I know my little girl, even though she is all grown up. You seem somewhat uneasy beneath the surface."

"It's nothing that won't settle out with time."

"What is it? Are you sick again?"

"No! It's just love-life problems and not even really that."

"Which means?"

"Which means… I found out this guy I thought I liked has been just lying about everything to me over the last couple of months. Once I got over the shock of the news, I felt betrayed and let down.

Mom, how can somebody just pretend like that? I mean how could he carry on, without even a hint of the truth or any remorse?"

"What did he say, when you asked him?"

"I haven't told him I know, yet."

"I think the only real answer to your question lies with him. It's not going to be resolved until he explains."

"Mom, I am so angry with him. I don't want to talk to him or hear any explanations."

"But you just asked me a question that shows that you do want an explanation."

"Okay. Maybe I do, but not from him."

"When the right time comes, you'll have the chance to get your answer."

"That's fine, but for now, I'm putting it behind me. I was going to ask you if it would be okay for me to come and do some sketches at the school."

"It shouldn't be a problem as long as you get permission from the adult staff and don't put any facial details of the students on drawings that you plan to sell. It would be too complicated to get consent from all of the parents. Just change the shape of the nose or eyes, so that no one can claim it's someone specific."

"Okay. I understand. I'll ride in with you, tomorrow. How's everything going with the school?"

"Great! It's amazing what God is developing there. We have a new project with blind students."

"Really? So, you have all the things—Braille and recorders and all the other things I don't even know about?"

"Yes, we do and we are getting more *things*," Kathombi laughed, "even art."

"You have art for blind people?"

"There is this movement to mainstream people with disabilities. The idea is to stop putting limits on people just because we don't see how it could work out. We need to let them try and, perhaps, show us how it can work. When Jessie Kimani, our art teacher came to me with this idea, I agreed to try it out; and we have had some pretty good results."

"Now, *that* sounds interesting."

"Yes, it's this texture and surface shape thing. Jessie will be able to explain it a lot better, but this is how I understand it. She has given each paint color a different texture by adding different grades of synthetic sand, silicone beads, I think. There is a grid made of a very thin but strong thread so that they have a reference as to where they are on the canvas. There are also different textiles cut in different shapes. We use the material from old sacks made from sisal and some from the newer ones made from that soft synthetic material. They select the shape they want from the model, and the volunteers in the class cut it out for them. They color the shape and then place it, by feeling the outlines of the textured lines of the dried or still wet paint on the canvas."

"That's ingenious."

"Wait until you met Jessie. She will impress you with all of the details, which I can't begin to explain. Anyway, they love it and have created some very beautiful projects. A few of the students made enough money from the sale of a few projects last month to pay their school fees. They even bought some pretty unusual new materials to work with. What's the most important to me is that their studies have improved and they're enjoying school. It is causing a renewed interest in art for all the students."

"I would love to see this. This would be inspirational to schools all over the world. I wish that there was a way to make a documentary of this project as a model to others. Maybe we could get authorization from those few parents before I go."

"You're right. There are a lot fewer-- maybe fifteen students in total. We could send out request forms tomorrow."

"I will try to see if I can have Joe help me get a camera. In the meantime, I can watch and map out what we need to focus on tomorrow."

"Oh. I neglected to say that they have art two days a week, so you'll have to wait and go the day after tomorrow to see."

"That's fine. I would come every day to see everything if you let me."

"That's no problem at all as far as I can see."

"Great."

"I am so proud of you and your new book. Your dad told me about how this all started when you discovered you couldn't draw in the hospital and decided to start writing again."

"Yes. It was something quite unexpected. It's so funny. I was lying there, thinking how devastated my life had become and that I just wouldn't tell Dad such bad news. Instead, I found out, not only was he not disheartened, but he had the idea to make something good of my bad situation. As it turns out, the idea opened a whole new world. The poems turned out to be as impacting or more to people as the drawings ever were."

"You get that from your father, you know. I don't mean the idea of the poetry book, but the poetic gift as well. He used to be quite poetic when he spoke. He still is at times."

"You two have hidden all these things for so long, I feel like I'm meeting new people sometimes."

"You thought we were Mom and Dad, same old folks, never changing? That's your problem. We're human beings and we do change in some ways over time by growing better because of experience and lessons. It's just like your drawings: the more time you spend putting detail into a relationship the more alive and beautiful it becomes. Please don't spend such a long time away from home again, or next time you may find that you don't know anybody when you come."

"That's a scary thought."

"It would be even scarier if nobody knew you."

"Whoa. You're right. That would be scarier." Joy had to agree.

Her imagination went into overdrive as she saw herself in the future standing in front of family members who, one after another, denied knowing her. The scene was erased by the present sound of keys in the front door lock.

"That's your dad coming in, now. You talk to him while I get dinner on the table," Kathombi said as she stood to her feet. "Your Great Grandmother Martha may be almost ninety-three years old, but she is still the queen of the kitchen. She needs some help with a few things sometimes. You know, when Joe and Faith, little Hope, and you were all here for dinner the other day, she was so excited."

"I haven't eaten that well in a very long time. Don't Joe and Faith come by pretty often?"

"Yes, Joe does, but you know, Faith has been pregnant and not feeling well, and then for a short while, there was the new baby to deal with. They left when the baby was just two months old, to see Faith's grandparents and you. That took a month. This time, finally, they are coming as a family. This fifth-generation child named Hope is a very precious thing to her."

"Wow, it's true. Imagine five generations. I'm glad Joe had little Hope before she died. I hope you are taking plenty of pictures. What a blessing for her to see Hope."

"It is a blessing."

"Good evening, young ladies. Marshall entered the room and first kissed Kathombi, then bent to kiss Joy's forehead. "So, what's the blessing we're discussing today?"

"I will let Joy bring you up to speed on the blessings and I will help Grandma get dinner on the table." Kathombi patted Marshall on the shoulder as she left for the kitchen.

"So, what have you been up to?"

"Mom and I were talking about the new project with the blind children for art."

"It's terrific, isn't it?"

"It sounds almost unbelievable. I can't wait to see what she's been telling me about. I'm going in with her to see how it's done. There are so many things she's mentioned; I think I'll go in with Mom every day this week to see everything."

"Oh yeah? That's very good. A lot has changed since you were here last. You know, with the birth of Hope, she's been thinking about finally adding a pre-school section in a couple of years. It hit home with commented that Hope would have to wait a long time before she could take advantage of the quality education that was available at her own grandmother's school."

"She's right, and there are more on the way. Is there room for all of these changes and additions?"

"A New Song School keeps rearranging itself, delivering bright new melodies with engaging refrains for the audience's delight, regularly."

"I see, and on that note, I must add that Mom was also telling me about your poetic side. Then as if on cue, you just throw out a line like that."

"Ah yes, I don't think of it as a poetic *side*. It's more like a couple of small *stripes* on the side. I used to get inspired sometimes and say some things that were so beautiful they surprised me. You know, your mother would encourage me to write poetry, but I didn't think I was fully gifted. Now being around numbers, formulas, and machines all the time, words are becoming more and more of a foreign language. I was so happy to see that just maybe with a gene or two, I had passed a real ability to you. It didn't start with me, this *verse and terms delightful* thing. You should try to spend some time with your great-grandmother. She used to be able to find a way to say things in a catching way. My grandpa would admire her ability 'to turn a phrase' openly. Yes, that's one of the things I remember clearly. Then again, he also had a poetic side with his phrases that were so descriptive. I think all the time about the things he instilled in me through his teaching and the example in the life he lived. I hope that I've been able to pass some of that passion, love, and giftedness on to you guys so that you can pass it on to your children."

"You have given a lot to me. My life reflects so many of the lessons I've learned from you. This passing it on to my kids, however, is a whole other issue."

"What do you mean?"

"It's just that I don't see how I am ever going to get married."

"Why do you say that?"

"It seems like when with great difficulty, I find someone I like, they turn out to be something different from what they seemed to be."

"Okay, Joy, what is the story behind that statement?"

"I'm just making a point."

"No, you're dancing around the point. Come on, now."

"Well … okay. Dad, I met or re-met this guy I used to go to school with here at the academy. He was in Los Angeles doing an internship at a big accounting company. He seemed like he had changed a lot since high school, really matured, and was a very nice and enjoyable person. It seemed that he liked me, and I was thinking maybe this was going somewhere. Well, I visited his parents' house on the way to Meru and met this pregnant young lady who said that he is her husband and she is carrying his child."

"Oh, no," Marshall said and contorted his face.

"Yes! Just like a punch to the head! It was all I could do to get out of there without making a complete fool of myself. The betrayal hurt so badly I was ready to explode. Then I was angrier than I have ever been. After a while, I started asking myself how I could have been so easily fooled. I must be an idiot. I don't know how I'm supposed to choose someone to marry. I can't trust anyone, including my judgment."

"That's not true. The right man will find you."

"When?"

"That, I don't know. But until you are one hundred percent sure, don't accept anything less. You'll know. God will make it clear to you."

"What if he finally finds me when I'm too old to have children?"

"If that happens, there're other options. I can think of three off the top of my head: You either live happily ever after without children. You adopt children that need the good home you can provide. You pray and ask God if He wants you to stand as a Sarah testimony to this generation. Whichever way it turns out, you will have to trust God for it."

"Why can't it be straightforward and easy like it was for you and mom?"

"You think it was easy? Did you know, the first time we met I knocked her down to the ground? It was an accident, of course, but it did not make it any less real. Or that she walked out of the restaurant on me the same night I had come back from the states to marry her?"

"No. You guys never mentioned this. Why did she walk out?"

"She was convinced that I was the wrong man for her."

"What? Why?"

"We had a seemingly irreconcilable difference in opinion."

"You two disagreed on something that severely?"

"It wasn't the only thing. It just goes to show you that it wasn't easy to start with, and it hasn't been completely easy along the way. The one thing we never forgot is we were right for each other. With God's grace for all of these years, we've continued to happily help each other to grow and become better, easy or not. I didn't know it at the time, but I came halfway around the world to find her. I wasn't looking for a wife. I was looking for a way to serve God through clean energy. He knew I needed help and sent the perfect helper for me."

"You two *are* perfect for each other. That's a hard act to follow. How do I find this man?"

"It may be at the moment you least expect it, tomorrow or long after you should have given up hope. Just don't settle for someone else just because he is the only one available. There are a lot of things worse than being an *old maid*, as we used to call it. I would have hated my life if I had married someone who I had to fight with every day, or I was not sure if they were looking out for my good or not. It would have been even worse if I had married someone who divorced me and kept me from seeing my kids peacefully and or having the chance to lovingly impact their lives."

"I guess so. I know I would hate to be in either of those circumstances. How do you tell ahead of time that someone is a liar?"

"You pray. You spend time with him once he's past the basic eliminations. You visit his family. You pray some more and you listen to what God says. Most of all, you don't put yourself under pressure to make a decision. Sometimes you have to open your mind to possibilities that you didn't even know existed."

"What do you mean?"

"When I first started the windmill project, my only thought was to find open, non-inhabited areas that had a pretty constant wind. Here, that meant desert wasteland areas. Now, there is new technology and some people who had no deserts. They were courageous in trying new ideas and looking at new possibilities. Because of these two things we could not foresee, we are now looking for off-shore areas to set up windmills, not in deserts, but over water. We are even hoping to use the off-shore power generated to help pump water to the desert wastelands for irrigation and perhaps, to turn desert areas into productive agricultural land. That's what I meant. Sometimes, our expectations keep us looking for success in places that limit us from seeing even bigger opportunities. Then again, God's timing is always perfect."

"So, it would be okay with you if I never got married?"

"Honestly, Joy? My first choice, of course, would be for you to be happy and married. But if I had the next best second choice, I would rather see you happy and unmarried than married and unhappy."

"You always make everything so clear and simple."

"The basics are usually clear and simple."

"The table is set and dinner is served clear and simple," Kathombi announced as she entered the room with Grandma Martha.

"You all come on now, while the food is hot. Joy, I made something special for you."

"Grandma Martha, everything you make is special. You are spoiling me terribly. What am I going to do when I get back to my normal life in the states?"

"You know my answer to that, child. Move back here, to Nairobi. You can be spoiled every day until it becomes your normal life."

Joy saw her mother glance quickly over at her dad who gave a knowing look in return.

"Now, there's food for thought, later on. Right now, Grandma Martha, my stomach is so hungry I can hardly think about anything else. She linked her arm comfortably through Grandma Martha's and they slowly walked toward the table followed by her parents."

Chapter 7

IT WAS NOT UNTIL the third day after she arrived back home from her month-long trip to Kenya that she had enough energy to start unpacking the various sketches and putting them in order. It had taken almost two weeks. Peter's system had indeed saved much time as he had promised when putting the first book together. It had, thereafter, become the basis of keeping everything in a quickly retrievable arrangement. Sitting at the counter in the studio, she placed sketches into stacks depending on the subject and intended use. When she came to the many sketches from different views of JoJo's hut, one, in particular, caught her attention. She closed her eyes and allowed her thoughts to return to the many visits to JoJo over the years. The memories of playing with her brothers and listening to the stories about past times and 'why we do things this way' or 'why we never say things like this' began to swim through her mind. A few minutes later she opened her eyes and looked at the picture again. *It was a pitiful-looking remnant when you just glanced at it. It's what you can't see in the picture that makes it special. Who knows, it might be another book in the making: It's What You Can't See.*

The phone rang. Distracted, she neglected to let the answering machine screen the call as a message, as she had been doing for the last two weeks. If it turned out to be a client, she'd call them back immediately. If it was Kyle, she'd simply erase the message. Not paying attention to who might be calling, she picked up the receiver. She paused having forgotten what the greeting was supposed to be. She combed through her memory for the phrase—

"Joy? Joy, are you there?" Kyle spoke, not quite sure of himself.

Joy panicked and hung up without saying anything. How dare he call her? She sat staring at the phone afterward. She jumped when the phone rang again. Not willing to go through the same thing, she did not answer. The call went to the answering machine, and Kyle left a message. This was a much less traumatic solution she decided.

The phone rang, but Joy waited for the call to go to the answering machine. She'd hoped he would get tired of calling or begin to understand that she was not going to answer him. Instead, Kyle had begun calling as many as ten times a day, leaving messages for her to call him. He was beginning to anger her because he took up so much of her time to erase the messages. The phone stopped ringing and the message machine recording came on.

"Hello, you have reached the Visions of Joy Studios. Sorry, we are unable to answer your call at this time. Please leave a message and we will return your call as soon as we can." She waited now to see who it was.

"Joy, what is going on? I know you're back. Why are you not returning my calls? I'm starting to get worried. Anyway, I'm coming up to your house tomorrow, so I'll see you then." The call ended.

"No, you won't see me, Kyle. I have other things planned, sorry." She said to the answering machine as it reset.

The phone rang again and Joy waited to see who it was. The recorded message played again.

"Hi, Joy. This is Peter. I was calling to see …"

Joy quickly picked up the receiver. "Hi, Peter. Peter this is Joy. Sorry, about that. What's up?"

"Hi. I was wondering since you seemed to have such fun the last time if you wanted to spend some time this weekend with us?"

"Sorry, Peter, but I promised to finish these sketches over the weekend."

"You can't put it off for later?"

"No, I can't. I have to drive out to the dam in Castaic and get a feel for the setting from the viewpoint of a tourist by Thursday."

"You're working for a tour group?"

"No. There is this developer who is trying to get investors for his resort project. Instead of taking staged photographs, he decided to have some drawings to add a natural touch."

"Can't you drive over after school one afternoon and make some quick sketches?"

"Don't start trying to tell me how to do my job, Brother. Why don't you come out here to the dam, today? I wouldn't be able to visit much, but it's supposed to be good weather and should be a nice outing."

"I think we'll wait and just make it for another time when we can have your attention."

"As you like. Hey, by the way, the sketches of the carousel turned out wonderfully in watercolor, and I got some good ideas for another verse book about children."

"That's great to hear. I thought you were just sketching to pass the time. You were working?"

"Not working, but having a good time in my way and just wanting to share it."

"Okay. Maybe we can try for two weeks from now."

"That sounds good. I'll put it on my calendar and call next Thursday to confirm. Tell Natalie I said 'Hello'. Oh yeah, I forgot to tell you that I went to the art school and met her friend. Wambui is a wonderful person and passionate about the school and the students. It was very interesting, and I am thinking about spending some time each year there to teach a couple of classes during my school breaks or something. So, we will see how things turn out, but tell her thanks for the contact."

"I will let her know. She'll be happy to hear that, for both sides."

"Talk to you later."

"Bye."

Replacing the receiver, the answering machine caught her eye and her thoughts went back to Kyle. She erased the message he had left.

"Can you believe the nerve of that guy, still keeping up the charade?" she muttered. *Focus!* She reminded herself, placing a pack of sharpened pencils in the carry-pack she was preparing for the trip to the dam.

This was a little unusual to have a commercial or advertising job. She had accepted it because it was so near her house and was promoting a natural resource—something dependable and lasting—not like some people. *Focus!* The carry pack was complete. It would be good to be outside for work. She reached for the soft wide-brimmed hat. The weather forecast said it was supposed to be sunny and warm tomorrow.

From the quick driving tour around the dam and lakeside, she chose three spots that seemed the most promising to come back to for sketching. Starting with the spot the farthest away from the main road, she parked in a small upper lot and unloaded her easel and carry-pack. Once her equipment was set up, she began her usual preliminary—leaning back, she took a deep breath with her eyes closed. She listened and inhaled to hear and smell for the thing her eyes might miss. It was, in fact, sunny but cooler than her hilltop backyard. When she opened her eyes, she was glad that she had come early enough to see the place without the crowd of people. People moving about distracted from the main lines and background. She would have to work quickly because people were definitely on the way.

As she was finishing the background sketches for the first spot, a car arrived and stopped in the lower parking area a good distance from her. Annoyed, she turned her back to the car to avoid being distracted. After a few more quick definition lines, she was satisfied. Fortunately, the group of five people had taken their time to exit the car and slowly make their way along the path that would lead them past her position. Packing up her equipment to head back to the car and the next selected spot, she heard traces of the group's conversation. Their pace would bring them right in front of her within the next two minutes. Not feeling in the mood for pleasant conversation, she finished packing, shouldered the carry pack, and began walking toward her car in the direction away from them. The breeze carried their conversation.

"That's very interesting. I've done a bit of traveling myself, and I'm just fascinated by different cultures," one of the females said.

"Fortunately, the world is full of them," one of the men responded, and they all laughed.

Joy froze at the last comment. Without turning around to see him—the voice and the chuckle were both familiar—she knew it was Kyle.

Perhaps it was her sudden stop that caught his attention. Before she could start walking again, he called out, "Excuse me. Joy? Is that you?"

She was unable to answer, unable to breathe or move. *I cannot believe that months of strategic avoidance maneuvers have come to an end with a surprise encounter. What Can I do?* After what seemed like hours, she was able to take a deep breath, force a smile to form on her face and turn toward the group.

"Yes? Oh, Kyle! Imagine seeing you here. Hello everyone. I hope you're enjoying the lovely weather, today. Unfortunately for me, today is all about work. I'm off to the next spot so that I can finish before sunset. I hope you have an enjoyable day." She turned her back to them again and continued toward her car. As she walked, she breathed a sigh of relief that she had been able to manage this unexpected situation. Her feeling of relief was short-lived, as the sound of footsteps, quickly gaining on her, signaled Kyle's approach.

"Joy, wait a minute. Please!" he called.

She stopped as dread overshadowed her, but did not turn to face him.

"Joy, please," he said close behind her. "I deserve an explanation. I have tried to call you, to see you, to find out ... what happened? You never answer my calls. I decided to make an uninvited visit up to your house today and leave a note after I dropped this group off. I don't know what more I can do." He stopped as he was just a yard from her back.

"Why should you do anything at all?" she said still not facing him.

"Before you left for Kenya, I thought we had something special. I thought maybe, I don't know ... Joy what happened? If I did something wrong, I deserve to have the chance to explain or apologize. You can't judge me and come to a decision to lock me outside forever without the opportunity to know what I'm being accused of. Don't you have anything to tell me?"

"Yes, I have something to tell you," Joy said slowly turning around to angrily face him. She was not prepared for the look of sheer desperation on Kyle's face. It caused her to hesitate for a few seconds, but then her anger rose again. He is really a good actor, she thought. She checked to see that the four other people were still out of earshot before she continued. "Things really did change between us when I went to Kenya. Do you want to know why? I had the pleasure of meeting your pregnant *wife* when I went to pay my respects to your parents. I was shocked to realize what a despicable, lying, self-centered person you are. Now that I know, I want nothing more to do with you. There! Now, you know why. So kindly leave me alone and let me continue my work." She turned and walked at an even more rapid pace than before.

"Joy, wait." He caught up to her side again. "I don't know what you're talking about. I don't have a pregnant wife. I don't even *have* a wife ... and I am not a liar."

This time she swung around immediately to face him. "I don't think that Leah would lie about something like that, and she was definitely pregnant."

"Leah?"

"Yes Leah, remember her? You know the one, who had to leave the house in Nairobi where you lived together. She's the one who is carrying your soon-to-be-born child. She's now staying with your parents until you return from this internship for the wedding."

"Wait a minute. Leah is not my wife. She was a visitor in my house in Nairobi for two months, while she was looking for a job."

"I see. So far, the stories are the same, so the critical part is whether you are going to tell me that the child she is carrying could not be yours because you never slept with her."

"I ... well ... it's a little complicated," he said looking down at the ground.

"I see. Well, Kyle, that little complication is a little baby, who will be born in a month with your name. That's what changed things between us. I thought we had something special, but I found out it was a farce—a very painful farce. But don't worry, I'm okay now. The pain is gone... and I want *you* to be gone as well. Don't call me anymore. Don't leave me notes. Don't try to visit me. Just leave me alone!"

"Joy, what you're saying ... what you think is true about me is based on a lie. I refuse to let you decide you want me gone out of your life, because of something which is not true. I'm going to get to the bottom of it. My parents never said anything about this to me. Leah... I have not been in contact with Leah since I left Kenya more than five months ago. But what you are saying she told you are lies... all lies, and I'll prove it."

"I was there. I *saw* her. I don't believe you, Kyle, and I certainly don't want to hear any more of what you have to say."

"I can't believe this is happening to me."

"That makes two of us." Joy turned away from him and hurried toward her car. The sting of tear welling up in her eyes made her want to run. This time she arrived without interruption. Mechanically loading her equipment into the car, she focused on the details of placing each piece. While looking down she squeezed her eye shut making the tears drop into the car trunk instead of rolling down her face, before slamming the trunk closed. She quickly opened the door and got in, started the motor, and forced herself to focus on the road as she drove to the next spot by the lakeside below. It was the only way to stave off the great wave of emotion threatening to overwhelm her. She parked in a distant corner of the parking area, well away from any one of the few cars that had already come.

"He's not going to waste another second of my life!" she screamed in her closed car as she pounded the steering wheel. The sobs came uncontrollably. When her breathing had slowed to normal and tears no longer filled her eyes, she resolved to complete her planned sketches as best she could before leaving. She sighed, blew her nose, checked her face in the rearview mirror, mirror, and declared and declared herself a disaster. "I am down but not out," she said as she got out of the car, and unloaded her things.

Despite feeling a little detached from the beautiful, warm, and sunny day by the scenic lake, she managed to complete some good sketches. She even smiled as she paused to nibble on her sack lunch, watching as two toddlers discovered the joys of mud. By the time the sunset's magentas and golden oranges faded to the grays and browns of dusk, she had created the promised portfolio for the developer and a couple of sketches of the mud babies for herself.

"So, Little Sister, you seem like you are back to normal."

"If I had known that having it out with Kyle would make me free of the anger and sadness, not to mention the telephone calls from him, I would have agreed to confront him sooner. Mom was right when she said he was the only one who could answer my questions."

"What happened, exactly? You haven't mentioned or explained any of this to me."

"It's not important."

"What do you mean, it's not important? Come on, out with it! I want every messy detail."

"I can't believe you want to hear or see something messy."

"I'm learning. Like it or not, relationships are messier than they are nicely arranged and orderly. Hey, none of this trying to distract me. Come on, sit and speak."

"Okay. You asked for it." She went through the entire Kyle-Leah-Kenya saga.

"Wow. Ouch."

"Yeah. So, I decided to just cut myself off from him. You know, like a tourniquet to stop the bleeding. I could not understand how or why he could do such a thing."

"Understandable."

"Yeah, but then he started calling me throughout the day leaving messages. I never answered them, hoping he would finally leave me alone. About two months ago, when I was doing those sketches at Lake Hughes and the dam out in Castaic, I ran into him."

"What? Then what happened?"

"We had it out. We were practically yelling at each other. I told him to leave me alone forever."

"What did he say?"

"Oh, he tried to act like the things Leah had said weren't true. He said he would bring me proof."

"And?"

"He has not called once over the last two months."

"He just left it like that?"

"I guess he is still trying to get to the bottom of his problem. He certainly has not contacted or proven anything to me. Anyway, that was two months ago, and I've been at peace ever since. The time should be over for his internship. He should have gone back home by now. He's probably married. That's the end of the story."

"Hmmm."

"Hey! Don't say that like you think there is more to come."

"We can't see the future until we get there. I don't know, but it just seems strange that he would hold so tightly to his claim of innocence if he wasn't," Peter said.

"Don't you start trying to defend him! In love and war, you are guilty until proven innocent."

"Fortunately, God is not like that towards us."

"But He is! He knew we would mess up. So, from the very beginning, He planned for Jesus to come and clean up the mess. He forgave us in advance because He knows us better than we know ourselves in the messing-up department. He can see our hearts and our true thoughts and intentions."

"Thank God for that," Peter said.

"Amen! Unfortunately for us, when we are offended, we can't see someone's heart or read their thoughts as He does. People can just tell us anything, and we're left to wait for the proof in the surrounding circumstances."

"Unfortunately, as well, many times circumstances don't give all of the answers at once. Clarity may come gradually over time, maybe even years after an event."

"That's true, but people can't wait years to make a decision, Peter."

"We make the best decision with the information we have at the time and hope for things to turn out well."

"The biggest part of hoping for the best is to remember to be as forgiving to the other person as we expect them to be towards us."

"Yes, of course, but forgiving doesn't mean I forget and give you the chance to do the exact thing again. If I know you have a fault or weakness and don't make allowances for that I am provoking you to sin against me, again. That's not good for *you* or me," Joy said.

"But isn't it possible for me to change? Can't I become stronger in my area of weakness, to the point that I would not sin against you given the same circumstances at a different time?"

"Yes, but before I opened the door to that possibility, you would have to prove that you had become stronger. You'd have to show that you had changed."

"Of course, but how could I prove it if I'm not around you because you have walled me off?"

"That's a good question, Peter."

"I think the answer is love."

"What?"

"Yes, you have to love me enough to let me hang around you, despite my weaknesses, until I grow stronger and you can see the proof. Love lets you make a decision about me without judging or condemning me forever," Peter said.

"That's what we learned in our family, huh? We always had to say, 'I forgive and I love you.' Did you understand that was what we were learning to do back then as children?"

"No, I don't think I understood for a long time after it had become a habit from Mom and Dad showing us. Although, I think it took you a long time to change, Joy."

"Me?"

"Yes, you."

"Not me, *you*! How many times did you scream in intolerance at the way I lived my 'artistic' life?" Joy said.

"Okay. How many times did you throw back in my face your disdain for how I lived my, as you called it, 'overly ordered' life?"

"True. You have this way of ... Fortunately I don't have to do that anymore, because you have become more human, even a little artistic. For this, I give credit to Natalie. I tried for years without success."

"I will say the difference is that she's much more patient than you are. She actually believes that I can do admirably good things. That really encourages me to at least try to see things differently and actually try new things," Peter said.

"She's blinded by love."

"Then her blindness has made me able to see more clearly. That's what I am talking about."

"Whatever she is doing has made you a better person. I feel closer to you. I actually like you more. It's not just that. I feel like you like me more, Peter."

"It's true. What I used to see as bothersome habits have turned out to be rare talent. Natalie absolutely loves your art. I'm proud to know you, Joy."

"Wow. She has really done a good job on you. I'm convinced that you should keep her. In fact, she's a very valuable person. If you don't keep her, I'm making a trade with her family for you."

"How can you say such a thing? You were doing so well."

"I'm just teasing you, Brother. I've grown quite fond of you over the years. I wouldn't trade you for anything."

"That is music to my ears."

"Okay. Enough entertainment! Aren't you here to take more pictures for the new book?"

"Yes, I am. But don't think that I'm doing this because you gave me all that money when your first book started selling so well. I'm really happy that I can, in some way, be useful to you. I have actually made you smile because of something that I've done. You always used to seem so disappointed," Peter said taking out his camera.

"Disappointed?"

"Yeah... or disapproving or something like that. I felt many times that I couldn't do anything in a way that pleased you. I was wrong just by being myself. Admit it, you've always thought that I looked at life from a cold and mechanical point of view."

"That's not exactly true, but I will admit that we've always been on different channels. I don't understand how you see things most of the time. I think you're not enjoying the beauty of life. It's frustrating to see someone you love missing out on so much happiness."

"But that's just the point, I'm not unhappy. I see things around me I enjoy and think are beautiful. Maybe it's not the same thing as you, but it's me that has to be satisfied with my life. Not you."

"I know that, now. I can see you are happy, and I'm beginning to understand people from your side of the universe. Peter, there is *one* thing I want you to be rock solidly sure of, though. I have always loved you, even at the times I did not like you. If I had to go through the problem of the tumor and the surgery, only to have the chance to have you closer in my life and my heart, it was well worth it."

"Wow. That is the nicest thing anyone has ever said to me."

"Enough of this true confession stuff. There's work to be done."

"Now, you are beginning to sound like me. I hope you have everything in order."

"Peter."

"Okay, okay. I'm just kidding. What's the title? Do you have any idea of sub-themes?"

"The title is: Through a Child's Eyes. It's about the idea that children have innocence because they don't carry emotional baggage—no grudges to avenge, no hatred to keep a close eye on, no anxiety bubbling up from pools of worry. In their lives, hope trickles down into every crevice of their being. They have no doubt that adults are performing their duties well and everything will be alright."

"How in the world are you going to show that?"

"I have sketches of children in different situations, where the adults are responding very differently than they are. For example, on this one, the mom and dad are anxiously looking out the window at the stormy weather outside—swirling winds, neighbors walking bent against the wind. Right in the middle, here's this little boy playing happily with his toys at his parent's feet."

"Okay, I get it. If I arrange them by the circumstances surrounding the adults, would that be okay? Or maybe it should be by the emotion on the parents' faces."

"Yes. I think by the adult expressions. The circumstances may not always be so clear."

"Okay. I'll organize the new sketches into groups, get your confirmation, and then start taking pictures. How many do you think you have?"

"I'd say around fifty."

"Okay. That's doable."

"Good. I will leave you to work. I have a couple more poems to work on." She consulted her watch. "What do you say? Shall we aim to finish by noon, or, at least, take a noon break?"

"That sounds fine."

"Lunch is on me. You choose the place."

"By the time we drive into town, I'm a third of the way home. We should take two cars, and I could continue from there."

"That's almost defeating the purpose of lunch together if we can't talk on the way. I know what. I'll treat you to lunch at the Café, right here at the junction."

"That's a deal. When I passed by on the way here, I saw the banner announcing that fresh strawberry pie is in season."

"Mmmm! That sounds very tempting."

Chapter

8

"A LAZY MAN'S LOAD!" Joy declared out loud. She was struggling to carry the huge portfolio she'd prepared for the national competition, topped by two blank art paper pads in one hand and the handle of the basket full of paints and brushes occupying the other. She smiled at the thought of her father's frequent comment during her childhood when he saw her trying to carry too much at once in order to avoid having to make two trips. Just as she reached for the door handle the phone rang. She jumped at the unexpected sound. It was enough to unbalance the load and it fell, crashing down in front of the studio door.

"No quick solution here," she muttered shaking her head at the mess. She hurried to answer the phone behind her.

"Visions of Joy Studios."

"Oh, I'm so glad that I reached you. Joy, I need to see you." Kyle said with confidence and happiness.

Hearing Kyle's voice was the last thing she had expected or wanted. "Kyle, I am on my way out—"

"Joy, I told you that I was going to get to the bottom of this. I went back to Embu to confront her."

"Kyle, wait a minute. Where are you calling from? I thought you were supposed to finish your internship over a month ago."

"I was supposed to finish. and go back, but the company had another project they thought I could help out on. They extended my work visa another six months. I asked for a two-week leave for personal reasons. I had to see what was going on. I couldn't wait one more minute to clear my name with you. Well… I have the true story now, and I'm just waiting for the lab test results. She blocked me from testing the baby. It was just a swab of the mouth, but she made me get a court order to force her to do it. That's when I knew she was lying about everything else. I mean, when you think about it, she should have been more than willing to have the baby tested to prove she was telling the truth. **She** would have gotten a court order for me to submit to testing so she could prove that the baby really was mine. I got back last night and all I could think of was you and letting you know that you can trust me. Joy, I was telling the truth!"

"Kyle, I'm really happy for you, but it really doesn't matter …"

"Doesn't matter? What are you talking about? Joy, I love you! I know you were opening up to me. I was so happy, and then this witch tells you all of these lies, and you close the door to me, completely. That's not fair. It's not fair that one evil person can cause me to lose the most valuable thing in my life. It's not only you," Kyle's voice trembled. "She made my parents think I had suddenly become someone who was thoughtless and irresponsible. Her family was angry that I could be as heartless and immoral to make their daughter pregnant and then abandon her. She had everyone I love and respect thinking the worse of me, when *she* was actually the one who was heartless, immoral, and the liar."

"If you had not slept with her, she could not have involved you at all. You have to take responsibility for that."

"I know… and I am willing to pay for my mistakes. If the test says that I am the baby's father, then I will take full responsibility. That's why I did the test. As I said, I'm willing to pay for my mistakes, but not for the cover over mistakes of others. There is another man in this picture, but she is hiding him in order to make me look bad. There's one thing, however, she didn't count on."

"What's that, Kyle?"

"The truth will come out eventually. Can you meet me for coffee? I'll drive out there today."

"Look, I was just heading out the door when the phone rang. I have a full two days of activities … and you must be exhausted after that long flight. Why don't you take a couple of days to rest? We'll talk again after the weekend."

"Joy, why are you still closing me out? Did you hear anything I said?"

"I did. I was listening. Get some rest and we'll talk."

"I'll be on campus Monday for my job. I will find you, Joy. You can't run from the truth forever," he warned as he ended the call.

Joy stood still holding the receiver as the empty line hummed for a few seconds. She wondered what he meant exactly. However, that was not the present problem. She hung up the receiver and sighing walked back towards the door and began picking up the thing on the floor.

∞

"The results are finally here and I was right—the baby is not mine."

"What happened?"

"It was very sad. Leah's mom made this a court case, you know. She was incensed that I was refusing to accept to pay any of the costs for the pregnancy ahead of time. I didn't believe Leah was telling the truth. Her mother didn't know I had requested the court-ordered paternity test. Leah didn't tell her **own mother** anything. I had to go back, when the judge got the results."

"This is really costing you a lot of time off from work and money."

"That's true, but I had to go. The judge had ordered me to appear for the results and the final ruling."

"I see. So, what happened?"

"We were all there, me with my parents, Leah and her parents in front of the judge in private chambers. As soon as the results were read proving that the father wasn't me, her mom looked like she went into shock. She stared straight ahead at the wall for about a minute. Then she turned to Leah and asked very calmly, who the real father was. I guess that was the last straw for Leah. She broke down crying and started telling everything, admitting she had a boyfriend in Embu and became pregnant by him. She didn't discover this until she had been shipped off to stay at my place. Once she found out she was pregnant, she told her boyfriend who refused to accept responsibility. She became desperate knowing her parents would be devastated by the scandal. So, she hatched this plan to trick me into thinking the child was mine, hoping to cover her tracks."

"Wow. Just think. She tried so hard to cover things up to her parents but ended by exposing everything to more people and being humiliated for lying in the process. Lying never pays."

"When I look back, it was such an obvious trick, but at the time I couldn't see it."

"What do you mean?"

"When I got home that night after a really hard day, she had cooked a really nice meal—all my favorite things--- and bought this expensive bottle of wine. The house was immaculate, proof that she had made an extra effort to clean it up. There were even fresh cut flowers for the table," he chuckled. "She had never done that before."

"You should have known she was planning something."

"Yes, I was kind of suspicious at first. When I asked what was going on, she simple stated that she wanted me to know how much she appreciated all that I had done, trying to help her find a job and everything. She made this elaborate show of serving the dinner and wine and kept asking if I liked it. Every time she asked, she would pour more wine. I didn't want to seem unappreciative of her efforts, so I kept drinking and eating. Then she suggested that we sit on the sofa for coffee, I was so drunk by that time I was not thinking well. She started touching me and saying that she really hoped that I understood how grateful she was."

"Kyle, you don't have to explain all of these details."

"I know, but I want you to have **all** of the details."

"Suit yourself."

"You are right to think that was right there, at this point, if not long before, I should have run from the scene. I should have locked myself in my room or gone to stay with a friend."

"Yes. Anything."

"But I didn't, okay. I was distracted by the thought of how badly she would feel if she thought I did not appreciate all that she had done to say thank you. I ignored that inner voice warning me to escape… because I was too busy proving that I was a wonderful person. I stayed right there… like a bull's eye target, just to prove that I was a nice guy to graciously accept her appreciation to me. I was soon oblivious as to when the line was crossed. It struck me as odd later that she seemed so lucid and was so clearly persistent. I felt regretful immediately afterward. In shame, I stumbled off to my room. The next morning, I was so embarrassed, I didn't talk to her and avoided her after that. I gave short answers to any questions; leaving early in the morning and returning late in the evening, going straight to my room."

"A little late for that."

"Yes, I admit that. I was like a prisoner in my own home. She never said a word about it and she never cleaned the house or cooked for me again."

"Of course, why would she? She had gotten you to swallow her hook, line and sinker."

"I didn't know what to do and couldn't ask anyone for advice without exposing my shame. My chance for escape came when all the papers arrived for me to leave for my internship. I told her she would have to move out because I was leaving the country. She pleaded with me to leave her the keys to try to find another place by the end of the month. After I cleared this with the owner, I just waited, thinking I was being freed of the whole situation. The next time I heard her name was from you, that day at the dam."

"How is that possible? She was living at your parents' home."

"I tell you, she was very clever. Once I left, she carried out the rest of her plan. Knowing it would be hard to reconcile the pregnancy timing while I was there, she waited for all of this to become blurred and started building her case with my family."

"What do you mean?"

"She told them the same story she told you. She knew my mom would make me 'do the right thing' by her, especially being the daughter of one of her best friends. To think that all Leah cared about was saving her reputation in the eyes of her parents. The way she had things set up, whether we got married or not, she would have me sending financial support for and giving legitimacy to this baby. At the same time, she was making me seem like a horrible person. She is really evil. How could she think she would ever succeed by destroying my life and reputation with a lie?"

"You have to admit your actions did help her out and she almost succeeded. For six months everyone in your world thought she was your fiancée slash wife."

"I don't think she ever planned to marry me. She must hate me to do what she did."

"She must also be mentally deranged. She wrote me a letter through the school address, threatening me."

"She did what? You never told me that."

"It was a month or so after I got back from Kenya. I was so angry at you; I wouldn't have told you anything. She is very cunning, at least. She called me a 'marriage wrecker', a 'husband stealer', an 'instrument of evil'."

"Oh, my goodness. The *nerve* of her! How dare she say that? She was the one who was the conniving and lying 'instrument of evil'."

"Oh, yeah. She said that you had called her denying the baby was yours because I had told you to do so. She even asked, 'What kind of person tortures a pregnant woman?' and then she asked questions like, 'Can't you find someone who is willing to *settle* for you in America? Why would you try to steal the father of my child and beloved husband while I am in this weakened condition?' I felt horrible."

"She is pure evil."

"She even wrote 'God will judge you for putting the health of an innocent baby at risk out of sheer selfishness' … and 'if I am so stressed and the baby is born early it will be your fault'. Can you imagine? I felt so bad, even though I knew I wasn't doing any of that. I thought she was really suffering because of what she thought I was doing. Then she wrote that if I didn't stop trying to steal her husband, she would curse me. I could not even bring myself to answer her letter to set her straight. I just got angrier at you."

"I could feel that, I was so frustrated. I had to wait until I could prove my innocence, there was nothing I could say in my defense. Can you see now she said that to make an excuse for the baby being born 'early'? She didn't want people to think that the baby was conceived before she came to Nairobi."

"Did you ever, for even one moment, think about what you would have done if the baby had been yours?"

"I spent a lot of sleepless nights wondering whether I would have to pay dearly for that single indiscretion and be, in some way, tied to the woman for the rest of my life. I prayed so *hard*. Anyway, I am glad that it's all behind me and I can hold my head up in front of you."

"You are very fortunate. Not everyone gets to walk away clean from such a situation. Some with the same amount of regret as you, maybe even more, will spend the rest of their lives watching, under duress, the results grow up in front of them or paying money in support for years."

"It's very true. I know and thank God every day. I also pray for her. She's in a terrible situation, right now."

"I don't want to seem cold-hearted, but it would have been better if you had prayed for her situation before you contributed to it. You set yourself up, you know?"

"I know… and I plan to be more careful and less trusting of people's intentions."

"Sounds like a good plan, but don't you think … you need more than that? I mean isn't there some major change in your life so that you never end up in that situation again?"

"As I said, I'm going to be less trusting of people. Short of avoiding people altogether, I think that's going to do the job. Oh yeah. I need to pray more and pay attention to the warnings God sends. Believe me. I have learned my lesson."

"Umm …"

"Joy, what made you decide to go to Tunis, for six weeks?"

"It wasn't any single thing, Peter. It was a little bit of wanting to get away for a while a little jealousy of Mom and Dad's trip to Victoria Falls and wanting to travel to places I've never seen. I'll be helping young artists there and contributing to international understanding. There is also the obvious fact that Tunis is the only location my school is offering."

"It seems sort of extreme to me, but I am content that you'll at least be here for the wedding and Natalie will be happy."

"Peter, you guys will have started your trip when I leave. Remember your honeymoon will be during two of the project's six weeks? Natalie was showing us the brochure for Victoria Falls. Looks like you were also bitten by the jealousy bug after Mom and Dad got back from their trip there."

"This was not decided based on jealousy, Little Sister, but pure interest. Did Mom and Dad tell you about the upside-down rain?"

"No. What is that?"

"Joy, I did a bit of research and this is the simple explanation. The water from the river falls over a steep drop from a that stretches for I think it said about a two-kilometer distance. Along the edge at various spots, incredibly large volumes of water fall far into the gorge, making a huge amount of constant and violent splashing back up into the air. The splash rises as a sort of heavy mist over the surrounding area. As the water falls back down to the ground, it gives the same effect as rain. So, when you visit the falls, you wear a raincoat if you don't want to get soaking wet from water droplets falling from a bright clear blue sky. There is so much 'rain' the surrounding environment is the same as a rainforest."

"Wow. I want to see this. Okay, I'm setting it as a new goal to reach there within the next five years. It sounds extraordinary. Only God could think to make something like that, just to let you know He's able to deliver from the opposite or the reverse way we expect or think logically."

"That's what we call a miracle, Joy, isn't it?"

"In most cases, it is. Maybe, when we think we can explain something scientifically, we classify it as a highly unusual event. We don't call it a miracle. I was talking to Joe the other day. He said he would still call something a miracle, even if it was something normal, but happened at a time that it was not supposed to. It has to be in answer to prayer, for the benefit of a believer, or as a testimony to an unbeliever. We were talking about the widow whose oil and flour never ran out so she and her family didn't starve. That's God's miraculous provision quietly, low profile and daily."

"It's very different from Jesus calling Lazarus to life from the grave after days of being dead and in front of a big crowd."

"Yes, Peter it is very different, but also a reminder that you just can't put God in a box or a formula. You can only be sure that He will use whatever it takes to get you to the next step along your journey. My problem is that I'm not always sure which way the next step is. Sometimes, I feel so lost and think I'm moving in the wrong direction only to find a short time later that I'm closer to my goal than I thought."

"Yeah, I know what you mean, Joy. It's hard for me to believe that I once thought that Natalie was a decoy to my happiness sent by Savannah."

"Speaking of Savannah, she seems happy about all the wedding activities. She's taking her duty as maid of honor very seriously. All bride's maids are ready to strangle her because we see her trying to run in every decision."

"You don't have to tell me. I made Natalie promise not to give her the ring until the morning before the ceremony. I would find it very hard to forgive her if she misplaced it and only realized it when we were all at the altar."

"She is more *artistically ordered* than me."

"Yes, she very definitely is. It's hard to get annoyed at her for long, because she is so engaging and sincere. She can make anyone feel at ease and she is always willing to help you if there's a problem."

"She got that from her dad. Uncle John is just like that."

"You're right. She acts like him, but she looks just like her mom."

"But her mom is the one who has the artistic bent. Looks can be deceiving."

"Her mom's artistic bent is well ordered, and Aunt Sylvia is very organized."

"Even talents are given in different groupings and combinations."

"Yeah, I look like Grandpa Karima, and everyone thought I would be artistic. Remember my art set that you destroyed?"

"Yes, Peter! That day is one I will never forget."

"You and me both!"

"Now you, see? That's a perfect example of what we were talking about, before. I felt so badly, with you screaming and carrying on, but it was the opening of the door to my life's work as an artist."

"I know. And when you had to replace my art set, you used the competition prize money you won for the picture you made to buy me an abacus. How did you decide on that anyway? I had never seen one before I unwrapped your gift."

"I don't think I had ever seen one before the morning I bought it, either. I didn't even know what it was. I remember walking through the toy store and seeing this little boy sitting on the floor in the middle of the aisle. He was sliding the different colored widgets across the rows and then putting them all back again. I was intrigued that it had colorful moving parts and yet, everything could be quickly put back in perfect order. I just knew that you would like it."

"I did. You know, I still have it? It's on my desk at work."

"Really? That's great! You let that be a constant reminder. Just remember all of this when you have kids and don't prejudge them."

"Don't worry I'll remember. Isn't it funny that you chose an abacus for an accountant?"

"Nothing happens by accident in God's kingdom., Brother."

"That's right! I'm getting married to the most wonderful woman in the world. I probably would not have met this woman, had I not been an accountant."

"Don't forget, you met her at your father's best friend's house. This has been in the making since before you were born," Joy said.

"That's pretty comforting, you know. God cares enough to arrange all of that."

"Yes. It would be more comforting for me personally if I could see the person, he has arranged for me."

"Don't worry; you will see him soon, maybe in Tunis," Peter said.

"Soon, yes. Soon? When is soon? I remember how excited I got two years ago when this evangelist said he had received a message for me from the Lord: I would be getting married soon. You would think that *soon* would be before two years, wouldn't you? Did I miss him?"

"You couldn't have missed him. Maybe God's *soon* is farther away than ours."

"It must be, at least in my case. I don't think I will meet him in Tunis, but I am looking forward to all the other things I'll see and do. They have a lot of beaches in Tunisia, too."

"Hey! What about my wedding? That happens first, you know," Peter said.

"I know, Brothers. I will be here for Natalie. I have to go down to the church next week so that I can check it out and make sure I know my way around. People are going to think I should know since I live pretty close, and they are coming from so far away."

"It's not very hard to find. It's right there on Crenshaw, one of the city's major boulevards. Uncle John's house is not far away. Neither is Dad's old school. Just across the street from the school, there's the new hotel where a lot of our guests will be staying. I made reservations for Grandma Martha and Mom and Dad in the hotel downtown where the reception will be held, to make things easier for them."

"I'll just stay with Grandma Martha, to help her and to spend some extra time with her. It's a rare treat. An extra car couldn't hurt, either."

"They'll get here the week before so they have the time to rest up before all the activities start. It's kind of sad that she doesn't have friends to go and see while she's here."

"How do you know that she doesn't have friends? Of course, Miss Washington died a few years ago, but she had other people she knew around where she used to live. Maybe we could ask Dad for names of people we could contact for her and surprise her."

"I will leave that to you. I feel like I'm starting to get stressed, already."

"That's fine. I have been thinking of going out to do some sketches of what the old farm—turned into the residence for the Suffer the Children Foundation Claire's Corner—has become. I keep thinking about the swing on the porch. Can you believe that we all climbed on the swing with Dad and Mom to watch the stars? I don't remember if it was bigger than the swing on the porch at home. Anyway, if they are going to be here a week before, maybe I could drive them out there."

"The wedding is on Saturday, but there is a rehearsal on Thursday and a big dinner right after the rehearsal on Friday evening. Maybe she can go to her old church on Sunday if she's not too tired."

"That's a very good idea, Peter. I'll call and see if Dad can help me out with as much information as possible."

"Good luck. Don't book Joe for any of your running around. He's my best man and we have a lot to do and catch up with. I just know when he gets here things will start falling into place."

"We always used to depend on him to manage things. He's still very good at it if his business success is any indication."

"Yes, and he will be here to help me that entire week. Joe and Faith will be saying with me, just to make sure he is not hindered by any other distractions."

"Okay, I got it. Joe's your private property for the week."

"I hope everything goes the right way."

"It will. You have Natalie helping you out. She's running things, and you're the one helping her."

"You're right of course," he sighed. "I just have to keep reminding myself. I will be so glad when Pastor Green says 'I now pronounce you man and wife.' I can breathe a sigh of relief. It will all be over."

"What do you mean it will all be over? I've been told that's when the work begins."

Chapter 9

JOY STOOD HOLDING HER bouquet. She watched with teary eyes as Peter and Natalie exchanged vows. The wedding had gone exactly as planned. Every candle, flower, note, and ring was on time and in place. She found that she also breathed a sigh of relief at the ceremony's ending words.

After pictures were taken, the bridal court was whisked away to the reception. Once she was sure Natalie was okay, she left her with Savannah and searched for Grandma Martha. She found her quietly sitting at one of the reserved tables. Her ever-present handkerchief dabbed her eyes now and then as her joy spilled over.

"Hello, Grandma Martha. How are you doing?"

"Oh! I'm fine, just fine. You know I never thought that I would live long enough to see my great-grandchildren, much less to see them married and have children of their own."

"We are so glad that you are here. It's a blessing for all of us."

"Thank you, Joy. God has been so good to me. You know, I was an only child. I never would have imagined that one day I would have so many relatives that it would sometimes be a challenge to remember all of their names. It's such a wonderful thing." She softly patted Joy's arm.

"Yes, it is."

"You look lovely, Joy."

"Thanks. I had to dress up for the wedding you know."

"Not as much as when you're the bride."

"True, but I may never have that problem."

"Problem? I remember my wedding day. I had to sneak out of my house, knowing it might be the last time I would see it. As I had packed my small bag, I was torn between the desire to avoid attracting attention by carrying a big suitcase and the desire to carry as much as I could. It was so difficult having to choose what to carry out of a room full of things. Fortunately, I didn't have much time. I compromised by wearing all three of my favorite dress, one on top of the other. I didn't have a white dress, so I chose the light blue one to wear on top. It was my favorite. You know, it was the very color blue that you all have on today."

"That is interesting."

"Yes, and it suits you well, my dear."

"Thank you, Grandma Martha. You are just full of compliments, today."

"I think you should tell someone when they look nice." She smiled, and then her attention turned to someone coming up behind Joy.

"I agree with her, Joy. The wedding was very nice, and you look so beautiful."

"Thank you, Kyle. I didn't see you at the church. I'm glad you were able to come."

"I would not have missed it. I stayed an extra week to be here. It was well worth it, to see you so lovely and happy."

"Thank you, again, Kyle. Grandma Martha, I would like to present a friend and former classmate from Kenya, Kyle Bundi Kinoti."

"It's nice to meet you, Kyle."

"It is a pleasure to meet you, Madame. You have a wonderful granddaughter."

"Oh, we call her Grandma Martha, but she is my father's grandma, so she's my great grandmother."

"Sorry, Madame."

"No, that's okay. Everyone calls me Grandma."

"It was a pleasure to meet you, Madame. I'll talk to you later Joy," Kyle said as he nodded his head and walked away."

"Huh! Who was that, Joy?"

"Kyle went to the academy with me, and he's here on this internship program."

"What I mean is, who is he to you, and why is he trying so hard to prove something?"

"Why do you say he's trying to prove something?"

"My eyes may be old, but I could see his attitude and your response. He's never going to win you over, is he? What did he do to make you so dislike him?"

"Wow. You could see all of that? Well, let's just say he did something that made me think I could never trust him. I don't know why, just how I feel. He's a wonderful person. I like him and he's a lot of fun …"

"But God has not given him a place in your heart of hearts?"

"That's it. I could not have said it better. I tried to tell him, but he is determined to prove he's the one I should marry."

"People want to marry and even fall in love for many reasons. There's no way of using logic to undo that. That feeling that you have that he's not the one for you is going to have to be so clear in your mind that it can't be changed with a moment of pity or a "maybe if."

"Why do you say that?"

"I have known many young women, who just before meeting their true mate, became so fearful of being alone, they condemned themselves to mediocre or marriages which ended in divorced lives. For the rest of their lives, they were wondering what if they had decided to wait? That poor young man, Kyle, will be forever proving himself to you and feeling like he has not quite managed to do so unless your heart changes."

"Thanks, Grandma Martha, you're a jewel still sparkling at ninety-three years old."

"You run along and do all of the bride's maid things. We'll have time to talk more tomorrow, after church."

"Yes. I forgot to tell you that I'm taking the same flight with you all to Amsterdam. Then our paths separate. I head for Tunis and you all for Nairobi."

"I heard about you going to Tunis. Why?"

"My school is doing this international outreach thing, and I decided to go and see how I could help. I needed a break and it's just for six weeks."

"You're running from that Kyle, huh? Why go halfway around the world and not come home? They won't do an 'outreach thing' in Kenya?"

"I never thought of that."

"Your dad first came to Kenya, because he wrote a project proposal to his school. I don't see why you can't try the same thing and come back. There's nobody you're running from in Kenya is there?"

"No, but Kyle will be going back in a little while."

"You need to stand firm and let him know. These days, physical distance is not a good protection barrier. People can get on an airplane and be anywhere in a short time."

"That's true. Well, things are getting clearer by the second. If only for that reason, I should move back home just to talk to you more."

"That would be nice."

"We'll talk more, later. I see the troops are gathering up in front."

"I'll be here. I have no pressing engagements."

"I remember you used to always be flying off to parts of the world."

"Yes, I know. That was a wonderful time in my life. Came along just after Grandpa Joe died and I didn't know what I was going to do with myself. It turned out that Sarah and I did so many wonderful things for so many wonderful people. Sarah Washington was a brilliant and big-hearted friend." Grandma Martha suddenly chuckled at a memory. "We finally got so old, one day we looked at each other and decided it did not make sense to spend so much time in the air getting swollen feet. Claire's Corner was full and it was time to move on to other things. She was a dear friend, and I was so sad to hear about her passing away. As usual, she did a good job in making sure that the work would continue. I still get letters from kids who we brought over, even now. They're all grown and working in big jobs back at their home countries, but still take time to write."

"I want to hear all about this, later. Grandma Martha, I love you so much. I want you to know that I feel so fortunate that you are here to share the wisdom you've been storing up for all these years. You must think we are very childish and ignorant, running around making every mistake we can think of."

"Oh, no! Child, I don't think that at all. After all of the things I've been through, I'm glad that anything I have learned can be of help to anyone. That's especially true with my family. You know the Bible says that the wise person, wisdom, herself, is easily entreated. The wiser you become the more approachable you are and willing to share with others. I find myself just shaking my head in awe. Imagine Jesus just taking time and sitting with children. He knew he was heading for the cross soon. He was aware of the immense task that he had to complete in such a short time, equipping the disciples. Mind you, this sitting with the children could not have been a onetime event. He didn't call them to gather round. They came seeking *Him*. Do you know how hard it is to convince children that they can feel free around you? No matter how hard a person might try sometimes, they just don't trust certain people. Then there are other people who they seem drawn towards. I've found that the people who children are naturally drawn towards are the people who everyone else is drawn toward because of their hearts. They've found the secret of happily giving away what they couldn't keep anyway. They've found the value in every soul, young or old. You remember that, now. It doesn't matter what a person *says* is important to them. You have to watch what they spend the coins of their life on, the minutes and hours of their life. Are they spent on things or people; for some sort of profit or as an investment in some sort of person? Oh, my goodness! Turn around and look; they're waving for you to go up there."

"Huh?" Joy said as she turned around. "Oh, my goodness, I have to go."

"You go on. We'll talk more, later."

Joy reached over and hugged Grandma Martha, and then gave her a light kiss on the cheek. "You're amazing," she said huskily and then darted up to the group complaining about her absence. Looking back at the table she had just left, she saw her mom and dad walk over and give Grandma greeting hugs and kisses, with her broadly smiling at them. A very distinguished Tana walked in and greeted everyone at the table. Faith rushed in with Hope in her arms. After giving hurried greetings to everyone around the table, she handed the baby to Grandma. It must have just been her imagination, but Joy thought, as she watched her grandma kiss Hope, that she seemed to glow and smile bigger than before. Her ever-present handkerchief dabbed her eyes again.

"You should let your father push this wheelchair. You're such a thin little thing."

"I'm stronger than I look."

"I guess so. It's such a bother. I only have to use a wheel chair in the airport. With all these long hallways, you do a week's worth of walking in a couple of hours."

"I know, but don't you worry. You're okay. Mom and Dad went ahead to get a place in the check in line and we can just take our time."

"Aren't you supposed to be going to Tunis with a group of people?"

"Yes, but I made my reservation a long time ago when I found out the flight you were taking. I wanted to spend as much time with you as possible, so I booked the same flights as far as I could. The others waited to book almost at the last minute. They'll be taking a longer route, not always on the same flights and paying more money."

"I *see*. You'll get there before them?"

"No. The funny thing is they left yesterday, but I'll arrive the same day. They have these long layovers between flights."

"Poor things."

"No. They don't deserve pity, Grandma Martha. It's only fair. If you don't plan well, then you have poor options."

"Joy, you make it sound like that's a good thing, but nobody should want things to be fair. None of us are blameless enough to ever come out on the good end of the fair stick. We deserve to die for the sins we commit. That's fair for you. Where would we all be without grace and mercy covering our sins? No, I never want things to be fair. I always want God's life-giving mercy, so I give as much of it to others as I can."

"I never thought of it that way."

"Now you can spread the word," she said as she did her shoo-fly gesture to Joy.

Chapter 10

When she alighted from the shuttle, Lionel was nowhere to be seen. She took a seat near the front of the orientation room and browsed the information booklet. Lionel appeared with the second group of shuttle passengers and made his way to the seat beside her, just as the guide began the session.

"The purpose of this security orientation is to help you avoid foreseeable problems. It is not a guarantee that all will go well or as planned. You are in a foreign country. That may seem like it is too obvious a thing to say, but it will perhaps be too easily forgotten as you become familiar with people at your residence or participate in activities with friends. Local friends may be able to advise you as to behavior to comply with to guard your safety in specific situations when you are with them. However, when you are not accompanied by local people, there are even more stringent general rules to guide you. This is because your very appearance may draw attention to you. If you have to speak, even your knowledge of the French language cannot hide your foreign accent. Are there any questions so far?"

"I would like to know if there is any advantage to not having a foreign accent, but just a normal California accent." Lionel's joke caused some scattered chuckles across the room.

"No," the guide said sternly and continued. "I would like to start with a little of the country's history."

The guide went on for the next thirty minutes in a monotone that threatened to put the audience of twenty Americans to sleep. Joy had to use her elbow three times to prod Lionel back to attention as his head began to nod. Watching out for him helped her to stay awake.

"The following points are important to focus on for the females in our group. If you do not rent a private home, the student residence, where you are staying, has a curfew of 9 pm. At this time, the doors are locked, and no one may leave or enter. If you are delayed, for whatever reason, from arriving before this time, you are advised to stay the night where you are or make other arrangements with a friend. The residence makes no exceptions. In addition, you must never be on the street walking alone or with a group after 10 pm. It will be assumed that you are a prostitute. You will be arrested and placed in jail until the next morning. This is a very dangerous situation as you can imagine. There is no 'One phone call' or reasonable treatment. Prostitution is illegal, but tolerated in the red-light district known as *abdallah guech*, located down one of the alleys, near the market area."

"Wow. That's good to know," Joy whispered.

"Don't worry Little Sister, I'll take care of you," Lionel reassured her.

"You don't have to worry about me. I'll make sure I'm inside before 8:30 for the next six weeks. The rest of the time, I'll be pretty occupied with classes and tours," she replied.

"I figured you would be one of those careful ones. I plan to e n j o y myself, go everywhere and see everything," he shot back.

At the end of the session, the speakers had asked them to break up into two groups for a city tour.

"Is it okay if I ride with your group? I'm hoping they pass by your residence. I want to be able to find you if there's any problem."

Joy could only smile in response as she reflected. *He seems like a nice guy, even though I don't know him well. He must have a younger sister, for him to so easily address me that way. He looks and acts nothing like Joseph or Peter.*

She had first seen Lionel at the art institute during the orientation meeting for the participants in the overseas program. He was notable for being the tallest man in the room and the only one walking with a cane. It was difficult to guess his age, but he had a few gray hairs. She had overheard him say that he had been injured in the war. It was during rehabilitation therapy sessions he had discovered his love for photography. After using the GI Bill to obtain his degree in art, he had decided to teach. He had applied to the art institutes because of the opportunity for promotion. He said that his last position for five years had 'led nowhere'. She noticed his conversation was punctuated with profanity and when he had excused himself to go for a smoke out on the terrace, Joy's mental line placed him on the other side of people to get to know better. He on the other hand had sought out her company from time to time on campus. When they arrived in Tunis, he managed to stay frequently by her side at staff orientation meetings.

It was not surprising that their paths crossed often, as they taught in the same department at the same institute. Some of the same students were in both of their classes. At the end of the third week, Joy received an invitation to a party hosted by a group of students from sub- Saharan Africa. Jamila explained that it would begin at 6 pm to be sure everyone would arrive before nightfall. She also asked Joy if Lionel could escort her there and back since he knew the location, and it was on the way to his own lodging. Joy had agreed.

Lionel arrived with a rapid stroll, ten minutes later than he had promised. Seeing her annoyance as he approached her sitting on the stairs at the residence entrance, he started his defense before even greeting her.

"I'm sorry. I had to stop to buy some drinks for the party. It took longer than usual. Don't worry you'll be there on time. Don't stand there giving me that look. Come on or we'll be even later. It's not far from here." He continued walking without slowing down as he passed her.

"Oh, you!" she said, jumping up from her seat on the stairs. She had to trot to catch up with his long stride. He walked rapidly despite the cane assisted limp, looking straight ahead a and saying nothing.

"I didn't buy anything for the party. I didn't know I was supposed to."

"You're not. I usually bring some wine or whiskey for myself to drink. They don't have anything but sodas and juices at their house. So, I bring my own."

"I see."

"You don't drink, either, huh?"

"No, I don't."

"Then you don't have to worry. They always have enough of everything."

"How often do you go there?" Joy asked frowning.

"It's more often recently than before. There's this girl I like …"

"You are not fraternizing with the students, Lionel?" Stunned Joy stopped walking.

"Hey, she's a grown woman!" Lionel stopped and stared at her. You know, most of the students are older than you? They're my age." He started walking again, leaving her behind.

"Really? No, I did not know." She trotted to catch up.

"It's good that you'll have a couple of hours to just sit and talk with them. You made them quite happy when you accepted."

"Really? And how would you know that?"

"Yes, really. And I would know that because, unlike you, I spend a lot of time talking to people. It's how I learn things."

"I see."

"Maybe I could tell you a little about a few of the people that will be there tonight. You know, to help get you up to speed in the human arena."

"Okay Lionel, go ahead."

"I'll start with Fatu; she's the one I'm sweet on. She's pretty fair in photography, pretty fair looking, too. She has a big kind heart and is very quiet spoken. That is unless you mess with her in the kitchen. She is the best cook I have ever met. You can give her anything and, with her box of spices, a few onions, and tomatoes, she'll throw down a meal to compete with the finest restaurants in the world. She's the only female in the house and that's probably why. Most important of all is, for some reason, she has taken a liking to me."

"Okay and so there is one female and how many men?"

"At the house, there are seven bedrooms altogether. These are occupied by six men and one by Fatu. Depending on money and logistics, there may be, from time to time, four to five other people, who will sleep on the sofa or floor in the living room."

"I see," Joy said frowning.

"But the party is not just for those who live there. They've invited all of the African students coming from other countries. I think there are four other female students, like Jamila, and a lot of male students. I found out that it's hard for women to go to the university or other countries because it is so expensive. The focus is to educate the men who will be the main supporters of their families."

"That's interesting."

"Yes, it is. Then there is Daoude, who is like the big brother of everyone—gives advice and rules the house. He's pretty smart, actually a genius in photography, but doesn't talk much."

"If he's the same one I'm thinking about in my techniques class, he does have a good eye for combinations and effects."

"Then there are Maurice and Abu, really nice guys, very talkative and fun. I guess I've never discussed anything serious with them. The other three are not in any of my classes, so I don't know them well: Yusuf, Suleiman, and Babu. I think they are science majors, but nice guys. The rest you will have to find out on your own. Anyway, I think you'll have a good time. Even if you don't, you'll have done a good thing by honoring their invitation."

"Thank you for the orientation. I hope I will enjoy myself *and* meet their expectations."

"Just be yourself, Teach. This is not an exam. You can practice your French and stuff. You're pretty nice when you relax."

"What do you mean relax?"

"Well, we've arrived. Put on your happy face, Little Sister, and plan to have a good time, like me." Lionel adjusted his package and began to climb the entryway steps. The door was unlocked and he entered. Joy followed him quickly, only to find a long stairway up to the next level, inside the entry hallway.

Daoude must have been watching from an upstairs window because he was halfway down the long stairway which led to his home before Joy closed the entry door behind her.

"Welcome, professors!" he said as he warmly shook their hands. "Please follow me."

When he reached the landing, he opened another unlocked door revealing the presence of fifteen people scattered about the living room in small groups. They made their way over to greet the two professors with a handshake and then returned to their previous activities. A group of four was sitting around a coffee table, playing cards. Their exclaims and game comments made loud and excited punctuations in the dull roar of the conversations across the room.

"Hey Little Sister, I want you to come and greet Fatu. She must be in the kitchen. After that, you're on your own."

She followed Lionel again across the room, then down a short hallway to the right and through the first doorway. The ambiance suddenly changed as the women in the kitchen worked busily preparing food. There was serious work going on in sharp contrast to the group in the other room, waiting for dinner, but enjoying themselves.

"Welcome, Prof Anderson. Hi, Lionel. I'm so glad you have come. The food is almost ready. Give me a few more minutes, and we can talk while we eat." Her French was slowly and clearly pronounced for Joy's sake.

"Thank you for inviting me, Fatu. I'll see you in a little while," Joy made an effort to reply as clearly.

"Yeah. Let us know if you need any help," Lionel smilingly offered as he placed the package down on the corner counter

"You! Get out of my kitchen!" Fatu yelled playfully.

Back in the living room Joy rotated from group to group. In addition to the dinner conversation with Fatu, Lionel, Daoude, and Yusuf at the only real table in the room, she was able to spend some time with everyone she had seen, as they helped clean up after dinner. When people began to leave, she looked around for Lionel, but did not see him. She looked for Daoude, to ask his help and finally saw him enter from the far hall door.

"Daoude, have you seen Lionel?"

"No, I haven't. Let me look for him." Daoude re-entered the far hallway.

Joy sat on the couch, now that the card players were gone, and waited. Twenty minutes passed. *Where could he be? It would not take ten minutes to look in every room in this house. It was 8:20 and time was running out.* Looking around her, there were four guys left in the living room.

Daoude rushed into the room smiling toward Joy. "I've found him. He is with Fatu and says he'll be here in a few minutes."

"Thank you, Daoude."

"No problem. Would you like something else to drink while you wait? I am making some mint tea. It's almost ready"

"Well, if Lionel is coming now. I'd better not."

"It's ready in two minutes. I'll bring it." He rushed out of the room toward the kitchen.

She watched the hallway to the left where Daoude had come from and where she was sure Lionel would emerge any minute. She waited another ten minutes. There was no Lionel and no Daoude. Now, she was angry *What was wrong with these guys?* She stood to go to the kitchen, when Daoude appeared smiling. He had a small kettle in one hand and a tray of small glasses in the other.

"I told you, it would only take a few minutes," he said sitting down beside her.

"Daoude, I really must get going! Can you please get Lionel for me?"

"Yes, I will. He said he was coming, but I can try to find him again. In the meantime, here is your tea."

Joy was not in the mood to drink tea, but when he presented the glass to her, she realized he was not going to move until she accepted it and drank at least some.

"Thank you." She accepted the glass and took a sip. "It's very good, thank you. Do you think you can go to get Lionel? If I don't leave soon, it will be too late for me to get in the residence."

"Oh! Yes, I see. Let me see if I can find him." He stood, drank his teas in quick sips, smiled, and walked into the hallway and out of sight. Fifteen minutes later he returned alone.

"Where's Lionel?" Joy asked. Her eyes now narrow as she realized she was caught in a web of deceit. Before Daoude answered, she knew Lionel would not be coming to walk her home.

Even if I asked someone else to escort me, there were only seven minutes left before curfew. If we left right now and ran full speed, it would be too close to call. I did not pay close enough attention to find it in the dark myself.

"I know he's got to be here somewhere, but I can't locate him," Daoude shrugged his shoulders and smiled weakly. "He is not answering my calls and there is no response to my door knocks. I'm sure he'll be ready to go soon. He knows you are ready to leave.

"Daoude, I was wondering ..."

"Just a moment, let me see if I can find Lionel or see if Fatu knows where he is." He stood and rushed to the hallway again out of sight. Whoever was lying or whatever game was being played didn't matter anymore. With him went all hope of leaving safely before the morning. She looked over at the four guys sitting on the other sofa and room chairs and wondered why they were waiting.

Daoude rushed to her side and softly said, "I am sorry Prof., I found him with Fatu, but he says your residence is closed now and that there is nowhere else to stay."

"Okay, I'll just need a blanket and I'll sleep here on the sofa."

"I'm afraid that space is already taken," he said as he nodded toward the young men.

"What?" She remembered that Lionel had said as much on the way to the party. "Oh yes, of course."

"You can stay in my room. There will be no problem."

"That's very kind of you," she said in as grateful a manner as she could manage. Her thoughts however were otherwise. *What choice do I have? Absolutely none. What a mess.*

"No problem. Let me show you." Daoude played the epitome of a good host.

She reluctantly followed him down the hall to the last room.

"Here you are. I hope you will be comfortable," he said graciously. He closed the keyless door behind him as he left and his footsteps retreated down the hall.

Well! Here we are, she told herself, glancing around the cluttered room. *Obviously, the sheets were not changed. I'll just sleep in my clothes under the blanket, on top of the sheets.* She quickly set her watch alarm, turned off the light, and arranged herself on the bed. She was almost asleep when the sound of the door softly opening startled her.

"Who's that?" she called sharply.

"It's me, Daoude. I waited until you were settled to come to bed."

"Oh, I thought …" She caught herself from finishing the sentence out loud.

I had thought he had offered me his room for my sole use. It really doesn't matter what I thought, does it? I am in his world, in his house, in his bedroom, and in his bed. I am an alien in this territory and not entirely clear about the pathway that has led me here. I have to step now, with extreme caution.

"Are you comfortable?' Daoude asked.

"I am fine," she replied, but all the frustration of the evening peaked at this point and stinging tears forced their way through her resolve. She tried to sniff quietly as Daoude sat down on the other side of the king-size bed.

"Oh, you are sad. You miss your boyfriend? Please may I comfort you?"

"No," Joy sniffed. "I'm fine. I don't need or want anything, except for morning to come quickly."

"I understand… If you think of something later let me know."

"Yes of course," she said with false confidence. She willed herself to sleep.

Joy woke up with a jerk at the sound of the broadcasted call to prayers from the mosque's minaret. She stealthily rose in the morning shadow to ready herself to leave. Slipping noiselessly from Daoude's room, silently negotiated the hallway in the darkness she soon stood in the living room a short distance from the snoring young men on the couch. She made her way over to where she could see the street below through the window next to the front door and waited for the sun's first rays to show. She quickly slipped outside and hurried along the streets. She made a few wrong turns at first, but managed to regain her sense of .direction and sighed with relief when she saw familiar buildings and increased her pace. She arrived at the dormitory residence in a relatively short time. As she turned to run up the steps to the entrance, someone call her name.

"Joy, there you are. I was so worried."

She turned and drew in a sharp breath of surprise. Kyle was standing up from where he had been sitting on the corner at the top of the steps.

"Kyle?"

"Thank God you're all right. I was so worried when I came last night straight from the airport and they told me you were not yet in. I decided to wait, but when they closed the door and said no one could come out or in until sunrise, I decided to go to the hotel and come again early this morning. What happened?"

"What are you doing here?"

"I came to see you."

"To see me? Why?"

"Can we go to the café on the corner and sit down?"

"I am really tired, Kyle."

"I can imagine, after being out all night."

"Wait a minute! What is that supposed to mean?"

"I don't know what happened. You tell me what it means."

"It means that another friend betrayed me. That's what it means."

"Come on, let's get some tea. You'll feel better with something warm in your stomach. I need to hear about what happened.

"You are so bullheaded. It is quite annoying. Just …"

Kyle stood between her and the front door, smiling sheepishly.

She didn't have the strength to argue anymore. "Okay."

As they walked to the café on the corner, Joy began to tell the story of the previous night. She continued after they paid for the tea at the counter and sat at a quiet table in the corner. Kyle was right. The warm tea in her stomach did make her feel better. It was also comforting to share her experience with someone who seemed understanding.

"That's pretty bad. Sorry, you went through that."

"I know now who I can't trust; lesson learned."

"Unfortunately, all everyone else in the house knows is that you spent the night with Daoude in his bed. They can assume anything they want about their professor, especially in the light of your colleague Lionel's behavior."

"What do you mean by that?"

"Well, it's just like me. Daoude can say anything and you have no proof that he's lying."

"It's not the same."

"I have your version of the story, but what if this Daoude says something else? What if he says that he had sex with you?"

"Who would it make a difference to, besides God?"

"What if your future husband was here and heard that?"

"So, what if he did? He would have to either trust me or decide not to marry me. In which case, he would not be my future husband."

"You have me still feeling bad for having done something "questionable" while I was drunk. You don't even drink and you have no qualms about something that is highly questionable. I bet in all the time that you would have continued to refuse me, you would have never mentioned this episode. How can you sit in judgment still? After all I've done to prove myself to you, you don't trust me."

"I'm not sitting in judgment! And you are right. if you were not here this morning to ask me why, I would never have told you about what happened last night. I don't expect you to beat up Lionel and Daoude or to comfort me. Why would I tell you some useless information?"

"You would tell me...so I would know that you know how it feels to be the victim in a situation that could ruin your name... no matter what really happened. So, I would know that you understand how I feel."

"I do understand, Kyle. I have understood for a long time."

"Then prove it!"

"What?"

"Prove you've understood. Prove that you're not still holding something against me for that *one* mistake. I came here to ask you to marry me. I spent all of that money and time and effort to show you that I wasn't just hanging around you because it was convenient or because we were in the same city. I came here to convince you that I really love you and want us to spend the rest of our lives together. Joy, marry me."

So, this is the moment that the choice is made. Will I live to regret having turned down the love of a lifetime or live to regret agreeing to marry the wrong man? He's right he has made quite an effort to prove his point; to show he loves me. It seems the perfect beginning to a lifelong love, but it is not perfect because of one problem. I don't love him. I don't love him because I don't trust him. Somehow, I know that will not change.

"No Kyle, I cannot marry you, I will not. I am sorry, you spent all of that money, time, and effort to come here… I thought that I had made my answer very clear back in LA."

"I spent some time at Peter's wedding talking with your Uncle John, and he told me how he had flown to Paris to convince his wife to marry him right then and there."

"Yes, I know the story about Aunt Sylvia."

"Anyway, after I heard that story, I was inspired to show you how much I care, how much I really love you I'm sorry that you were not convinced, but it was worth it for me. I would have done anything to take the chance that I could persuade you. You are worth it to me. I guess I am just not worth it to you."

"Kyle, please! Don't think that this is a question of being worthy. If it were only that, there would be no question. You're a wonderful, intelligent, talented and kind man. You will be a fine husband and father. You're wonderful with kids."

"Then, why won't you marry me?"

"I can't! It would condemn you to living in constant fear of me thinking you're a failure. You're a great guy, but I can't live every day for the rest of my life, wondering if you will make the same kind of mistake again and put everything at risk."

"I *won't!* I know what it cost me in time and heartache, and it is something I will *never* allow to happen again."

"That's great! I hope for your sake, it's true."

"It is true. I promise… It's not right that you expect someone to be perfect, to never have made a mistake. People, especially men, are human, and that means they will make mistakes."

"I know that. I have made mistakes myself to prove that to be true. That doesn't mean that I have to give up my right to have the best chance to be happy in a relationship. I should be able to choose as much, as possible, what I feel comfortable with. I don't expect my husband to be perfect, just as I hope he does not expect me to be perfect."

"What is it that you are not comfortable with?"

"I know for sure that I do not handle or deal well with this particular kind of this lack of exercising good judgment and discernment. At least I know that about myself. Do you know why you have to *ask* me to marry you? Why don't you simply make an order and have a computer select me? Why you don't you go to a store and pick me off the shelf and then pay for me at the register? It's because I have to *agree* for it to be a marriage after the wedding. Right now, I choose to say I don't agree that we could be happily married."

Seeing the hurt and desperate expression on Kyle's face tugged at her heart. The words Grandma Martha had told her at Peter's wedding strengthened her resolve. "*No*, Kyle, for the last and final time. I will not marry you." Joy stood to her feet and started to walk toward the residence.

Kyle quickly moved to walk beside her. "If you keep refusing to accept love, you will end up old and alone. Is that what you want?"

"No! That's not what I want, but I know this: If the choice is to live making two people miserable or to live in misery all by myself, then I choose the latter. In the mean time I will keep my heart, ears and eyes open to see who God will call into my life. I trust Him to do the best for me. Look," she said stopping to face him. "I'm doing far too much talking, right now and … Anyway, there is really nothing more to say. Good-bye Kyle." She reached out to shake his hand.

Kyle looked down at her hand as if it were some foreign object. He looked up at her face, then over her head. He suddenly threw his hands up and shook his head. "No! This is not goodbye. I am not giving up. This is wrong, Joy. You'll see." He turned still shaking his head and walked away in the opposite direction.

She let the breath out that she had been holding, worried that Kyle would not leave. Relieved that he had gone, she walked back to the residence. She turned to climb the entry stairs, and heard her name called for the second time this morning.

Lionel walked up to her smiling. "Joy! I was afraid you got lost. Hey, Little Sister you left out this morning before I had a chance to say I'm sorry about last night."

"Lionel, I don't believe you are sorry. I believe you had planned for things to go exactly as they did. You are really, really ... I don't know the word! I don't have anything more to say to you, and I don't want to hear anything you have to say." She continued to walk up the stairway.

"If you had ever been in love, you would understand. Sometimes the feeling erases everything and every other thought."

"What?" She descended the stairway again to stand in front of him. "Listen! I love a lot of people, but it is a *real* love, Lionel. It's not some lustful frenzy that makes me forget promises and responsibilities."

"Okay, I'll let you cool off." He began backing away. "We can talk next week."

"Don't even try to ..." She stopped in mid-sentence because he had turned and was hurrying down the street. *The nerve of that guy*, she thought as she hurried up the steps. Just as she was about to push the door open, she heard Kyle call her name, again.

"Joy, wait!"

He is insane, she thought as she swung around to face him.

"Joy? I'm going to leave this afternoon and I thought maybe we can at least spend the rest of the morning together. I mean I did come all this way."

"Don't take this as a lack of appreciation for your efforts, but I am very tired and I just want to get warm, get bathed, and get some sleep." She pushed the doorbell.

"Okay. I can appreciate that. I'll go and let you go and do all of those things. I'm leaving, but this is not goodbye. I want you to know that. You'll see," he said as he turned and walked away.

"This *is* good-bye Kyle. *You* are the one who will see," she whispered to his retreating back. The guard asked, through the intercom, for her to enter her code. The release buzzer sounded in response, she pushed the door open and finally went inside.

Chapter 11

The phone rang and Joy tried to quickly chew the English muffin in her mouth as she walked to answer it. Swallowing, she answered. "Hello, Visions of Joy."

"Are you rested now? You were so tired when you got back on Tuesday."

"Yes, Peter, I am fully rested now. The trip was just incredible."

"Our was amazing. Hey, we have to get together and exchange trip stories."

"Yeah, that would be nice. You want to come up this weekend? It will be my treat for both of you. I can cook Friday night and we can take a picnic lunch up to the lake on Saturday."

"That sounds very relaxing, and just what we need."

"Okay, I'll see you Friday."

"What time is dinner served?"

"Try to be here by 7:30."

"Good. See you Friday."

⁂

Joy watched as Peter looked over the dishes on the table with a frown.

"So, you went somewhere for only six weeks, and it changed how you eat?"

"It didn't change how I eat. I'd say it added some things to my list of favorites. Come on have a seat, you guys. When I got home. I looked in the international food section of the market and was happy to find some of them. Like this for example. It takes twenty minutes to cook from start to finish and it's wonderful for a different texture and taste. Use it kind of like you use rice."

"What is it?"

"It's couscous. Take a little bit of everything then add more of what you like: chickpeas, chicken, vegetables..."

"Ah! I see this on menus sometimes. I have always wondered what it would be like, but never had the courage to try it."

Joy watched as Peter and Natalie followed her example and dished the food onto their plates and tasted

"Well? What do you think?"

"It's pretty good," Peter said savoring the grain in his mouth.

"Great! I really came to like it when I was in Tunis. It actually has very little taste, until you put some kind of sauce on it."

"You'll have to teach me to prepare it now that my husband has taken a liking to it."

"I would be glad to do so, sister-in-law, Natalie. It's really simple. But I was going to suggest that you tell him if he wants a Maghreb dinner, he has to drive you up here. That way you get a free dinner, he has a happy stomach, and I have a pleasant dinner with nice company."

"Sounds like a win, win, win situation," Peter said with his mouth full.

"This marinated chicken is wonderful, too. The chickpeas and ... I'm coming to spend a weekend with you to learn how to make all of these."

"You are most welcome."

"I feel an over indulgence in the making."

"No! Don't give in to the temptation. You have to save room for my *piece de resistance*. We have a special rice pudding for dessert."

"Choices! There are too many good choices."

"Okay. If there is no room for the pudding tonight, I will make it a part of tomorrow's picnic lunch."

"That's a great idea, Little Sister. It's supposed to be sunny tomorrow and should be pretty nice at the lake."

"So, what kinds of things are there to do?"

"There's lots to do in the water: paddle boats, fishing, water skiing, parasailing, swimming, canoeing. Wait, I have sketches I can show you. Let's eat then talk."

⁂

"Are you sure I can't help with the dishes?"

"My dishwasher will be so happy to have a chance to flex its muscles. It will take me all of five minutes to put everything in. You go get your pictures ready."

"You know your brother has everything filed in albums by the day and place. That's what's in the sack."

"Well, mine are not yet filed, but I do have them in stacks of where they were taken."

"That will have to do."

"Oh, I have some sketches of people and the souks, that's the marketplace."

"That's what I would like to see."

"Then you shall. I'll be right there. On second thought, you can go to the studio and get the three sketch pads next to the phone. You can start looking at them and choose one that you would like to have. How's that, for a treat?" When there was no answer, she turned around to see Natalie rushing down the hall to the studio.

⁂

"Your sketches are captivating. I mean I can feel the joy of this older shop owner in the souks watching this child."

"I like that one too. It was his grandson, and I would pass by this shop each morning walking up to the university. He would babysit while his daughter did her morning shopping. He was always so happy. He told me it's what made it worth getting up early each morning, knowing he would see the smile on his grandchild's face."

"How sweet? Who's this?"

"That is one of the most interesting young men I have ever met, Hammed. I think he was the youngest shop owner in all the souks. He was by far the most ambitious and intelligent. He told me he started as a sheepskin curer. He would go to the slaughterhouse each day and purchase the skins, take them down to a secluded part of the beach and soak them in the seawater, dry them on the rocks and then soak them again until they were cured. Then sell them to the leather bag makers. He had saved money with the wild idea of becoming one of the people selling bags to townspeople and tourists. His father died, and his older brother became too ill to work. When he first proposed to his brother that he could take over the shop, his brother had laughed. Then he showed him the money he had saved, his brother was shocked and then convinced. Instead of selling the shop to a friend, he agreed to take the money as partial payment and let Hammed pay the rest over time. Because he knew leather and all the leather dealers, he was able to make a good business. I was very impressed by his salesmanship. More important was the fact that he opened my eyes."

"He opened your eyes? How could he open your eyes? Joy, you see more detail in something simple than millions of other people."

"He would play this guessing game with me."

"What is the guessing game?"

"Let her tell the story, Natalie," Peter said walking in. "She's an artist, remember? She's not going to leave out any details."

"You can't tell when Peter is complementing or insulting you, sometimes," Joy said.

"You just have to assume he's insulting you."

"Then, for your sake, I will explain the guessing game. From a distance, he would guess the nationality of a person, by the way, they walked, looked at things along the way, and dressed. As they neared his shop, he would greet them in their native language and beckon them to come inside. Mind you, he knew how to sell bags in six languages. They would be so happy to hear their own language, they would answer his beckon and usually come in and buy something. I asked him why he didn't call everyone. He explained to me that he watched them as they walked down the path to see which type of things caught their attention. If they were interested in bags, he knew he had a customer. If not, the chances of making a sale were much lower. He was so good, he would tell me the nationality and how much he would make on the sale. You know what? He was usually right."

"How did you get to be such friends?"

"One day as I was passing by, he asked me what country I was from. He was surprised when I told him and a little disbelieving. I asked him why. He said that if I were a real American, my walking pace would be quicker and that I would not just walk by never looking at anything in particular. He had watched me carefully for a few weeks, and I had perplexed him—one of the rare times he was not able to guess a nationality. So, he decided to ask, in case someone like me ever came by again."

"That is a fantastic story."

"Even more, he was already training his younger brother Abdul to be able to do the same things, and I played the guessing game with him when Hammed was busy."

"Here's another shop owner, Abu-Bakar." She pointed out another drawing. "His family had been coppersmiths for generations. They would hammer out a platter, blacken it and then engrave it with a very detailed drawing or story. They were very intricate and fine drawings, beautiful work. I brought one back with me."

"I think I saw it next to the phone, leaning against the counter."

"Exactly! Okay, now. Did you choose the one you want?"

"I need more time. I'll look through them again." Natalie sighed. "Peter, you go ahead and show her the pictures from our trip to Zimbabwe."

"Okay. I will go straight to the ones from the falls. We can work forward or backward from there."

"Start with the day you went to the falls. Where did you stay?"

"We stayed at a place called the Tower of the Rainbow. It was near the town center, so we walked into town a couple of times to shop for souvenirs and eat something different from hotel food. At the same time, it wasn't far at all from the falls. After breakfast, a van came to pick us up and took us to the other side of the small town to the falls."

"That sounds convenient."

"It's striking that this little sleepy rural town is sitting right next to one of the most magnificent natural wonders in the world!"

"You can't even tell there's anything like it nearby, from the hotel."

"When you're there at the falls, you have to yell to be heard. It's called Victoria Falls because Livingston named it after his queen of course, but the real name is something like 'the mist that thunders'. When we arrived, the van parked across the street from the national park entrance. There is an entire strip mall of shops renting plastic raincoats and rubber slippers in all kinds of bright colors. Our guide told us that we should rent them, even though it might not seem like we would need them. When we saw him take his personal rain poncho out of the van, we were convinced. Standing in line to go in, we could hear a sound just like you hear when you're approaching the cataracts of a fast-moving river. I was standing there talking to Natalie and started feeling these little droplets on my face now and then. I knew it was sunny and hot, but I couldn't help looking up. I could see these small drops falling like the sprinkles before it rains, but the sky was bright blue and sunny. We were so glad that we had rented the raincoats, just a few minutes later. As we walked along the path beside the falls, it started to rain. I mean, heavy rain in spots."

"Wow!"

"And we kept looking up at the sky, as if things were going to change."

"I couldn't help myself. It's not true that 'seeing is believing'. I kept looking up, because I was getting soaked, completely drenched with water falling from above without a cloud in the sky. The context was so unusual; I had to confirm the fact over and over again. Several separate falls combine to make the national park and form the Victoria Falls. In some spots, the depth of the drop is so great that the mist obscures it and you can't see the bottom. The amount of water falling changes depending on the season, you know, and whether it's been raining or not. We took these pictures, Joy, but they don't capture the experience of being there—standing in the rain from below surrounded by the deafening roar, out in the middle of nowhere. It's just indescribable!"

"Wow! Sounds like you were moved."

"It was one of the most moving experiences I have had from a natural scene on earth. It was second only to staring into space at universes beyond the Milky Way."

"Even *I* got goosebumps standing there. I agree with Peter, it was quite moving. You know what I was thinking? If I can be overwhelmed by one of God's creations in one part of the world, how much more should I be overwhelmed by the One who made it and all the rest of creation and the worlds beyond."

"How humbling it was to stand there and remember that He still cares for us as if there were nothing else in creation to be concerned about."

"I am even more determined to get there, now. Can you tell me how we could have lived so near for all those years and not know about this, Peter?"

"We heard about it but never bothered to discover the details. We were so busy, caught up in our daily goals and activities, we didn't look beyond the sunrise and sunset where we were. I think people all over the world have heard about Victoria Falls. I wonder what percent of those who have the means have come to see it."

"Don't we kind of do the same thing with God?"

"What do you mean, Joy?" Natalie asked.

"I mean, we've all heard about God, but how many of us limit our experience in the presence of God's awesomeness or limit our exposure to His vision for our lives. We only ask Him to help us in our limited daily responsibilities and the needs that we can see? What about the other things which He wants to lead us toward, beyond that? Perhaps there is a life somewhere that will amaze and move us deeply."

"Joy, do you believe we limit God in our lives by not letting Him show us what He has created for us?"

"Do we have to make the effort to go where His promise leads us?"

"I don't know, but I don't want to limit God in my life. I want to go as far as He says I should go—to be moved and amazed."

"I do, too."

"Me, too."

"Let's help each other to do that by reminding each other. You two have each other. Until I find my mate, I especially need your help. Is that a deal?"

"That's a deal," Natalie and Peter chimed together.

There was silence for several minutes. Joy thought for a while about possibilities and what that would mean.

"I have a feeling I will be heading home soon. I don't know for how long or to do what. That's just what I feel. It seems like I would be going backward or limiting my horizons, but we will see."

"I think so, too." Peter agreed.

"I was going to say that, but it's not home for me. We passed through Nairobi and spent two days with Mom and Dad. It was my first time and kind of scary, but Peter was always by my side. I think it's doable."

"We have to remember that if it's what God has in the plan, it is more than doable. It's wonderful."

"Yes, you're right of course. It *will* be wonderful. Thank you for the very first reminder in our new deal."

Later that night, Joy had an idea that would not let her sleep. She finally threw back the covers and went to the studio desk, looked for a business card she had filed away, and dialed. The phone ringing at the other end sounded so far away. She had second thoughts about the call and was about to hang up when the ringing stopped.

"Hello?"

"Wambui? This is Joy Anderson. I came by to visit the school last year …"

"Yes, I remember. You were here visiting your family. You're Natalie's, friend right?"

"Exactly. I wanted to see if you would be willing to consider a proposal?"

"What kind of proposal are you thinking about? You mentioned a couple of ideas when you were here."

"This is bigger than anything we talked about. I will give you a brief overview of my thoughts. If you are interested, I can send you an email with some details. What I need for you to do is to see what you think is possible and write a detailed outline. I will take it, refine it to reflect the interests here, put a budget with it and submit it as a proposal intention letter. If they are interested, and I will do everything to assure that they are, we will have to work closely to finalize a proposal."

"No problem. If it benefits the students, I will do my best."

"Okay, in brief, I would like to see a regular interchange between the schools. That is, students coming here for exposure and more training as well as students from here going for a semester at a time to get exposure and training in cultural artistry. There would also be instructors from here for a semester at a time to teach subjects like the latest filming techniques and for them to learn some cultural aspects of the visual arts and instructors from there coming here to give classes on African art and to learn techniques."

"That sounds wonderful."

"Great! I will send you an email with some more details. In turn, you can see what the possible numbers and times would be and specific activities. Don't limit yourself. Think big! We can always start as a pilot but the full scale needs to be appreciated. Once I refine it with the budget, I will send it to you. You can look it over and give your final approval before it goes in."

"This is exciting! I'm waiting for your email. It will be a top priority when it arrives. We have needed something like this badly, Joy."

"So have we, Wambui. So have we. I have thought about this quite a bit, so I should be able to get it to you this week."

"The sooner it arrives, the better."

"Okay, bye."

"Bye." Joy did a little happy dance. *It has been a long time since I've done a happy dance. I'm going to call Dad and let him know. First, though, I'm telling Peter and Natalie because we have a deal!*

Three days later Joy tapped the send option on email and afterward said a prayer that Wambui would respond soon. Almost immediately, she responded that she had received the email and had been working on her own a little, based on what Joy had explained. She predicted that she could complete her part over the next four days.

Joy did another happy dance. *That's twice in the same week. What's going on?* She picked up the receiver to make another call to Natalie and Peter.

She returned from the church cell group, she found an email from Wambui with all of the needed information. It was late but she could not resist the temptation to start finalizing the details for the proposal intention letter. The time flew by; and when she next looked at the clock, it was 1:30 am. The letter was finished and sent it off to Wambui for final approval. *Let's see Wambui is in tomorrow afternoon with the time zone difference and should be able to glance over the letter to send it back the same day.*

I'll be a mess in the morning, but I will be satisfied that the ball is in their court. She yawned as she rubbed her eyes. Tomorrow is Friday anyway, **a** pretty light day for me usually. She calculated that there would be plenty of time to print the letter out and get it over to the administration building by late morning or early afternoon. She yawned passionately and shuffled off to bed.

Despite going to bed so late, she was up at the usual 6:30 and went straight to the computer. Wambui's response was there. 'Confirmation is given for green light, as is.' But there were also two emails from the book publisher. In the first one, there was a report on her books sales with a notice of a deposit. The second offered an advance on the next book proposed.

Wow! I may be able to finance this myself if this continues. She consulted her watch. It was too early to call Natalie and Peter. She'd have to settle for an email for the time being. Just as she tapped send, she yawned passionately, again. The coffee shop would be the first stop when she got to campus. Her first class was at 8:00 am.

Chapter

12

"The whole town is talking about this new program, Joy. It seems like I am always congratulating you for something wonderful you've done."

"Thank you, Kyle. I hear that you are due congratulations as well. Where is it that you are off to this time?"

"I'm off to Brazil for a year this time. I figured I might as well get all my traveling in while I still had no family responsibilities."

"That sounds like good reasoning. Best wishes. I hear it is an amazing place. Don't forget to visit the falls."

"The falls? Why?"

"You'll know when you get there, but here's a hint: There are only three places in the world that have anything like it."

"Okay... Well, wish you all the best on this new project. Remember if you need a good finance/accounting consultant, there's one waiting to help."

"Thanks, Kyle, but I think we have that covered." She smiled in the direction of Peter as he approached.

"Hi, Peter. So, you're back as well? Nice!" He smiled and shook Peter's hand.

"Yes, I had an amazing offer that I couldn't refuse. It's a start-up foundation, a sharp learning curve for me with one set of national laws superimposed on the other. I think that there will be national branches soon to keep things simple. My brother tells me that he knows a good lawyer to negotiate the course for us to get settled officially here for the foundation."

"Congratulations, and all the best."

"Thanks, and the same for you."

"Sorry, Kyle, for the interruption. I'm going to have to take her away from you," He grabbed Joy's hand. "I came to get you. We need you for …the program."

"Okay. Thanks again, Kyle. If I don't see you again tonight, have a safe trip."

"Thanks. I'll be back in a year and I know there will be even bigger things going on."

She walked away toward the front with Peter. "What program are you talking about? This is an open house. There is no program."

"I know, but Natalie told me to rescue you and bring you straight to her."

"Where is she?"

"Right back here," he said pointing to the front curtains.

He pulled the curtain slightly aside, creating an opening for Joy to pass through. Natalie was waiting just on the other side.

"Oh Joy, thank you for coming. I know that Kyle is an awkward situation at best, so I figured I would send Peter to rescue you."

"Thanks, but I was okay."

"At the same time, I have some news I wanted to share with you; but I didn't want to tell you in front of everyone."

"What's wrong?"

"It's not bad news."

"What is it?"

"I just found out that we're going to have a baby."

"Oh Natalie, that is wonderful news. Congratulations, you two!" She hugged them both.

"Thanks. We haven't told anyone else yet."

"Your secret is safe with me."

"We're going over to Mom and Dad's afterward to tell them. You want to come?"

"Oh, I promised Wambui that we would meet afterward. Tell you what: If the meeting doesn't last too long, I will stop by the house hoping you're still there."

"Okay."

"Aren't they supposed to be coming here, tonight? I thought they told me they would come by for moral support -- my first open house and all."

"Yeah, I saw them. They just got here, even Grandma Martha."

"Really? Let me look for them. I'll see you both later." She hugged Natalie, again and walked back through the curtain.

She did a general visual sweep of the room and spotted them near the front door. One of the helpers arrived with a chair for Grandma Martha. She seemed to sit down heavily, and then began looking around the room her elf. Joy began making her way toward her. Their eyes met, and she smiled in greeting. Joy signaled to her that she was coming over to her, and she nodded her head.

"So, how do you feel?" Grandma asked after she hugged her.

"I feel great. I wanted to thank you for your wonderful idea. This is all because of a proposal to my school. I can be here, and it's counted as me being there. There are two other instructors with me. We are the guinea pigs. Very happy guinea pigs, mind you. I think if those two come back alive, others will sign up. The students who came with us just dived right in. They already have a field trip scheduled for a visit to the wood carvers."

"That's great. Their lives will never be the same. They don't know anything, yet."

"No, they don't know anything, yet. They won't even understand all that they learn here at first, but if they are wise it will become a very good part of them."

"That's why you're here, you know."

"Why do you say that?"

"God gave you the idea and the favor to make it happen. But unless there is someone here with the right mind and heart, it won't be all that it should. You're the right one, Joy. That's why you're here; but don't forget that the people with you are also the right ones for the part that they will play or for what they will learn, to be used in the future."

"I hope you're praying that I listen to God's guidance."

"I am."

"Good. Do you want something to drink?"

"I was hoping they would have something good to eat."

"I'm warning you to be prepared for disappointment. We're running this on a shoestring, so the drinks are good, all fresh juices, but the food is not. It's those little appetizers, the ones that are just one mouthful each."

"Oh, then I will take some mango juice please."

"Okay, I'll be right back."

"Joy, you spend time with the other guests. Ask Natalie to bring it to me."

"Okay." As she walked away to look for Natalie, she thought. *Natalie's secret would not be a secret for much longer. In fact, it was as if Grandma knew already.*

She looked back over her shoulder at Grandma. She was sitting quietly and watching Joy as she crossed the room. She smiled again at her, and then Joy turned to quickly find Natalie.

She found her talking with Wambui and told her of Grandma's request.

"Wambui, excuse us a minute, please. Don't leave. This will only take a second."

"Sure."

She pulled Natalie quickly to the side. "I have a warning for you. I think God has already given Grandma the news."

"Seriously, you think she knows?"

"I just don't want you to think I told her anything, but she asked for you specifically."

"Okay, thanks for the warning." They walked back over to Wambui.

"I'll go get her juice and be right back, you two."

"Okay. So, Wambui, we can talk a little now if you want. It seems that people are more interested in talking to each other and looking at the art than asking us questions."

"I think that's good. The program is not about us. It is about the students and their work that fills this room."

"You're right. What did you want to talk about?"

"I wanted to know if you think it would be better to try to keep the regular schedule with all of these field trips."

"I think that it's good that they want to go see firsthand how things are done, but they have to keep the regular schedule and have to get the field trip approved and scheduled. We could easily have people everywhere with no control over the activities."

"That's true, but the local students know where the other artists are and when."

"Maybe we can give one morning a week for free time to do group field trips or individual field trips. The rest of the time they are to be in scheduled activities or have specific permission."

"I'll redo the schedule to reflect that change. I think, for safety purposes, if they plan to be off campus on the free morning, they have to give details of the activity before they leave and a contact number."

"I agree."

"Good, that's basically all. I made the schedule for the instructors who have come; and the students chose their subjects before they arrived, so they have a schedule as well. Attendance will be taken and marks will be given in the form of a transcript when they leave at the end of the semester. I did negotiate a freight allowance for all the things they will want to take home, like primary materials, their own work, purchases, gifts and souvenirs. I hope they never forget this experience and have plenty of reminders and things to share when they return home."

"That's a great idea. I hope you didn't forget that I like to have my classes early so that the rest of the day is free to help or advise."

"I didn't forget at all. You start every day at 8:00 am and you have two to three classes per day. Of course, like we said, if we give them one morning free for field trips, the schedule will have to change a bit. You will have to be free to go with them since most of these trips will be a large group on the bus, unless someone arranges for an individual trip."

"Could you try to make the other two instructors free the same morning so that we can have the option of going with three different groups or all going together to see something interesting."

"Good idea."

"Deep breath, Wambui. This is going to be a great four months, and it doesn't start officially until Monday morning. That means we have the whole weekend to tie up any loose ends. You have three instructors and six students from America. If the American students have their way, they'll have the Kenyan students speaking American slang like pros, by the time they go to California next semester."

"I know. I heard some lessons going on."

"You'll be going back to that side of the world for the first time in four years. Isn't that what you said?"

"Yes, although it seems like a lifetime ago."

"You won't be in Vancouver, but it's not far away. What is it you wanted to focus on?"

"I want to focus on stained glass techniques. The other instructor, Mr. Mithuri, going this time is a specialist in beaten copper tableaus and inlays."

"I remember the instructor for glass etching was really interested in learning how he does that. This is all so exciting."

"Yes, exciting is the word."

"I'm going to leave right after we close. I need to stop by my parents."

"That's fine. I'm not hanging around either, now. I'm glad we were able to talk."

"I'll stop by tomorrow to see if there is anything I can help out with."

"Okay, see you then."

Joy looked over the room and spotting Natalie, went to give her an update.

"Natalie, I already had the meeting with Wambui, so I'm coming right over to be with you and Mom and Dad although, again, I am the fifth wheel."

"Why do you keep saying that? I don't feel that way. I consider you a part of our life, especially since the deal."

"Thanks. Things did change a lot when all of us agreed on that."

"You should ride with us since we have to come back past here to go home and so do you. Just leave your car, and get it on the way back. That way we can spend the driving time talking."

"Okay, that sounds like a good idea. What happened when you took Grandma Martha her juice?"

"I don't know what was going on. She just thanked me and asked how I was doing. You know, all the usual things, then she just smiled really big and said that was very nice. She invited us over for dinner any time we were free, every night until we really got settled in, if we wanted. She was really nice. When she finished her juice, she handed me the glass and thanked me again and I left."

"I think she didn't want to scare you off, first thing."

"Yeah, that's probably so. Anyway, everyone will know before the night is out. Joseph and Faith are coming over, too."

"We haven't all been there at the same time in years. This is really a grand occasion."

"It is, at least, for me."

"It is for all of us. Maybe you will have a little boy. We will have one of each sex in this fifth generation, to start with."

"Either way, I'll be happy."

"So will all the rest of us."

As Peter guided the car to exit the expressway on to a familiar city street he, Natalie and Joy were caught up in their own reflections of the night's events.

"That was wonderful, you guys!" Joy called from the back seat over the roar of the car's motor.

"I can't get over Grandma Martha," Natalie mused

"I told you not to be surprised if she already knew you were pregnant."

"But how?"

"If you spend much time around her, you'll find yourself asking that a lot."

"I guess so."

"Joy is right, Natalie. I'd forgotten how unnerving that can be... Hey Joy, did you see how happy Dad was?"

"Yes, but you know he has always loved kids. He thinks he's one himself. You're right, Peter. It was good to see him so happy. Yeah, and then I laughed so much at you and him with your happy dance!"

"Yeah, what is that exactly?"

"Oh, it's this thing Dad made up when he first came here and saw that there were traditional dances for everything. He didn't know any back then, so he decided to make one up so that 'his tribe' would have its own dance. Mom still laughs so much every time he does that."

"I know. You would think she would be bored with it after all these years."

"It was fun, although it was my first time. Following you guys around the living room, I really felt it was a dance of rejoicing."

"It was! We were all so happy."

"That's why it's called the happy dance," Peter said parking his car beside Joy's.

"Well, here we are and on that happy note, I will say good night. See you Monday morning, Peter."

"We'll wait, until we see you start your car. Why do you always buy these questionable cars, Joy?"

"You know, I will only be here part of each year, and I have my other car in California. Why spend a lot of money on a car which I will use only part of the year and for short distances. I don't plan on making any long trips. Good night, Sister-in-law."

"Good night, Joy."

The car started without a problem and they both pulled out of the parking lot. Joy turned to the left at the corner. Peter honked as he turned to the right. It wasn't until she was halfway home that Joy remembered she had left her new mobile phone in the office.

"Why did I even get that phone? I spend more time looking for it than using it," she said to herself. Then she thought, Am I talking out loud to myself like Dad always does? That cannot be a good sign. Anyway, I'd better go back and get it. Otherwise, I'll have Peter or Dad coming to my house when they call to make sure I have arrived safely and there's no answer.

Back at the campus, she made sure the key to the office door was in her hand before she opened her car door, then walked quickly to the office building's side door in the dark. Grasping the handle to insert the key her pulse quickened as she found it already unlocked.

Chapter 13

HESITANTLY OPENING THE DOOR, she went inside, slid the deadbolt closed behind her. The thought crossed her mind that doing this meant she was possibly locked in with a thief or worse. She quickly reasoned again that it also meant that if a thief had seen her enter, he would not be able to just follow her into the building. She listened and heard nothing. "Is there anyone here?" she called out. There was no answer.

What was I thinking I would gain by that? Only someone who is supposed to be there would have answered. She walked cautiously down the hall to the office where the light was on. That's interesting. I made a point of turning it off when I left. Intending to surprise the intruder, she jumped in front of the open doorway, her arms raised in protective Judo style, but the room was empty as far as she could see. Relieved, she crossed the room and was almost at her desk, when, she heard a sound behind her. Swinging around with her arms raised again, she scanned the room, but there was no one to be seen. Confused, she dropped her arm again. Just as she was beginning to chide herself for hallucinating, out of the corner of her eyes she caught sight of a familiar movement in the far side of the room on the floor. She walked closer to investigate. It was a baby lying on a blanket, making playful sounds with hands and legs moving. She went even closer and became even more confused to see the baby clean, well dressed, and obviously happy, but all alone. There was a frantic pounding on the door she had entered just moments before. She picked the baby up and walked quickly back down the hall.

"Yes? Who is there?"

"I am Miriam, the cleaner. Please open the door."

"Oh, Miriam, wait a minute!" She had seen Miriam in passing a few times talking to Wambui near the end of the workday. Joy positioned the baby on her left hip and slid the deadbolt open. The door was immediately pulled open and Miriam quickly pushed two empty trash bins inside and removed the work gloves.

"I was so afraid," she said, eagerly reaching for the baby. "I thought someone come, locked the door and gone. I left just for little time to carry trash bin to the alley. My keys are inside. I don't know what I would do if my baby left inside." She closed her eyes, hugging the baby close to her.

"I'm so sorry I gave you a scare. I left my phone and when I came back to look for it, I found the door open. I thought someone had forgotten to lock the door and then I found the baby."

"She not crying? She is good baby, very quiet child. That's why I name her Salome."

"No, she was not crying. She was very quiet, but, Miriam, why do you have her here? She should be asleep at home."

A frightened look flashed across her face as she darted past Joy and down the hall carrying a bin with one hand and the baby with the other.

"I almost finished. I take her home soon," she called over her shoulder.

Joy was obliged to follow her as the elusive phone was still to be found, hopefully on the office desk.

Miriam was putting the baby back on the blanket when Joy entered the office. She stood and walked quickly to take the bin to its place in the broom closet, standing open, further down the hall.

Joy found her phone but was reluctant to leave the office with the baby in the corner and Miriam busy in the other room. She was drawn to the playful baby and picked her up, again. Making funny faces and sounds her, she was delighted when the baby laughed with huge bright eyes and looked for more entertaining expressions. Miriam rushed into the room.

"I'm sorry she disturbing you."

"She's not disturbing me at all. I'm disturbing her, actually. She is such a happy baby."

"She is, even when she has little to be happy for."

"Miriam, you didn't answer my question earlier."

"I do not have anyone at home to keep her. I am alone."

"What about your family or friends?"

"I not from this country. I spend time working here or making small tapestries I sell. Please, I finished." She reached and took the baby. "Now, I will go."

"I can drop you off, if you like. I came back for my phone and I found it." She said holding the phone up for Miriam to see.

"No. I fine, thank you. I don't want make trouble."

"It's not trouble."

"No, thank you. I need this job. I walk home myself."

"Miriam, why are you afraid? I just want to help."

Miriam stared at the floor as she stood holding her baby. She turned away sharply and scurried to pick up the baby's blanket, the bag and keys on the floor.

"Look, I am not forcing you. I am going back out to my car. You can do what you normally do. If you choose to walk away that's fine. I will drive away after you leave. If you want a ride, you can come over to my car and get in."

"Why you want take me home?"

"I'm partial to babies and would just like to help, that's all."

"Okay, I ride with you."

"Great! I heard you mention that you make tapestries. Could I see them one day?"

"Yes, I will bring one Monday afternoon and leave on desk. I come when everyone is gone."

"That's okay. I'll leave a note for you on Tuesday."

"Thank you." She smiled for the first time.

On the way home, Miriam told her that she had entered the country as a refugee after crossing the border. It was not war she had fled from, but an abusive husband who had promised her parents to let her continue school. Once he paid the bride price and married her, he had taken her far from her home. There he refused to let her go to school saying there was too much work to do. Even when she stayed up late to do everything required of her, he had still refused. He said he found her too stupid to go to school, and it would be a waste of his money. Soon she was pregnant and hopeless. Once the baby was born, he started to beat her. Whenever she asked to go to school or he thought she was showing her sadness, she would get such a strong slap; it would often knock her to the ground. When the baby boy named Josef was one year old, her husband decided to take another wife. He became suspicious of Miriam, and placed her child in the charge of the other wife. This meant that she was blackmailed into submission. She could only see her Josef if she did all that was demanded of her by her husband and the new wife. It was worse than being a slave for the next year. Her heart broke when Josef began to call the other wife Mama and began to give small commands for Miriam to do things as he had seen the other wife do. She decided to kill herself, but then found she was pregnant again. So, she decided to run away instead. She knew this meant that she would never see Josef, but he was no longer her son. She thought she would die of sadness if the new baby was taken in the same way.

"How did you get away?"

"They don't think that I leave my son, so they leave me free to do the work. One day, I take the money for shopping and walk the way to the market, but I not stop at market. I walk for five days. I use market money to buy to eat and ask nice people give me water. When I drink water, I ask way to border. When I crossed, I ran to refugee camp. I only want to rest and get strong because I decide to come to Nairobi and find way to go school. It take so long because I pay for transportation across big desert areas. I not let anyone know I have things very expensive or they try to beat me or kill me for take it. You know they very poor. They not know I have gold bracelets, so I have good idea to make tapestries from old sacks and knitted clothes that people threw away. I just needed a part of sisal sack and the sweater with holes no one wanted. I take them loose and wash the threads. I draw design on the sack and sew small pieces of thread through, one by one and tie knot to hold there. I find right color when I can. Sometimes, I just use what I have. In Marsabit when Salome born. I stayed and made tapestries there. I sell them to tourists and save enough travel to Nairobi. When I get here, I walk around the streets and see the institute. After, I come and sit outside and watch people come and go. Miss Wambui say hello to me, when she leave every day. Then she ask me, one day, what I looking for. I ask for job cleaning because I not want her think I was beggar. She laugh and ask how old my baby. When I tell her two months, she very kind and give me chance. I come in the days first so she can watch me. When she see I am good cleaner, she let me work night. I can do other things ... sell my tapestries in day. Now three months pass, I have small house, safe, warm, for Salome."

"Wow! I am anxious to see how this tapestry looks. It sounds like something we call latch-hooking in the states."

"Here! Let me go here. My house inside."

Joy did not even look where she was pointing as she slowed to stop the car at the corner Miriam indicated. There was no use asking any more questions about her house location. Joy had already gained more territory than she had expected into the life of this fearful but, at the same time, incredibly courageous young woman.

"Work on tapestries and sell during day and clean at night. I almost save enough start school."

"Oh, I never asked what it is you wanted to study."

"Art! I love all kind art. Thank you." She scrambled out of the car and waved goodbye.

Joy waved back and drove away.

Normally, Joy would leave her place of work and be on her way home, as soon as she could. However, over the last two months a couple of times a week she had found a reason to be in the office when Miriam came to place Salome on the blanket. Salome was beginning to turn herself over and at times managed to work herself close to the blanket edge.

"She's not going to be safe in here for much longer, Miriam."

"I know."

"Maybe I can find a used playpen for her to stay in when you're here. Would that be okay?"

"Miss Joy, please. I don't want to be trouble." She frowned

"No trouble. I think I saw one in a shop in town when I was looking for something for my niece."

"Thank you." She smiled.

Salome was growing and soon began pulling herself up to stand in the playpen. She cooed and smiled often, coaxing Joy to take a few minutes to pick her up and play with her.

After three months, Miriam asked her to watch Salome one Saturday so that she could do something special. She didn't say what it was and Joy did not ask. She took Salome Friday night with the few supplies of baby things. The agreement was for Joy to meet Miriam Sunday morning at the office before church time. Miriam was not a Christian but had talked many times at length with Joy about God.

It was hard work having Salome all day, but Joy decided it was totally enjoyable. On Sunday Joy waited at the appointed time, but there was no sign of Miriam. An hour later it was time to be at church but still no Miriam. There was little choice but to wait. She had no real idea of where Miriam lived. Anyway, she would not be at home, knowing Salome was with her at the office.

"Where is Mommy?" Joy said. Salome prompted by Joy's words, looked up at the door expecting to see Miriam. She looked back at Joy confused "Sorry baby, she's not here, yet."

It was two hours later that Joy answered the call to her cell phone, "Hello?"

"Is this Miss Joy from the art institute?"

"Yes, this is Joy."

"This is Nurse Margaret from Nairobi hospital. There has been an accident involving Miriam Abdullah, and she gave you as her closest relative."

"Yes, of course." Joy felt her stomach quiver. "What happened? Is she all right?"

"She was hit by a car this morning, not far from the hospital. She is in serious but stable condition and would like for you to come to the hospital."

"Yes, of course. I'm on my way." She said and stood at the same time. Taking a deep breath, she grabbed Salome and the bag and rushed out to the car. She hurriedly secured the baby, in the child's seat as she thought how fortunate it was, she had gotten the seat for the times she had baby Hope. Salome grabbed her hand as she snapped the last buckle in place.

"Tisst!" Salome said mimicking the sound of the buckle click.

"What a smart baby you are!" Joy tickled her to distract her for the second it took to finish and close the door.

Salome laughed.

Joy went around to the driver's seat and put the key in the ignition. Her thoughts were jumping from concern to concern: Miriam's possible condition and injuries, Miriam's job, care for baby Salome during the coming school week … She glanced at Salome in the rearview mirror. She was quietly studying the buckle lying against her chest.

Wait! Let me call Natalie and Mom. She found her mobile phone in her purse. "That's a miracle," she chuckled as she dialed Natalie's number.

"Mio" Salome tried to say 'miracle' and chuckled as well.

"Hello?" the phone answered

"Natalie?"

"Yes, what happened to you today? We didn't see you after church. We're already at Mom's, but Peter has to go to a meeting in a few minutes. Where are you? Are you on your way?"

"No, I … Natalie something has happened to Miriam. She got hit by a car and she's at Nairobi Hospital. Can you and Mom meet me there?"

"Yes! Oh, my goodness. Yes, we'll meet you there."

"Thanks." She hung up and started the car.

They were in the hospital lobby when she arrived.

"Thanks for coming. I am so scattered. I did not ask where she is."

"We just got here ourselves; but we did ask the information desk, and they said she's in the ICU, bed two," Natalie explained.

"ICU? Okay, let me go see her. Can you hold the baby, Mom?"

"I think I can do that."

"Thanks." She said handing the sleepy Salome to her mom.

"Poor baby," Kathombi cooed as she took the baby.

"Here, Natalie, the bottles and everything else are in there," Joy said frowning as she handed her the baby's bag.

"Okay, we got everything. Now, go. It's that way," Natalie said.

Joy rushed down the hall in the direction she had been given.

Nurse Margaret gave her a quick briefing and then led her to bed two.

When she saw Miriam, the memory of her own surgery with the pain and discomfort washed over her like a flood. For a moment nausea and a faint feeling overwhelmed her, and she leaned against the chair to steady herself. When she looked up again Miriam was just opening her eyes.

"Oh, Miss Joy, I so sorry. I on my way …"

"Don't worry."

"How is Salome?"

"She is fine. You know she is a good baby," said to comfort her.

"Yes, she is no trouble." Miriam smiled weakly.

"How are you?"

"They say my leg broken and I loss lot of blood. They think I be okay, but I not be okay, so I write these papers."

"Miriam? Why are you worried? You will feel better tomorrow, I'm sure they know what they—"

"Please, Miss Joy, take Salome make her your daughter when I die. I want her have heart like you. She need to live with someone who loves her. I write this paper, say I have no family and don't know father. Nurse sign too, witness. She see me write and sign."

"You are going to be all right. They said you are going to be alright."

"Miss Joy, you know Jesus, you tell me about?"

"Yes, of course, you're right. We should pray."

"No, I no mean pray, now. I already pray. Jesus tell me that hear me pray. He want me get ready go with Him."

"What? You have a broken leg and a concussion, and you should be fine …"

"I tell you something, listen… very important."

"I'm listening, but—"

"I save money for school, but now it helps you take care, Salome. I put in my good shoe at house. Here, I make map my house, from where you stop at corner first night you take me home. One thing else." She took a deep breath.

"Yes?"

"My gold bracelets and earrings. I hide them since I leave my country. I never wear them; people don't think I have something to steal. I wrap in newspaper and tape in lampshade."

"How far away is your home country? You never told me where you are from."

"Better you not know. Better my mom think I dead already for her stay safe. Please tell Salome she Kenyan. She born November 5 at Marsabit."

"Let me bring Salome to see you. Then I will bring her again tomorrow and every day until you get better."

"Please," Miriam said softly and pressed the papers into Joy's hand.

"Okay, I will keep them for you," Joy said as she reluctantly accepted the papers. She stuffed then into her purse as she walked back down to the lobby.

"Mom, let me take the baby to see Miriam. I think she needs some encouragement. She's thinking she's going to die."

"Why?"

"She said Jesus told her, but the nurse says otherwise. I don't know. It may be some of the medication she's been given."

"We'll go with you."

Kathombi carried Salome, Natalie carried the bag and Joy led the way back to Miriam's bedside.

"Oh baby, good baby," Miriam exclaimed when she saw Salome.

Salome was delighted to see Miriam and wiggled to get down to her. Kathombi held her out toward Miriam as close as she could without letting her soil the bed. Miriam just clapped her hands and smiled, while making playful noises. She made no movement to take the child in her arms. Finally, Salome laughed and calmed down in Kathombi's arms.

The nurse came in and saw the group, she empathetically shook her head from side to side. "I'm sorry. The baby has to go out, and there should be no more than two visitors, at one time," she softly said.

"We were just leaving, Sister Margaret," Joy assured the nurse and then turned to reassure Miriam as well. "We'll be back this evening, Miriam. We'll let you rest for now."

"Oh, Miss Joy. I forgot to give you the keys."

"I will give her your valuables, Miriam, don't worry," the nurse assured her.

"Thank you, Sister."

She nodded to Miriam and then turned to Joy.

"Please wait for me at the desk and I will show you where you can sign her things out from the safe in admissions. You will need to fill out some information forms, as well, in case we need to contact you. I just have to make sure everything is in order." She turned and checked the IV drip and the arm where the IV entered. She began to straighten the bedsheets.

"Okay." Joy turned to usher her group toward the door.

"I'll take the baby back to the waiting room. You can find us there when you're done," Kathombi said as she also turned to walk through the door. Natalie was close behind.

"Okay, it shouldn't take long. Thanks, Mom. Thanks, Natalie."

Carrying Miriam's handbag, Joy joined them in the waiting room a few minutes later.

"Mom, could I ask you to take Salome home for a little while. I want to hurry over to Miriam's place and get her things. Worrying about them is the last thing she needs. As soon as I'm done, I'll come by to get the baby."

"No problem at all. I can't promise that your father will let you take her away too quickly. Take your time; she looks like she's due for a nap anyway. Take care of Miriam's things, and then come by for dinner. We live closer than you to the hospital. Didn't you tell her you were coming back this evening? You're going to need someone to take care of the baby again when you come back here. No, there is no hurry."

"And if Mom and Dad get tired, I need the practice. My baby will be here soon."

"I'm convinced, already. All right then. I'll see you soon."

"Everything was exactly as Miriam said she left it, fortunately. She lives in one little room with a bed and table and all the while she has all this money she's been saving up. That's discipline, Dad."

"From what you told us about her life, her dream to go to art school has been the driving force behind several unusual accomplishments."

"I know. I wish I could bottle that and sell it to parents in the states … well everywhere."

"Ah! *That* you can't buy. It's spiritual and given freely."

"Speaking of spiritual things, I was so surprised to hear her say that Jesus told her to get everything ready because she was going to be with Him. You know, I've talked with her several times about Jesus. She always politely listened, but I didn't think she was taking it all that seriously."

"That's why we just tell people of our love for him, and let God do the rest. We never know how seriously people are taking what we say."

"I guess so."

"Here she is all clean and dry, again," Grandma Martha declared as she accompanied Kathombi carrying Salome into the living room.

"Here, let me have her." Marshall held out his arms and Salome reached toward him. "Good girl."

"Don't you get her all excited, you hear? She's close to going to sleep."

"Okay, Salome. Grandma says we have to be quiet, so you can sit here and watch all the other women in the family."

"Now hold on Dad; she's not ours —"

"Yes, she is. You said Miriam gave her to you."

"I know, but I doubt that when she's back to her normal self, she is going to abide by that. She loves this baby more than she loves herself."

"Salome knows where we live now, so she can come by whenever she wants some of Grandma Martha's good food or play with

Grandpa. Isn't that right, Salome?" he said and tickled her. She laughed in response.

"She can't even walk. How is she going to come here by herself?"

"Good point but not a problem. You'll just have to bring her until she can come by herself. I warn you though, the time will pass quickly."

"Oh, time!" she looked at her watch. "I am going to miss visiting hours if I don't hurry. I'll be back soon. I just need to reassure her about her things and Salome." Joy jumped to her feet and dashed over to plant a kiss on Salome's head before heading toward the door.

"Joy, they said two can go in the room. I'll go with you. Your dad, Grandma Martha and Natalie are going to vie for baby possession until she goes to sleep."

"Okay, Mom. It would be good to have you and we won't be there long." She slipped her arm through her mom's and they walked out to the car.

Natalie waved to them from the kitchen window as the car backed down the drive way and drove away.

It was hours later that Natalie recounted to Joy what had happened next. She went back to the living room, where she found Marshall frowning. Before she could ask him the reason, he asked her a question.

"What is that sound?"

"Sound?" She listened for a few seconds. "Oh, it's Joy's phone. She always forgets it."

"I think you should answer it," Marshall sighed.

"Yes, you definitely should," Grandma Martha sighed as well.

"Okay." Natalie walked over and picked up the phone. "Hello. No. This is her sister-in-law. Can I take a message? Oh, no," Natalie gasped and plopped down on the sofa. "She's… on her way. She should be there in a few minutes. Yes, of course. Bye." She sat stunned.

"What's wrong, Natalie?"

"Dad, you are not going to believe this? That was the hospital. Miriam just died."

Chapter 14

"THANK YOU FOR COMING, today. I want you to know we were as eager to find out what happened in the death of Miriam Abdullah as well. Now you understand, because the death was unexpected and we did not have an immediate cause of death, the law required an autopsy. We would have recommended that one be done anyway, so we could have some answers." He picked up the report from his desk and scanned it. "She died from internal bleeding because her body was unable to normally stop the bleeding. She gave no history of having this problem before. The exam showed this was caused by severe liver dysfunction. Surprisingly, the liver was almost destroyed by cancer that would have killed her in six to eight months."

"She had cancer?"

"Yes, a particularly horrible type of cancer. She was fortunate to have died quickly of something else, beforehand."

"I couldn't understand why God would allow this woman who had endured so much to get to the point where she could finally realize her dream only to be robbed of it all. Now, I see it was God's merciful intervention so that her end would not be filled with suffering that had marked her life before."

"You could say that. I did not know much about her life. What is important is that we have an answer for the reason she died. Of course, I mean the physical or medical reason. We are always looking for information to allow us to improve our care. You can imagine this was quite a concern for us."

"Yes. Well, thank you, Doctor Mwangi." Joy stood to shake the doctors' hand.

"Again, let me express my condolences for your loss."

"Thank you. The funeral is on Saturday out at my family's village in Meru."

"My prayers will be with you and your family."

"Thank you."

"I'm sure she would have been happy to know that she was laid to rest in the family plot, with all of our other dear family members," Kathombi mused.

"I don't think she would have been half as happy about her getting to be with the dead family as she would have been to know that Salome is happily in the arms and hearts of the living family," Marshall said as he made a silly face at Salome to make her laugh.

"Oh, my goodness. Dad, what am I going to do about Salome? I mean I am supposed to go back to work in California a month from now."

"Yes."

"You know how I've said I am waiting for a husband to find me, and that I am ready to start a family."

"Yes."

"I am obviously not and I have to admit it. I've signed a contract that is going to prevent me from taking care of this beautiful child, no matter how much I want to. What would I do if someone asked me to marry him tomorrow?"

"I have no idea about the details of how it would be resolved. I do know one thing is true. Even if it had to be through a miracle, there would be an answer. God is never caught by surprise, and His plans are infallible. Why don't you ask Him?"

"Yes. Maybe now that the funeral and all of that business is done, I can turn to get further details about moving forward. I don't know."

"Then you are in a wonderful position."

"I said I *don't* know; I have *no* idea how I am going to pull this off."

"I know, Little Sister. *I* say you're in a wonderful position because you don't have to worry about getting rid of a wrong idea. You can hear clearly and obey, immediately."

"Leave it to you, to somehow find the positive in being lost."

"It's all in how you see things."

"If I could at least get to stay for the summer, I would have the time to work all of this stuff out. The other instructors could escort the students back home. I don't even know how to get a passport for Salome to go back with me."

"If you stay for the summer, you have three more months to work all of that out. You'll have to formally adopt her first, I think. You should ask Joseph's lawyer to guide you or refer you to someone who can," Marshall said.

"That's a great idea. What if everything's not done by the time I have to go? Do you think I could leave Salome here with you?"

"We would have to see how that would work out."

"I would hate to miss her birthday, though. Oh Dad! This is hard," Joy said.

"Life always is. You know what they say in situations like this? They ask the question: "How do you eat an Elephant?""

"Yes, I know the answer: One bite at a time. I'll call Joseph," Joy said and stood up.

"Joy?"

"Yes. Oh, right! I should pray first," Joy said sitting back down.

"Yes, and I think Salome needs to be changed." He held the baby up and she reached out for Joy.

"Ah, I see. Only play, no work from you." She took Salome from him and gave her a kiss.

"I'm only thinking of you. I know how to do it with years of practice. I changed your nappies, Little Sister. You on the other hand have not had the chance for much practice, so you need the opportunities."

"Oh, thanks for thinking about me." She turned and scrunched her nose at him as she left to go down the hall to her old room where she had left the diaper bag.

∞

"Here she is, all changed," Joy announced on her return a few minutes later. "Dad, could you hold her, while I call Joseph?"

"Sure. I have to get back to campus in two hours. Until then, I'm in charge of the baby. I forgot to ask how your classes went this morning."

"Good. The kids these days are so smart and not afraid to try new things. They are really enjoying themselves and venturing out to new media. It's really heartening to see. This will send ripples out from this experience once they get back. California will never be the same. I can just see us being overwhelmed with applicants wanting to come next time."

"When is next time?"

"It's supposed to be next September, but I was seriously thinking of trying to make this an opportunity for both semesters. It would be great to be able to arrange to be here in Kenya year- round and welcome the students and instructors on this side of the project. If I can get one of the other instructors to be in charge on the other side, it might work. Of course, there is a little fact that I would have to get the change approved."

"That's a very good solution. You will be here all, or at least most, of the time, and I can see this little darling every day."

"It's not a done deal. As I said, it would have to be approved first."

"So how do we get it approved."

"I think I would have to write a letter requesting a proposed amendment and then it would have to go to the committee. They would see if they think it is a change that would benefit the project and the school and …"

"Salome, did you hear that?" Marshall held Salome up in front of him smiling. "She said she just has to write a letter." Marshall made a funny face. Salome giggled and waved her hands. "Yes, she just has to write one little letter," Marshall said and Salome laughed.

"Okay, I'll write the letter today."

"Now, Baby Girl, you may think this is strange, but you will get used to it as time goes on. This being your first time, I don't expect you to do this perfectly; but you must at least try. Are you ready?" Marshall held Salome up facing away from him and stood up.

"What are you doing, Dad?"

"Little Sister, I am showing Salome how to do her first happy dance. Come on."

He held Salome out in front of him as he did his wild gyrations around the room. Salome, startled at first, began to laugh and wave her arms with Marshall's movement. She laughed even more fully as Joy joined in.

"What is all the commotion in here?" Grandma Martha said as she walked into the room. "I thought as much. So, what are we celebrating? Only one thing would make me join in, and that would be if Joy is going to stay here, and we can see her and Salome all the time."

"Join on in!" Marshall nodded his head as he continued to dance.

The baby, watching her, smiled wide-eyed with delight, then started laughing all over again. So did Marshall and Joy when Grandma started dancing.

It wasn't long before the three of them plopped down on the sofas, fully winded. Salome kicked her legs and waved her hands, ready for more.

"I knew you would get into the spirit of things, but that's enough for now, Baby Girl," Marshall soothed Salome.

"Whew, what a workout. It used to be so effortless." Joy sat upright. "After all of that celebrating, I had better go write the letter to get things started."

Grandma Martha's ever-present handkerchief dabbed her forehead wordlessly.

"Are you all right Grandma?"

"I feel absolutely wonderful. I have been waiting for this for a few years. I didn't know we would have an extra blessing, but I knew you should be here."

"Why didn't you say anything?" Joy said.

"You were in school and then you found a job doing what you like. I knew when the right time came, you would come back."

"I never would have thought this was the right time. I never would have imagined that I would have a daughter either, just months after arriving, and without a husband."

"God's timing is perfect." Grandma smiled.

"Well, I will write this letter and hope this committee accepts this project amendment. I think they meet every third Tuesday of the month, so that means they meet a week from tomorrow. I'll fax the letter in. Then, we'll just have to wait for the response."

"This sounds all too familiar. Doesn't it, Marshall, waiting for the answer to a proposal?" Grandma said.

"Yes, Joy, I could tell you about waiting."

"Well, let me get this letter written first, and then you can tell me about waiting."

"I think we will have to do it over dinner. Baby Girl has fallen asleep and I have to go to campus. You'll be here for dinner won't you?"

"Be here? She is helping me cook tonight. Kathombi said she had a meeting that would keep her late today. So, Joy, you are the assistant cook tonight. Natalie and Peter are coming over."

"Okay, that should be fun. Let me get this letter written and sent from the cybercafé on the corner. I have to puree some food for Salome. She's going to be hungry when she wakes up from her nap. Let me take her to lie down now. See you later, Dad." She took the sleeping Salome and headed down the hall again to her old room.

By the time she finished the letter and the amended proposal, Salome was awake again. That meant feeding her before she headed out to fax the letter.

When she returned with Salome and the finished letter on a thumb drive, no one was in the living room. So, she headed to the kitchen.

"There she is. I was just getting things set up."

"Grandma I'll be back, right after I feed Salome and dash down to the corner."

"Here, I already pureed some vegetables and some fruit. I'll feed her, while you run down to the corner with your letter."

"You are such a dear!"

"I'm just doing my job. This baby is the dear. Come on Salome, Grandma has something very tasty for you."

Salome smiled and reached out for Grandma.

"Let me put her in Hope's baby chair. There! Now you can feed her with ease. I'll be right back."

Salome was finishing the food that Grandma had prepared for her, and was happily babbling to Grandma when Joy returned.

"She is such a sweet baby," Grandma said.

"Yes, she is sweet, poor thing. Let me clean her up and we can get started on dinner."

"Did you get everything done?"

"Everything is sent off. We pray now and wait. In the meantime, I'll run like crazy to get all of the documents needed to make sure that Salome is safe and can stay with us as long as she needs to. That reminds me. I meant to check with Joseph about getting his friend the lawyer to help me get through the maze."

"Invite him to come over with Faith and little Hope tonight. We'll have a full house."

"Our full house is getting fuller. We'll need to get another baby chair, maybe a third chair before long when Natalie has her baby."

"Whoever would have thought that three babies would be in this house again during my lifetime? I feel like my life is so full, I could just burst!"

"That's so funny. I have never thought that you could ever be overwhelmed, by anything. You are always so sure of yourself with you and God doing insider trading on life. You're fearless, never fazed."

"My goodness, child. Who are you talking about? We need to talk about what actually goes on. I am afraid and unsure so much of the time. You know, I never got to see my mother and was distant from my father until he finally disowned me. At sixteen years of age, I left everything I knew and had held dear to marry and follow a man I had only known for a few months of Sunday afternoon walks in the park. We had a family for a while with a valley full of friends. I thought things were at the best point. Then my only child was killed by a selfish drunk, who asked the judge for leniency.

"We started over with a frightened and bitter little grandson, who we raised as our own child. Just when we began to think that we had succeeded, my best friend for more than fifty years and the love of my life ...dies. My "son" and the only family I had were on their way to the other side of the world. I tried not to show it, but I was afraid of being alone again."

"What happened What did you do?"

"I prayed, of course, but I prayed for what I could see as the solution. It was a poor solution at best. That's usually the case, you know. When we start depending on our own limited resources to see how things will turn out, we open the door for discouragement to easily attack our peace of mind. It doesn't matter what we knew for sure, even minutes before. Once we are discouraged, doubt rushes in like a flood and we can find ourselves drowning in despair. We can't see God's hand working to accomplish His plan because we are only looking for evidence that our plan is moving forward. I was like John the Baptist in prison. He had been the one who proclaimed Jesus to be the Lamb of God, but then he became discouraged in prison. He sent his disciples to ask Jesus if he was really the one. You know what I love most about that story?"

"What's that?"

"Jesus didn't get angry or disappointed that John was in doubt about what God himself had revealed about Him. He gave an answer which turned John's attention to what was being accomplished in the kingdom of God. After this, there is no more mention of John's doubt. When I came to the end of myself, God provided me with a wonderful distraction. Your Mom was suddenly placed on bed rest and restricted from travel and became a captive guest and company for me. Through her, I learned so much about Africa and a bit of Kiswahili. I thought this was all simply an interesting and entertaining pastime. I had no idea it would ever be an intimate part of my life. I also had no idea my life would change completely by helping your mom get in touch with one of her old friends. From the first day, I met Ms. Washington, my eyes started to open to see God's hand moving in that period of my life. I resurfaced from my despair and found I was ushered into an amazing time of world travel and philanthropy for orphans, which has given me a huge family, spread all over the world. What I saw as God's silence was actually my own lack of focus on what He was doing."

"That is so profound. You know, looking back over many times in my life, it is so obviously true. But how can knowing this is true, make it any easier each time to see past the physical things and focus on spiritual things? It's like I start at the first step every time."

"I think, sometimes, it may seem like you start at the first step, but just knowing how he has delivered you in the past really does make a difference in how fast you recover your correct focus. I was thinking a few months ago about how it seems that my lifelong friends are old and dying, and there's nothing I can do about it. I'm old myself, on the outside. I can hardly recognize the reflection I see in the mirror as someone I know. On the inside, I feel no different than I did the day I was married, except for one thing."

"Only one thing is different, huh? What is that?" Joy teased.

"I know I was born in a world that no longer exists. None of my family and friends are here and I'm surrounded by machines that were not even dreams when we were dreaming of the future. Social rules, clothes, shoes, education, expectations are practically unintelligible. So yes, there is only one thing I know for sure. Only one thing remains unchanged and totally dependable. That's the Lord."

"Ummm."

"I may not know what's ahead of me or what I will have to go through, but I know that He is there beside me, my eternal best friend and guide. More than that, He's the all-powerful God of the universe. So, He's able to comfort me in times of problems or bad situations, and change the situation if that would be the best thing for me."

"So, what you are saying is that the uncertainty of life is always at the same level although it may look different, your confidence in God has increased. So, you are confident that when things don't go the way you thought they should or the way you wanted it is still the best thing for you? You are really convinced of that?"

"I am sure that He won't let anything happen to me that would not be for my good. I remember that Jesus told the disciples to go to the other side of the lake, and then He went to sleep in the boat. It didn't matter what storm, wind, or waves showed up. They made it to the other side because that was the plan. It was what He had proclaimed. In my life, He has proclaimed that He will see me in eternity at the right time and that He is always 'with me' until then. When I remember that point, all my fear goes away. Yes, I may look fearless, but it's because of my confidence in Him. It has worked my whole life and *that's* a long time."

"I hope that I have a testimony like that for my life."

"Just keep on living, trusting God and you will."

Salome started banging on the table in front of her chair with the small spoon and was delighted with the sound. She started banging more rapidly, saying something unintelligible.

"Are we ignoring you, Salome? Just think, she is only beginning her journey." Joy took Salome out of the chair and walked over to grab a paper towel to wipe the baby's face.

"By the time she is your age, you will have a lot of good experience to give testimony to her, to encourage her on the way."

"I hope I will have done a good enough job that she is willing to listen."

"You don't need to worry about doing a good job or being a perfect mother. The secret is to live your love for her so that she is convinced of it. It's kind of like God's love. Whether we agree with or understand His decisions or ways, we obey. We obey because we are convinced that He loves us, and we can trust Him. Always be honest so you'll never be caught in a lie. Let her see that you are not perfect and that you learn from your mistakes so that she can learn at the same time. Children are unknowing and inexperienced at the beginning, but they are not stupid. They learn quickly. If you forget that, they will quickly leave you behind in disrespect. Realize that she is already a person and loved by God as much as you are. Most of all, never forget that your main responsibility before God is to teach her about Him. You have to know Him well to teach about Him. You understand that more clearly than most people because you are a teacher. You know you can't teach something which you don't know yourself."

"I will remember that. Thank you." She gave Grandma Martha a hug. Salome squealed with delight, as she was engulfed in the hug.

"You have been fed, little lady. It's time to get things ready for the rest of the family."

"I'll get her playpen. She can stay there while I help you. I brought it in from the car when I came back and left it in the front room. Please hold her while I set it up in the corner there for her." Joy handed Salome to her and quickly darted out to get the playpen.

❦

"You two have almost finished, I see. Sorry, I'm so late. The meeting lasted far longer than it should have, but everyone has to feel that they have been heard. You just never know what's going to provoke a lot of discussions," Kathombi said as she entered the kitchen.

"I've had a great time with Grandma Martha. I netted a lot of valuable life secrets and some recipe tricks to her famous cooking."

"I see. And how has Salome been?"

"She is doing so well. I have to take her to the doctor tomorrow morning when the class is on a field trip."

"Is she sick?"

"No. I need to see if she's up to date on vaccinations and everything and start making sure that she stays okay. I found a few papers from visits to a pediatric clinic when I went to clean out Miriam's place, so I'm going back there for the time being. Faith gave me the information about her pediatrician, too. Once I have all of her information and see how things go, I'll decide which place is best."

"Hello, Salome."

The baby pulled herself up to a standing position smiling in response to Kathombi's greeting. She held on to the playpen side, and she reached for Kathombi with the other hand.

"What a good baby," Kathombi said as she picked her up. "Let's go sit in the living room before Grandpa Marshall gets home and takes over."

"Go ahead, Mom. I'll be in to set the table in a few minutes. You already know about Peter and Natalie, but Joseph and Faith are coming, too. It's a full house today."

"That sounds wonderful. Come join me, Grandma Martha. Joy can finish up in here."

"That's right, you go sit with Mom. It's just a matter of turning down the fires and setting the table. I can do that."

"All right, then. That sounds like a good idea. I think I will go sit down for a while." She took a light hold on Kathombi's arm and the three of them moved toward the living room. She glanced back and smiled at Joy. "Thank you for helping, Joy. It has been delightful."

"I'm the one who got helped. Thanks for sharing."

"She is such a sweet child, Joy. I hope my baby turns out to be as easy going," Natalie sighed leaning on Peter beside her.

"I know. That's what everybody says, but it's not surprising. Her mother was quiet and easy-going. It's sad that she won't have any memory of her. I'll keep the gold jewelry for her, of course, but there's nothing physical to look at or to think back about and smile or laugh."

"She didn't have any pictures at her house? Maybe there were letters or other documents," Peter offered as possibilities.

"I didn't find any photographs of relatives or houses or anything. I hardly knew her and there is no family that she left any contact information about."

"What *do* you know about her? There must be something. Think about it," Joe insisted.

"I have been asking myself the same thing, but I only know what she told me in a few minutes' time on her way home one day and then during a few minutes in the hospital the day she died. Actually, most of what I know is that she was very afraid and did not want anybody back home to know about the baby or even that she herself was still alive. When we talked, it was usually about the baby and school."

"I mean she must have wanted her baby to remember something about her."

"She did mention that she wanted me to tell her she was born in Kenya and her birthday is November 5th. Oh yeah, she said Salome was born in Marsabit."

"There! You have something to go on," Joe said pleased with this bit of information.

"What? What do you mean I have something to go on?"

"You can go to Marsabit or send somebody. It's maybe an eight to ten-hour drive on some pretty rough roads at times. Once y o u g e t there, gather all the information you can—any official records, details from people who saw, heard about or talked to her. Write down anything they remember about her. It would even be good to take pictures of the place as it is today. It won't be the same in a couple of years or when she grows up. Put it all in an album to give Salome when she's older. It's not the same as a family album, but it is better than nothing."

"And now we can all see and understand why Joseph is so successful in helping people organize their business," Marshall exclaimed.

"You're right, Dad. Joe, that's a great idea."

"You shouldn't go alone, Little Sister. If you can wait until next month, I'll go with you. Right now, I have appointments for permits and registrations almost every day," Peter offered and then looked at Natalie.

"I'd love to go on this journey of discovery with you, but I have to go in for an ultrasound this coming Wednesday. It seems this is going to be a big kid and maybe is going to arrive earlier than expected. One thing's for sure, I don't want *my* baby to be born in Marsabit."

Everyone laughed at this.

"Speaking of babies, you will have to leave Salome here with someone. Your mom, Grandma Martha, and I are the take-care-of-Salome tag team."

"I have my hands full with Hope, and she can't go either." Hope, sitting on her mother's lap, looked up sharply at her mom when she spoke her name. Not getting any answer there, she looked around the room gone quiet. All eyes were on Joe, and she also switched her gaze in question to her father, sitting next to her.

"Well, it seems that I am elected, by default or consensus, to go with you, Joy."

"It was your brilliant idea. It's only right that you should see it come to life."

"Let me finish up a couple of things on Monday. Tuesday is a holiday. We could leave early Tuesday morning, make it to Isiolo by lunchtime easily, and leave for Marsabit after lunch and a good rest for my weary arms. If all goes well it should take another three to four hours. At any rate, we'll arrive well before dusk. I've heard that by the time we arrive in Marsabit, we'll be shaken to the core from the bad roads and parched all over from the desert wind and sun."

"As long as we arrive and get to collect memories for Salome, I'll be okay. That should be Tuesday evening when we arrive then. That gives us all day Wednesday and Thursday to gather information and talk to people. We could actually be back here Friday afternoon if all goes well. You are amazing Joseph Anderson! I'll only miss two days of work; I don't have classes on Thursdays."

"If telephone reception is decent, I won't miss any days." Joseph said.

"Thursday is our field trip day. I'll just have to be sure that one of the other instructors can cover my classes on Wednesday and Friday."

"Ask them to possibly cover Monday, too, in case you are worn out from the trip. You never know what might happen."

"You're right. It's always best to plan for the worst. You *are* very good at this."

"He's the best," Faith said proudly as she patted his knee. Hope, thinking it was a game, smiled and tried to reach over to pat Joseph's knee as well. She was caught from falling just in time by Faith.

"Be careful, Hope!" Joe cautioned.

"That's hope supported by faith," Marshall said with a chuckle.

"Ah," Kathombi said. "Let's see if the source of peace can be remembered through joy."

"Touché, Thom!"

"Yes, that was very nicely put."

"Yes, well done, you two."

"Bravo!" The groups proclaimed.

"This is God's kingdom coming on earth as it is in Heaven. I want to be there when we gather just like this with Him in Heaven one day."

"Spoken like the true queen that you are," Marshall declared, smiling at Grandma in admiration.

"Yeah, Grandma Martha that's the ultimate," Faith agreed.

"My prayer is that, too." Peter nodded with a somber expression.

"You can't copy Grandma Martha." Joy said with a frown.

"Yes, he can; prayers are not copyrighted. We can all pray the same thing, can't we Salome?" Kathombi said smiling at Salome on her lap.

Chapter 15

"Mom! Dad! Grandma Martha! I'm home." Joy called as she used her foot to push the door closed behind her. She let her overnight bag drop to the floor and hurried over to the sofa to lay the blanketed, sleeping, tiny baby down before she plopped down at the other end.

"Hey, quiet! I just laid Salome down for her nap. She's been a bit fussy.... You're back a little early, aren't you?" Marshall whispered as he appeared from the hallway.

"Grandma and I are heating up supper," Kathombi said as she appeared on the other side of the room from the kitchen. "We just got home a few minutes ago. So…How was it?"

"It was just amazing, and I met a man named Amazing. I have so much to tell you." Joy sat up as they sat down on the other sofa facing her. "You know when we arrived…"

"Wait a minute; where's Joseph?"

"He said he'd see you tomorrow. He was so tired he just dropped me off and headed straight home to rest up for the morning. The telephone reception was not good. So, he is really behind."

"That's a shame. So, was the trip worth it, Joy?"

"Yeah...you should be just as tired as Joseph, but you seem excited, Little Sister. What did you find?" Marshall said.

"Well, I found that Marsabit is an entirely different world. There are so many miserable people in the refugee camp. It's not really a camp, as in temporary. Some of the people we talked to have been there for years. It is hard to imagine how they managed to keep looking forward to each day, expecting something different. There was this one man named Amazing, and yes that is his real name. Anyway, he runs an orphanage located between the camp and the town. He actually remembered Miriam, because she helped a few times with the children. He said she told him that she wanted to help so that God would bring people to help her child if she ever became an orphan. He even remembered her selling her tapestries in town to tourists passing through. What was really fascinating was the fact that she had even taken on a project of drawing some bright pictures on the walls of the little dreary orphanage eating hall with some old small cans of paints she found in the shed of the petrol station. Joseph took some photos of them. In fact, that's where he was when I came to ask him to—"

"What a minute! Did that just move?" Marshall asked pointing to the blanketed bundle on the sofa.

"What is it?" Kathombi also watched and jumped closer to Marshall when she saw movement again.

Joy motioned for them to calm down as she watched to make sure there was no movement too close to the sofa's edge or risk of falling.

"That's what I wanted to tell you about. This is a baby who was born while I was there in the refugee camp yesterday, on May 5th. I had come back to get copies of the records of Miriam's registration and the birth of Salome, but the secretary was late returning. While I sat outside the office waiting, I caught sight of this small woman. She walked in slowly from the desert side of the camp, quiet and all alone. She had this blanket wrapped around her covering from head to foot. I saw her ask a camp resident on the path something, and they pointed to the line of people at the registration office. She made her way over to stand at the end of the registration line. Glimpses of her face showed she was strikingly beautiful, although very thin, and rather sad. I just had to sketch her. I did this, of course, in secret not wanting to attract attention. I pretended I was writing something on my pad of paper. Before I could finish, she moaned, stumbled and fell down. A few of us rushed to help her. We thought she was sick or overwhelmed by the journey because she was all dusty. They called out to find if there was anyone who had come with her or who knew who she was, but no one responded. They unwrapped the blanket and used it as a mat for her to lie down on the ground. A cool cloth for her head and a cup of drinking water was brought, as someone went to find the nurse. She revived a bit, but seemed exhausted and in pain. The nurse arrived and we were surprised when she discovered the woman was in labor and about to deliver. There was not even time to move her as she quietly gave birth. Right there! It was the most amazing thing I have ever seen. The baby boy didn't cry much and was very small but was alive and appeared healthy, so everyone was happy. When the nurse tried to hand the baby to the mother, she didn't respond. The sad shock sunk in as we realized that in the midst of all of the joy for the new life she had brought into this world, her own life had ebbed away. People began making this ticking sound with their mouths and shaking their heads. The nurse, who had been smilingly trying to hand the baby to the mother, now, very sadly laid the baby beside the dead mother. To my shock, the nurse stood and began walking away. I jumped up and ran after her to ask why. She explained that without the mother the baby was as good as dead. No adult there had the strength, resources or desire to take care of another child."

"What? They were going to let the baby just die?" Kathombi asked.

"Yeah, I couldn't believe it either, Mom. Everyone walked away saying the same thing. The baby would die soon without his mother's milk or anyone to take care of him. I just couldn't walk away from that spot. I stood there, wondering what had gone so wrong with our world that no one would be willing to care for this defenseless baby. He didn't choose to enter such a hostile place."

"God help us!" Marshall said as he stood and walked over to pick up the bundled baby. As he walked back to Kathombi, he pushed the cover a little away from the baby's face. Cradling him he sat down next to her. Kathombi pushed the blanket even more away from the baby's face and caressed his cheek.

"I couldn't believe it, so I stood there and called out 'Isn't someone going to take care of this baby? We can't just leave him here to die', but no one responded. I didn't know what else to do, so I carried him over to the orphanage. Amazing was so sad to see the baby, but even he said that there was no milk to feed him and no one to take care of him. He was running around trying to make sure he had food and water for those already under his charge. He did not have enough money, time, or energy for anything else. Milk is very expensive apparently. He said he could not let the other kids starve in order to feed this baby who would probably die soon anyway. I ran with the baby in my arms to the market and brought a couple of cartons of that UHT milk. You know the one —treated somehow so that it will stay okay for a long time without being in a refrigerator."

"Yes, the yellow carton. Go on," Marshall said.

"I tried to find any woman, who might be willing to take care of the baby, now that there was milk to give him. Still no one would accept. I went back to the orphanage, bewildered again as to why. Amazing said it was because, once they accepted and became attached to the child, they would be responsible for buying more milk, when the small amount I had given ran out. I told him I was ready to give money so that they could buy milk for a year. He just shook his head and said it wouldn't make any difference."

"Why?"

"That was exactly my question. He explained again that it was complicated and would only become more complicated as the baby grew and needed other types of food. If I left money, he said a mother could not be expected to use the money to purchase food for this baby while she and her own children went hungry."

"Oh, I see," Kathombi said.

"I understood this was a difficult situation, but I was desperate to save this baby. I continued running around trying to find someone to care for him. Finally, Amazing pulled me over to the side and almost yelled at me. 'Stop asking other people to take care of the baby. Either you take the baby yourself, away from the camp, or you leave the baby there by his mother; and let the natural process take its course.' I was stunned, but I knew at that moment that I had to take this baby away from there. I went back to where Joe was taking pictures of the wall that Miriam had painted and asked him to help me. There were no baby bottles or nipples in any of the shops, so Joe took these little straws from the juice boxes and improvised by shortening them and sticking the straw into the side of the milk carton. I can tell you one thing for sure. This little baby boy is an amazing straw sucker. He will cry to eat again, soon. Anyway, I have to figure out what I need to do, but in the meantime, at least he will be alive. Amazing registered him as an orphan and gave me these papers to turn into the office here."

"Look, the baby's eyes are open. He's looking around. Hi Baby," Marshall said. He doesn't seem like he can see and he's not making a sound."

"You just wait a while, He has some strong lungs, Dad."

Kathombi and Marshall continued to stare at him.

"He is really tiny."

"So, what is little bit's name?"

"I didn't give him a name, Dad. I ... Maybe I'm as afraid as everyone else of getting attached and then being responsible for him for a long time."

"I'll get a bottle of warm milk for him. One of Salome's smaller ones should do," Kathombi said as she stood and headed toward the kitchen.

Joy watched the looks on her parents' faces and knew it was probably too late to believe this baby would easily leave this house.

"Well, Moses Anderson, welcome home," Marshall whispered.

⁂

"It is a big and very sad problem, but you can't go around adopting all the orphans in the world one at a time," Joseph reasoned.

"I know, but there has got to be something more that I can do than just praying that 'God bless all of the orphans, everywhere' and leaving it at that," Joy insisted.

"Like what?"

"I don't know."

"Well, you have a foundation. Maybe you should think of designating a certain amount every year for the support of some orphan-associated thing or project."

"I wouldn't want to take them to the states like Ms. Washington. That is too big an operation. And I could never open up a school like Mom, but dedicated to orphans. One school would not be big enough to make a dent in the problem, and where would they stay?"

"Maybe you could have a hybrid of the two or something completely different. What is it that they really need that you can provide? What if you were able to identify orphanages like the one that Amazing runs and supply the food they need and the cost of an education. They would have what they needed to be able to grow up able to support themselves and still live at home or rather in their own country. Ms. Washington had that other program for sending volunteers to teach in orphanages. You could choose the orphanages run by good people like Amazing and supply enough food so that the director can spend his time counseling and helping the kids plan for their future. At the same time, you could support the volunteers coming to teach them."

"Yes, and if there is a good school available near the orphanage, then we can pay the school fees for those who qualify to attend.

Mom has the best school in town. Did you know that there is a children's home not very far away?"

"No. I have always considered Clare's Corner back in on the farm site Grandma Martha gave to Ms. Washington, as a lifetime family contribution to orphans all over the world. I have never thought about any other orphans. Did you, I mean before you had these two pushed right into your life?"

"No, I think that I thought like you that our family had done a huge amount for the cause. For me, the issue of orphans was covered, by Grandma's contribution and all of her work. Oh, don't get me wrong. I always give in the benevolence offering, but I never felt moved to do anything more. I never even knew the situation about orphans, but now that's all changed. I am convinced there is something that I can and should be doing, at least, about orphans right around me. I don't mean Salome and Moses. They have a family, now."

"Okay then. We can visit the children's home you mentioned and get the details on how many children there are, their ages and how well they have done in school. Then we come back and talk to Mom."

"Great!"

"Just so we have a solid discussion with Mom, I need to know what kind of figures you are talking about."

"We would like to have … what's the term you used the other day, Joe? Oh yeah. We would like to have a diversity ratio of, let's say, five percent."

"So, if she has three hundred students, you want fifteen of them to be orphans, directly sponsored by Visions of Joy Foundation?"

"Yes."

"Okay. Is this the model you want to use or will it be different for each institution?"

"I think we can aim for five percent everywhere. In turn, we can ask the orphanages where we sponsor the volunteer teachers to have five percent of these who attend the class to be from the poor children in the surrounding community, and they will also be sponsored by Visions of Joy Foundation."

"I guess I could ask the next question in two different ways."

"What's the first way?"

"How many students do you want to sponsor in total?"

"What's the second way?"

"How much money do you want to spend each year on this?"

"I don't know. Peter told me that I have to leave a certain amount in the bank at all times to make sure there would be interest accumulating to use for the activities. I am sure he meant to add and pay his salary."

"How much is the interest you have to use for activities?"

"That's just the problem because it keeps changing. All the money from the book sales goes in, so it keeps changing each time we get a book deal. They just authorized an advance on the new book, of one hundred thousand dollars."

"Wow, I didn't know there was another one. I certainly didn't know there was that much money in books."

"Yeah, they refused the one about orphans in sad plights but accepted the one about orphans from horrible situations that have gone on to do extremely well.

"I was so impressed with all of those former Clare's Corner residents, who stayed in touch with Grandma Martha over the years. She let me write them for permission to write their stories, in brief, and show their before and after pictures… It's really inspiring. They are doing such wonderful things.

"Each of them has some kind of project helping orphans in their communities in some way. Some of them are quite moving. Take, for instance, the business major, who went back and started a women's hat factory. He said that before she died, he had seen his mother - like all the other women in his neighborhood - wear the same hat every Sunday for years. Hats were imported and so relatively expensive. When he was at Clare's Corner, he saw women who wore a different hat to church every Sunday matching the colors in their dress. When he returned, he had convinced a hatter and a milliner to come as business partners with him. They started in the dining room of this little house using the sitting room as the sales floor. Now he has shops in 12 cities and employs over a thousand people. He has internship programs for orphans 16 years or older. If they do well in sales, design or production, they have priority when he has a job opening."

"Sounds like another successful book, but there are no poems this time or sketches?"

"Oh yes, the book is in sections by the area of the world or country people come from and each section has a cover sketch and a poem. The cover of the book is also one of my better sketches. There is this child praying with tears on his face … anyway you'll see it. The book is called: *I Know God Hears the Prayers of the Fatherless*. The subtitle is: *He Touches People's Hearts and They Reach Out to Help*. That's the title and refrain of the book's main poem."

"So, is this money going to be added to the base amount, or is it for activities."

"I don't know. I haven't talked to Peter, yet. I just got the notice on Saturday."

"Okay. We need to have a meeting. All three of us need to be on the same page. We need to have you decide if the art activities or the orphan activities are going to have priority and to what degree. You need a business plan. Once those decisions are made, your finance/accounting department can arrange everything. You can even have a plan in case other books or other needs pop up. You shouldn't have to be making major decisions all the time."

"That sounds good."

"How are you providing the expenses of your two kids?"

"Oh, I make enough from my teaching job to handle everything, so far. As long as the institute thinks the project based in Nairobi is a good thing, my job is safe and I can stay here. It's so much cheaper to live here."

"Good. Do you want to meet here or at the institute or…?"

"Let's meet before dinner at Mom and Dad's sometime this week. I know they will have some good advice as well. That way we can have one meeting and everyone can have their say, including Grandma Martha."

"I sure hope she lives to be a hundred and fifty years old."

"Why do you say that?" Joy asked.

"She is just so full of good things…advice, both spiritual and practical. She's always calming things down and encouraging your heart. Once, thinking that I was making my little family a nuisance by hanging around Mom and Dad's too much, I sort of hung back a little. Then a few days later Faith says, 'Hope misses Grandma Martha. Do you think we could invite ourselves to dinner?' That night Grandma straightened me out about the importance of family at dinner time around the table. 'If you are busy or have another appointment that's one thing, but to think you are not always welcome is just foolishness! If you feel better bringing something to add then do it, but don't deny me the pleasure of seeing my great-granddaughter because of some pride issue you have.' After that, we go over to see her whenever we can."

"I know what you mean. Before Salome even began to call me Mama, she was saying 'Ga'ma'. That's what she called her."

"That Salome is a cute one."

"What gets me is Grandma Martha's endless energy. She never wears out. She always has more to give and always has time for everyone."

"It's just good to be around her. So! We'll meet Wednesday at six?"

"That's fine with me. I'll have to confirm with Peter, although Natalie stops by in the afternoon almost every day with the twins. I think she does it to have a break, but Grandma Martha is in seventh heaven with Little Marshall and Michael and Moses and Salome and, sometimes, a little Hope. Can you imagine five great-grandchildren all within a little less than two year's span?"

"You never know how fast things can change. You two went the fast route, with two at a time. We're going the normal route. You *are* coming to Hope's birthday party this Saturday?"

"Of course, I am. I can't believe that another year has gone by since Hope was born. That means it is also three years since my surgery."

"How are you feeling?"

"As far as my physical head is concerned, I feel fine. The rest—with my two new kids, moving back to Kenya, the difference in my career—has my emotional head spinning. None of this was expected to happen this year."

"It's been good to have you come back, and Peter, too. It just feels right. I don't know why, but I believe this is just the beginning of what's going to happen, and we all need to be here."

"I feel that, too. We'll see what God has planned," Joy agreed.

○○○

"So how are things going?"

"Kyle, it's good to see you. Has it been a year already?"

"It's been more, actually. I guess that means that you didn't miss me. Not counting the days?"

"I have been very busy. The fact that I am still here in Kenya speaks to the fact that a lot has changed since I saw you last."

"Several of my friends could not wait to bring me up to date on your activities."

"I see. Well, having to deal with the issues of two small children, I am not the overconfident young woman that you left."

"I never thought that you were over sure. In fact, I learned, while I was away, that you have a lot of wisdom."

"That's reassuring."

"Yes. I came here today to ask you to do something."

"Oh, come on Kyle …"

"No, wait. I am not going to ask you to marry me."

"Oh, you're not? What is it then?"

"I want to ask you to forgive me."

"Forgive you? Forgive you for what?" Joy was surprised.

"Well, first of all, I want to tell you something. Something happened while I was away that took the wind out of my sails. I had to stop and listen to what God was saying to me. That's what I wanted to tell you about."

"Okay."

"Let me start by telling you that I'm not proud of what led up to this, but I am proud of what God brought out of it."

"Okay, that's always a good starting point."

"About three months after I arrived in Brazil, I found myself in a situation that was very similar to the night I got into trouble with Leah."

"Kyle, you—"

"Now, Joy, remember what I just said?"

"Okay."

"This time I heard very clearly 'Get up, run from here and never come back.' So, I did. I jumped up immediately and ran. I don't know how I found myself standing in front of the hotel prayer room. I went inside and stayed until morning, praying… and maybe dozing a bit. When I came out, I had a plan."

"A plan?"

"Yes, a plan. Do you remember the day I told you about the paternity hearing for the child Leah claimed was mine?"

"Kind of…"

"You asked me a question. You asked if there wasn't some major change in my life I needed to make in order to never end up in that situation again."

"Yes, I remember that very clearly."

"Then, you'll remember my response. I said that would be all I needed to do."

"Yes. I remember that as well."

"The problem with that plan was, I was putting all the blame on other people. In my mind, I was the good guy being attacked by conniving women. It was like I had no part in being set up. Well, I learned sitting in that prayer room that night, I absolutely did have a part. If I was to be obedient to God's voice, not only did I have to get up and run, but I had to never find myself there again. I saw that the emphasis should not be on avoiding other people being there, but that *I* must never be there, again."

"So, what did you do?"

"I started analyzing it like I do when there is an accounting problem. What parameters did I have to put in place to assure the right results at the other end? Logically speaking, the problem could only happen in a situation where I was alone with a young woman and on my way to getting drunk and losing my ability to judge. It's not that every time I was alone with a young woman there would be a problem, but that there would be no problem if I wasn't. I had to conclude that if I never wanted to have that particular problem again, I could not be alone with any young lady who was not a close family member *at all*, day or night from that point onwards. Also, I could not find myself tipsy, at any time. My limit now is one glass of wine, if anything. That way, I will never even get close to being tipsy. God showed me, I had to do my part to make sure there was never even an opportunity for conniving people to find me in a weak position. Now, *that's* the answer I did not have for you or for *myself* before."

"That's wonderful. I am so happy for you and what this will mean for your life."

"I can tell you that having this plan is much more effective than letting the memory of all of the pain and misery I went through be a deterrent for repeating my mistake. The 'unset-up' is the answer. So… I've said all of that to let you know your refusal to marry me probably kept me from failing myself and God, again. I didn't know how blind I was, Joy, so I ask you to forgive me for being so prideful."

"You are forgiven, of course. I ask you, as well, to forgive me for my attitude."

"I forgive you, although I believe it was justified. That's between you and God. I would also like to know if I can sometimes volunteer to help with the activities at the orphanage. I want you to understand, this is offered whether you are present or not. It might actually be better if you were not there—so I can fully focus on the kids. Do you have play days at more than one orphanage? I would just like to contribute in a small way to something great."

"You are most welcome to come and help at the play days for the orphanage. We don't have enough volunteers. The kids don't often have a young man as a play target. You know, we have only one site for play days because we lack volunteers. If you are willing to form a team that will guarantee a minimum of people for play days each month, we can locate another site and you could be the lead. Just call the office and they'll help you set things up. That would be a wonderful thing. Thank you."

"Thanks, Joy, for the opportunity to be part of something good in this world." He stood up and extended his hand for a handshake. "I will do my best to make sure you get nothing but good reports about my work."

"I expect nothing less." She shook his hand in return.

Chapter 16

"Mom, how come Michael and Marshall have their birthday at the same time and Salome gets to go before me?"

"I told you, they are twins. You can call Auntie Natalie and see if they've already left the house on their way. Did you clean your room so that they can play in there if it rains?"

"Yes, ma'am."

Salome looked sideways at Moses. "Mom, he never does a good job when he cleans."

"Everyone cannot be as good a cleaner as you are, Salome, but he does a much better job in the garden than you. Have you seen the carrots he brought in for the salad? Everybody has something good to contribute to help our family do well. How do you think you can help each other, today?" Joy put the last touches on the cake's frosting and carried it to the refrigerator.

"I'll go pick a carrot, especially for you if you'll help me with my room," Moses said trying to sound sweet to Salome

"Okay. A big one, okay?" Salome agreed.

"Don't get dirty, now. You already have your best clothes on. Be careful."

"I will, Mom." Moses rushed outside to the garden in the backyard.

"You need to go to his room for your half of the bargain, don't you? Maybe next time you can go together so that you can show him how to do a better job."

"He doesn't listen very well."

"Maybe you need to say things several times as I do for you about your lunch box."

"I listen to you, well."

"You do?"

"Yes, I just forget sometimes."

"Please, go do what needs to be done in Moses' room. I need you both to come back and help me get the things on the table. People will be here in about thirty minutes."

"Yes ma'am."

The doorbell rang and Moses rushed in through the back door, dropped the slightly dirty carrot in the sink, and darted to the front door.

"Moses?" Joy's call stopped him in his tracks, and he ran back to stand with his urgent request in front of Joy.

"Mom, may I answer the door? It has to be Michael and Marshall. I've been waiting for them all day."

"Okay, but check first."

Joy smiled as he raced back out of the kitchen and through the living room to the front door. Too short in stature to look through the security glass, she saw him look through the key hole and yell out in delight. "Mom, it's them! They're here," he threw the door open and the three boys all tumbled to the floor, entwined in greeting.

Joy quickly dried her hands on the dishtowel and went to greet Natalie and Peter.

"Sorry, we're here early. The boys were so eager to come. We thought we would come over and maybe help you prepare things," Natalie apologized as she handed the two identically wrapped gifts to Joy.

"That's fine. Moses was pushing from this side for them to get here. They see each other every day in nursery school and every

Sunday at church. Saturday is the only day that they don't usually have a planned reason to see each other and it's like they can't stand it."

"I know, but I think it's a funny good thing when you think about it,"

"I agree with Peter, Joy. It means we have even more reasons to spend time with each other," Natalie added as Salome returned.

"Mom, I cleaned up very nicely, but they just came in and messed it up again." Salome was uncharacteristically upset and frowning.

"It's okay, Salome. Did you see Uncle Peter and Aunt Natalie?"

"Hello, Auntie Natalie and Uncle Peter." She gave them both hugs in turn.

"Thank you for bringing Mike and Marsh. Moses just kept asking about them every minute. Don't you want to have a little girl? She could come over and play with me when you come."

"Salome!" Joy exclaimed.

"That's okay, Joy," Natalie reassured. "Salome, we would love to have a little girl to come and play with you. We're waiting to see when God will decide to send her."

"Okay, that's nice. I will help you pray," Salome happily turned to look in the sink. She quickly washed the carrot Moses had promised her and skipped from the kitchen down the hall toward her room.

"You had better be careful when she prays, Natalie…" The doorbell rang again before Natalie could respond.

"Natalie, would you mind getting the door for me? I'm going to ask Peter to help me get the roasted meat out of the oven. It seems like everyone is coming early."

Natalie opened the door for Joseph, Faith, and their two children Hope and Richard. They headed toward the kitchen.

As soon as she heard Hope's voice, Salome came shyly to greet her. She hugged Joseph and Faith and reached out to the toddler in Faith's arms.

"Do you want to come with us, Richard?"

Two-year-old Richard scrambled down from his mother's arms to take Salome's hand. He reached for Hope's hand on the other and the three walked down the hall to Salome's room.

"She is always so sweet to think of Richard. She never forgets to include him, Joy."

"She has a very kind heart, but it is not hard to love the gentle family baby, Richard. Now, I am putting you all to work."

The doorbell next rang twenty minutes later at the arrival of Marshall, Kathombi, and Grandma Martha. All the kids ran in to greet them.

"Oh, my! Okay, everyone quiet. Testing! Where is Hope?" Grandma Martha called out.

"I'm right here."

"Okay, that's the oldest. Now, where is Richard?"

"Eya!" Richard confidently called.

"There! That's the youngest. Now, where is everyone else in between?"

"Here!" came the thunderous response from all of the kids.

"Okay, we're all here, so we can start the celebration."

"Yea!" everyone shouted, and Marshall led the long line of happy dancing. Richard got so tickled he fell down three times, causing everyone to laugh over and over again before they were finished.

The adults then gathered in the living room and the kids roamed from the backyard to their rooms as they finished eating and playing. Finally, the cake was brought in with candles aflame and the Happy Birthday song, causing Moses to glow as he basked in the love surrounding him. He closed his eyes for a few seconds to make his wish and then blew all four of the candles out.

"I hope you wished for good grades. You'll be starting at A New Song preschool this year, and there is not going to be any special treatment," Kathombi announced.

"Mom, how exciting. You're starting the preschool this fall, after all?' Joy asked.

"Yes. The final permit came yesterday. Everything will be ready in time."

"Yeah!" everyone cheered.

"That means the twins and Salome will be going as well," Marshall confirmed.

"That's wonderful. Congratulations." Peter cheered

"Halleluiah," Natalie declared. "Joy, this is definitely a carpooling victory!"

"Yes!"

"We're in the pool, too. Hope will be starting standard one, remember?" Faith said.

"That's the last of the building's classroom space. The campus is finally full and complete. Marshall, just think. After all these years and just in time for the grandchildren we didn't even think about."

"God knew, and He **was** thinking about the little ones, fortunately," Marshall said.

"And fortunately, you followed His direction. Mom, you are amazing."

"This," said Peter, looking back and forth between Joy and Natalie, "is a wonderful thing."

When Joy handed Marshall his portion of cake and ice cream, he winked and whispered to her. "Little-bit is becoming a fine young man. He really likes windmills, too."

"Is that so?"

"Yeah," he said as he leaned back and looked at the cake. "This looks good. Did you get it from Mocha House?"

"Sure did. I know it's your favorite, next to the orange dream cake." She smiled and returned to the table to find that Faith and Natalie had distributed all of the rest of the cake and ice cream. That meant only one thing. She saw Moses sitting patiently beside his empty cake plate waiting for the signal to open gifts.

"Okay, everyone, let's gather around for the opening of the presents," Joy called.

The twins, Michael and Marshall were the first ones to offer their gifts. Each presented a knee pad. Richard then reluctantly parted with the brightly wrapped small gift box he was to give, which held protective gloves. Hope followed with her gift of elbow pads. Salome gave a brightly colored helmet.

It was no secret that what Moses wanted most was a bicycle. It was very interesting to watch him smile as the gifts were presented to him. Every so often he looked at Joy questioningly as there was no sign of the wished-for object. She just smiled, trying not to give any indication that she thought anything was amiss. th

There was one more gift on the table from Grandma Martha. Moses ripped off the paper and found a bright, florescent, magenta, and green striped skateboard. Moses was transported by happiness for a minute. He had not been expecting this and did a short test drive beside the table.

"Rule number one: there will be no skateboarding in the house." Joy stated.

"Yes, Mom," he said as he bent down to pick it up and carry it toward the door. The twins jumped down to follow him.

"Rule number two: no skateboarding at all without protective equipment properly on the body," Joy stated.

Moses handed the board to Michael and rushed back to the table. He handed the knee and elbow pads to the other twin, Marshall, as he grabbed the helmet and gloves and headed toward the door.

"Oh! I guess you're not interested in seeing what Grandma Kathombi and Grandpa Marshall bought for you," Grandpa Marshall called nonchalantly.

Moses stopped in his tracks. He quickly handed the helmet and gloves to Peter who was in the line of fire and rushed over to Grandpa Marshall.

"Grandpa Marshall, I am very interested in what you and Grandma Kathombi brought for me. Yes, very interested."

"Oh, okay," Marshall suddenly started grinning and said in a loud voice, "then you can find it through that door. It's in the garage."

All the kids followed Moses as he ran excitedly to the garage. "It's here!" he yelled. "He really got it! Oh, look at that," Moses said seeing the surprise Grandpa Marshall had hidden in the garage through the outside door when he had arrived.

The other kids were jumping up and down and cheering in the garage.

"What did you find, Moses?" Marshall called out grinning.

Kathombi patted his knee. "Marshall, have mercy on the boy."

"It's my bike, Grandpa! Grandma! Mom! Mom, come and see!"

Joy walked out to the garage. Moses was sitting on the bike in the center of the group, just beside himself with joy. Everyone was touching the bike in awe. It was electric blue in color, with a zebra-striped seat. Salome was smiling the most. She had been the only child let in on the secret ahead of time. She knew exactly what Moses had wanted most and had asked her mom to make sure that he was not going to be disappointed on his birthday. Joy had assured her that he would not be. Despite the fact that they squabbled constantly, they always looked out for each other.

"Okay, this once, you can bring the bike in the house, to say thank you to Grandpa and Grandma."

"Let's go you guys," Moses said as he climbed off the bike and walked it into the house.

"Yea!" they cheered again as they followed him into the living room.

"Hold this for a minute?" he asked Salome.

She nodded her consent. As she stood holding the bike, Moses ran over to Marshall and hugged him first, then Kathombi. "Thank you, Grandpa and Grandma. It's what I wanted."

"You are quite welcome. Now, you go and enjoy your bike and skateboard. This is a party, so remember the importance of sharing with everyone you invited. Well, maybe not baby Richard. Look in the garage again, on the same side that you found the bike. There is an extra set of gear on the bottom shelf unwrapped. Remember Mommy's rules."

"Yes, Grandpa Marshall." The calm was over. The bike and the skateboard were marched outside, and everyone cheered the others on as they waited their turn.

"Dad you should direct movies," Joe commented.

"Yeah, you had the suspense peaking at a hundred percent," Peter added.

"He had almost made up his mind to be happy with the skateboard that I got for him." Grandma Martha pretended to pout.

"Now he can be happy with having his choice of either one *and* have a friend happy at the same time. It is the perfect situation: Eating his cake and sharing it, too." Marshall responded.

"Yes, wouldn't it be nice to be able to do that always?" Grandma Martha smiled.

"Sometimes I think so, but then I also remember the study done some time back when I was a student at UWC in Los Angeles. They found that the same result happened when a person thought that there was nothing to struggle for or, as at the other extreme, when the person thought that the struggle was for something unattainable. That person became despondent or depressed and started withdrawing from any activity." Kathombi commented.

"So far, Kathombi, there has never been a day I didn't see tomorrow as an opportunity to start or complete something that I didn't have time for today, and I have seen a lot of days. I have also seen a lot of things that seemed so overwhelming I didn't know how I was going to get through."

"What did you tell me once, Grandma Martha? You said, 'That's the life we face as long as we live.' Remember?"

"Mom, that's why you just have to know that God is with you in either situation, no matter what, no matter where, no matter when, in every situation," Joy said.

"Exactly, Joy. I can vouch for that. It's not just a belief of comfort that allows you to feel okay. God is not simply there to give you encouragement as you go through difficult times and he just sits there. No. He can intervene to bring a change in you or your understanding of the situation. He can also just change the situation altogether."

"Yes. There's always hope. Even better than that, we are sure that beyond what we can see and above what we can imagine, God has a plan to bring good into our lives, If anyone can plan well and successfully, it's Him."

"I pray, on this day, Little-bit remembers that all of his life."

"Amen!" Everyone said.

Peter came inside, "There is so much energy out there. I need a break."

"Faith and I will referee the kids outside," Joseph said heading toward the front door.

"Is anyone up for a game of scrabble? I'll set up the board," Joy challenged.

"Joy, you just love to be punished. Mom is the reigning champ, but I am the heir apparent. Peter declared. "Why do you always think that you can win?"

"Because, dear Brother, I believe it is possible."

"Okay, keep believing, Joy. Natalie, you keep score so that her belief is not aided by math mistakes in her favor."

"You did not just accuse me of cheating, did you?" Joy asked.

"No, I just want you to have your full concentration on the game and not be distracted by scorekeeping." Peter smiled.

"I see, always the thoughtful brother. I'll set up the game."

Friday afternoon was a quiet time in Joy's house. Each was to be someplace in the house, working quietly on something for two hours. It was okay if this ended up in napping, sometimes, or quiet discussions. Today, Joy was sitting in the den sketching when, out of the corner of her eye, she saw Moses enter and stand at the door. It was unlike him to be quiet or still for so long, so she looked up to see why. He was standing there with a paper in his hand just looking at her.

"What's wrong, Moses?"

"I have a poem I wrote for you."

"Really? Can I see it?"

He nodded his consent, walked over, and handed her the paper. As soon as she took the paper and began to read it silently, he sat down beside her.

Why
Why did God send Mommy to save me?
Why does He make her love when I am the bad me
Like she loves me when I am the good me
Like He loves me all the time too.
I think He saved me for a big thing for me to do
I am happy that my mommy does what God tells her to do
I hope she knows what big thing God wants me to do, too.

Joy stared at the paper. She frowned as questions crossed her mind. *God, how am I going to guide this child? This is a question that has perplexed me in my own life. How am I supposed to have an answer for him?* Taking a deep breath, she smiled at the little expectant face beside her.

"You know, sometimes the special thing that we are supposed to do is a secret between God and us alone, at least for a while. He will tell you before He tells other people. He gave each of us talents that allow us to do what He's planned. It's kind of a clue when we discovered that talent or someone points it out to us.

"Once you discover this clue, you should do your best to use it and look for other clues until you can see the picture clearly."

"What do you mean?'

"Here let me show you." She turned to a clean sheet on the sketch pad and drew a few scattered lines that didn't touch. She slowly continued to add one line at a time until Moses sat up with recognition.

"I know what it is," he said excitedly. "That's our house."

"You see. It wasn't clear at all in the beginning, but now it's clear and you can see yourself right where you belong. What made you decide to write a poem, today?"

"I don't know. I just started thinking about a lot of things. I see you write poems about things that make you feel good or very sad, all the time. I felt like maybe I would write a poem about what was making me feel confused. I felt better when I did, but I did not have an answer. I was going to hide it so that you would not feel confused like me."

"It's okay that people feel the same way as you do sometimes. Maybe they need to think about something a little more and you can help them to do that."

"Okay."

"So, now you have one clue or line on your drawing. Keep looking for others to appear."

"Mommy, what line or clue do I have?"

"Well, I think that it is the clue that you have the talent of poetry. You can write poems that show others how you feel."

"I do?"

"Well, you just did that without anybody asking you, right?"

"Yeah, that's right, I did."

"You will have to keep trying and watching to see how good a talent you have or how God wants you to use it."

"Okay, I will. Am I going to write books like you?"

"I don't know, you just might. My Dad, Grandpa Marshall, never wrote books, but he is a poet."

"He's too busy catching the wind."

"Yes, I guess he is, but it just shows that all of your talents don't have to be used by you all of the time. I didn't write books with poems until I was a big lady. I was too busy drawing. Then one day I couldn't draw, and so I started writing. Soon I was making books. It was not something I thought I would do. But God already knew I would need to do that to have the money to help orphan children."

"Mom, you should help Grandpa Marshall make money. Could you make pictures and poems about helping people with windmills? I don't think too many people know about them. He always has to be writing them letters."

"Hmm. I will talk to him about that. It may be a very good idea."

⁂

Salome and Moses came running out to the car from the schoolyard.

"Slow down you two. It's not like I'm going to leave you. What is so exciting today?"

"Mom, Grandma Kathombi said to tell you she is very proud of me. I am first in my class. And Hope is first in her class, too."

"Congratulations, Salome. And good for Hope."

"Grandma said to tell you she is proud of me, too, Mommy. I'm number two in my class."

"That's very good, Moses! I am proud of both of you. I can't tell you how glad I am that A New Song started a pre-school section, this year."

"I would be number one, but Muiti's science project was a little better than mine was this time. Next time, I'll do better and see if I don't get first."

"Sounds like a plan. It can't hurt to try harder to do better whether you get first or not. Did you see Auntie Natalie? I wonder if she already picked up the twins."

"Yeah, she left with Mike and Marsh just before you came," Salome reported.

"How come the twins didn't come with us today, Mom?" Moses asked.

"We have something special to do today. We're going to swing by Grandpa Marshall's house on our way home. I want him to see something. In fact, it's about your idea Moses."

"It's my idea?"

"Yes, the other day you mentioned something about making a book about windmills so that people would know about them and maybe help Grandpa build more of them."

"Really? Can I see?"

"It's not done yet. I need to talk to him to get a better understanding and do some research."

"I like research, Mom. I can help you."

"That's wonderful, Salome. I could use your help."

"I don't like research. What can I do to help?"

"I don't know, yet, but I think that Grandpa can steer us in the right direction. Do you know anything about windmills, Moses?"

"Sure. Grandpa has a whole lot of them, and he lets me play with them if I am careful. There are antiques and modern, and some are efficient and not efficient, others are adjustable and fixed. I know a lot, but sometimes, I get them confused."

"That's more than I remember or probably ever knew. We can ask him to help us."

∞

Moses was the first out of the car and into the house. "Grandpa Marshall! Grandpa, where are you? We are here on official windmill business and need your attention."

Marshall was coming down the hall from his bedroom when Joy and Salome came in the front door. "What's all of this noise about windmills?"

"Heavens, what's the noise about?" Grandma Martha came from the kitchen.

"Come on in and we'll explain," Joy opened the sketch pad and began the explanation. "A few weeks ago, Moses had an idea that we could help make the world more aware of the importance of windmill generated power by making a book about them. The proceeds could be used to help pay for poorer areas or countries to have a windmill project. I am ashamed to say it. Despite my many years in this house and being the daughter of one of the world's experts in the field, I know very little about them. I think today I found out that Moses knows more about windmills than I do. That's quite funny, in light of the fact that I have lived all of these years next to the expert, and he has only lived six. It just highlights the fact that quality time with someone about a certain subject makes all of the difference."

"Well said, Joy. So…"

"So… I would like to make this a family project. I can do the drawings, or at least, most of them. I can also write most of the poems. I will have some help in that area from Moses and whoever else has some hidden talents. What I need is information. Now Salome can help me in that respect because she can ably do the research on some facts with your help, Dad. I also need to have some insight into feelings about the windmills. Dad, you have all those old models still, so they must mean a lot to you. I need to know what it is and why. Any photos you have of your projects over the years would really help. I know you don't have a lot of time. We can do this slowly and Moses can give me the stories you have told him."

"Gladly. I am ready," Marshall said.

"Grandma, I know the old windmill is still standing behind the farmhouse where you and Grandpa Joseph first lived. I need to have your thoughts and memories about that windmill. Well… that's the idea. I know it doesn't sound like much, but I think it is wonderful. If we mix the facts and the sentiment, people will take notice. Once they buy the book, they can even give more by contributing to a fund. Even if they only buy the book for the pretty pictures, the money can be used to help others reduce pollution."

"I think it is a great idea. Yep, I like it!" Marshall said nodding his head.

"That's wonderful, Dad! What are we waiting for? Bring out the models!"

Chapter 17

"Did you ever think about orphans when you were little, Joy?"

"Not much. I really didn't understand much about anything in that arena. I remember I used to think that they were very special people because Grandma Martha had given up her home for them and was always flying around the world to find them. I remember thinking, once, that they had more people thinking about, praying, and caring for them than any regular child had with two lonely parents. I had no idea of the real misery that those children were being rescued from. Some of the residents at Claire's Corner seemed so nice and happy. When I look back now, I understand why some of them did not want to be around people so much. They were very courageous to take the chance they had been given and make a difference for themselves and for their home countries. I might have been afraid to go back, but, somehow, Ms. Washington inspired them to understand it was their duty to go back and make it so other orphans could escape from misery as well. Since I came back to Kenya, I have been faced with the orphan problem first hand, and I have begun to understand, really understand."

"Did you ever think that you would be in the orphanage business?"

"It is not a business. I keep telling you that. The foundation is a service organization. We are not here trying to make money, but we want to make the money we already have somehow help orphans."

"I know that. It's just a manner of speaking. When did you get so precise?"

"Sorry, I just want it to be perfectly clear to anyone, especially people who have not heard of us before."

"No, I'm the last one to complain about precision. I'm just making a comment on one of the things that has changed about you. You are so serious about this."

"I am absolutely, serious. Every time I look at Moses or Salome, I am reminded of how their lives could have been if they had lived to experience the life of an orphan in some of the horrible places we have visited. Even if I could forget, something like the other day would happen."

"What happened?"

"I was sitting on the sofa doing some sketches, and Moses comes in and says that he wrote this poem."

"He's writing poetry? He's only six."

"Listen Peter or you will miss the point."

"Okay, so then what happened?"

"I asked him if I could see it, so he handed it to me and sat down beside me."

"I was stunned ..." she was unable to speak for a few seconds. "Sorry, I get overwhelmed just thinking about it. It was asking a question about why God had allowed me to be there to save him. He thought it was so that he could do something important or 'big' as he put it. He was hoping that I could tell him what the big thing was."

"What did you do?"

"All I could do was to stare at the paper and ask God for guidance. How was I going to be able to guide this child when I don't have the answer to that question for my own life? I reached over and hugged him and then an idea came to me. I told him that God gave us clues so that we could figure that out. I started drawing this sketch making lines a s partial and unlinked as possible."

"What happened?"

"I kept adding more lines until he yelled out 'I know what it is! That's our house'. I told him that one day he would see what he is supposed to do just as easily as that."

"That's amazing. You'll have to come and do that for my kids. That's so clear!"

"You will never believe what he did next."

"What?"

"He had an idea for a book that we are all working on together, even Grandma Martha and Dad. It's about windmills of all things."

"Why windmills?"

"He thought that Dad needed some help in taking the technique to poor countries that can't afford to buy it themselves. He said that a book would help people see the importance of wind power and raise money for projects."

"He is one smart little boy."

"Smart, yes, but with a big heart," Joy whispered.

"Makes you wonder where this kid will end up. He's only six years old."

"The possibilities for all of our kids are so mind-boggling. Maybe we hold them back by not helping them explore their depths. Salome is so studious and serious about doing things well. She is very detail-oriented and has a strong gift for searching for things on the internet and in the library. She's like a bulldog that gets a hold of a tire and won't let go. She loves it and looks for reasons to search. Anyway, everyone is doing their part in this project and it is moving forward quickly. Did you know that Grandpa Joseph bought that farm because it had a windmill and a house on it? Their house was the first one in the area to have hot running water because he set up a system to pipe the well water to a small water heater?"

"No, I did not know that. It looks like I will be one of the first ones who needs to buy this book to learn about my own family."

"There will be a lot of family history in it, that's true, but there will also be a lot of Kenyan and East African history too. That's where Dad's projects have been over the years. There is some technical stuff, too. He is insisting that it's important so people will understand why desert and wilderness hillside or offshore sites are chosen and why and for which type of windmill for what kind of results. We'll all be experts by the time Dad gets through."

"Not a bad thing. Maybe this is just what Moses and Salome need."

"Yeah, you can always trust God to be working on more than one angle at a time."

⁕

"Okay, Joy. I understand what you want to have as the result, but I disagree that this is the way to achieve it," Joseph explained to Joy.

"Why?" Joy asked sitting back in her desk chair.

"For one thing, as I explained, if you do it that way you'll have to go through the entire long process of registration every time you have a new idea. Frankly, it will not only become a nightmare to manage, but it is a waste of time, energy, and money."

"Joe, give me something positive. What do you recommend I do?"

"The way to keep the accounts separate but under one roof is something Peter will have to help you set up. The way to have one foundation which has a broad mission through specific projects is something I can write up for you."

"Can you work with Peter to give one joint proposal that's clear and comprehensive?"

"I can do that. I will also have my legal advisor make sure that it is worded and structured to meet all of the legal requirements," Joseph promised.

"Okay. When can the three of you have that ready?"

"It's like I am in a dream."

"Why do you say that, Joseph?" Joy asked frowning.

"My little art major sister is in the process of establishing a multinational foundation and is asking for deadlines. I would have thought that it would have been Peter or me doing such a thing."

"It is Peter, you and your lawyer friend doing such a thing. I could never have done this by myself. Your little art major sister has the money, but as the result of encouragement from her father to try something different, and her mother's encouragement to persist with prayer. That is not to mention, the business advice and support of a brother who is a business organization genius and another who is a world-class finance/accounting expert and expert photographer. Add to that the fact that I have two of the most helpful sisters-in-law that backup, step for step, these two experts, and top it off with the amazing Grandma Martha and you see why God put this art major in such a family."

"Do you realize that you could pay both Peter and I normal level salaries with things as they now stand?"

"Is that true?"

"Yes, it's true."

"So, why not work for the foundation. Make it so successful that you have a job for the rest of your life or as long as you choose to work?"

"I must say it's very tempting. I have been getting so fed up with the business people coming in for so-called ***advice.*** What they really want is to find out how to do the ***wrong*** thing legally or, at least, in a way that they will not get caught. Faith and I were talking the other night. We both agreed that your foundation is the one bright thing in our work lives. Its vision and activities are transparent and undeniably good You aren't looking for a way to put one over on people. You have an accounting system that is clear and straightforward. It is exactly what it says it is. The work has proof everywhere of the people's lives that are being impacted for the better. You're not dipping your hand in the till, because you have a job that you enjoy and that earns what you need. You are doing this with your heart and because you believe it is the right thing to do."

"That is how it should be, right?"

"Yes, but unfortunately that is not how it is the majority of the time."

"I don't know what the future holds for me, but I will continue to do this as long as God allows me."

"Good! Let me ask my lawyer friend about the ramifications and discuss this with Faith and Peter, and Dad and Mom and …why don't we just have a family meeting to hear everyone's take on it, and then we can answer you as individuals."

"Okay. Let's meet next week, Tuesday afternoon."

"Fine. I'll notify everyone. Can I ask you something?"

"Sure."

"Where do you see all of this ending up?"

"I don't really know. I was thinking the other day that we could make a book for each of our special interests and have that book be the seed money for projects the foundation could sponsor and that we could continue to pledge a certain amount of money from our salaries for a general fund for emergency projects or special unexpected needs."

"Whoa! What do you mean a book for each of us?"

"Let's take you, for instance. We could make a book about young entrepreneurs that could fund a project for you to train young people to do business correctly, in every sense of the word. This would assure there are successful honest businesses being started. Of course, there would be awards or prizes maybe even an international competition, to attract more attention and provide incentives. I don't know, something like that with all the business kind of things that you are so good at. The book would be about young people here in Kenya or East Africa. You could find young people in other parts of the world to give it an international appeal. We could interview them to get some interesting quotes and briefly talk about what they're doing and how they are successful. And show how they are giving back to their communities. You know all that corporate responsibility stuff. I'll add some poems about inspiration, both given and received, and some sketches from the field, like how they got their ideas or how they started. At least their families, friends, countrymen, youth groups and organizations businesses, great and small, would buy a copy for their coffee tables and you could start your project."

"I thought I was the business genius."

"I got the prototype idea from Moses. You know he's the brain behind the internationally famous *Busy Catching the Wind*. It's in its second printing. We got a letter from way up north asking us to do a book on wind-generating power farms. I have a proposal in for it, *Harvesting the Wind to Feed Our Cities*. The cover is already done. At first glance it looks like a regular orchard with fruit falling from trees, then when you look closer you see that it's turbines with electrical charges, not falling but running, down power lines toward the nearby city."

"That sounds rather clever," Joseph said.

"Yeah, compliments of your clever father."

"Okay, so this multi-project with multi-funding streams under one accounting and general management seems a bit complicated and time consuming. Do you see hiring someone to run all of this that you can have a life?"

"I was thinking about that just this morning. That is, I was thinking about the complicated time-consuming aspect, not the having a life aspect."

"Why do you say that?"

"I know that I will be satisfied with whatever God puts on my plate, and that I'll have the wherewithal to do it correctly. I just have to be watchful that it's Him and not me piling it on my plate."

"Right. So, it's Tuesday afternoon. Let's make it at Mom and Dad's house, Grandma's going out less and less."

"I know and she's going to be one hundred years old in two weeks. Can you believe it?"

"I try not to think about it. We have never lived in a world without her, but she can't live forever."

"I am trying to make this a most memorable event."

"I heard. You come up with some very big ideas, Little Sister."

"Mom, how old is Grandma?" Moses ran in to sit beside Joy on the sofa.

"She is going to be one hundred years old."

"How old can you get before you die?"

"I don't know how old the oldest person in the world is, but it's less than one hundred twenty I think."

"What happened since Methuselah? My teacher says that people need to eat better food and exercise more. Maybe Grandma needs a bike."

"Wait until she hears your suggestion. I bet it will make her laugh."

"I like it when she laughs. It sounds delightful."

"Oh, such big words you are using since you've spent all that time over Grandpa Marshall's house getting the book finished."

"It's a good book, Mom."

"Thank you, but I did not do it by myself, and the idea was yours."

"I think Grandpa really liked making it and Grandma Martha, too. She told me some of the things she remembered were 'so old they had not seen the sunlight in decades'. Sometimes, I saw her crying; but when I asked her why she was sad, she said, 'O heavens no, I'm not sad. I'm just squeezing a few more drops of joy from an old story.' That meant she was happy."

"Really?"

"Yeah. When we went by there on Sunday, she gave me a big special hug."

"She did? Why?"

"She said that she was so glad that I loved her and that I had the idea for the book. She said my idea was 'a telegram from heaven'. I told her I didn't know what a telegram was. She said it was like an email without a computer, straight from God to give us direction."

"Oh Grandma, she will find a clear way to explain things no matter what."

"Yeah, I understood after that. She said it was God's way of letting her tell her and Grandpa Joe's story in a way that would help a lot of people. She said 'Little-bit, only God could have made that happen'. Then, she hugged me."

"Awww!"

"You know what is funny?"

"What?"

"Grandpa Marshall told me 'Thank you', too. He said he always wanted to be able to help poor people to have electricity with windmills but didn't know how it was going to happen. He said that it was 'a telegram from heaven', too. I knew what it meant this time, because of Grandma Martha. So, I told him I agreed and I said 'God can always get a message through!' I said that because that's what Grandma Martha said."

"Oh my. What did he say to that?"

"He just laughed and hugged me again."

"Sounds like you have been getting a lot of hugs."

"That's nice to get hugs. It makes you feel funny; but when you see that everyone is smiling, you know it's a good thing, Grandma Martha, especially."

"Yeah. Her hugs are very special."

"Mom, she told me a secret."

"She did?"

"Yeah, she said when I grow up to be a man, one of my 'most happy thoughts will be about this book and all of the treasures that are inside'. She said for my children, 'it will be a hidden treasure', so I have to save a copy for them. She said it was very important. I asked her if she would save a copy for me and she said it would be better if I asked you to do it. Can you help me do that Mom?"

"I would be glad to do it. When we go over there this Sunday, we have to ask her to write something special inside. We will each do that, me and Salome, too."

"Does that mean she is going to die? Is that why she didn't want to do it?"

"I think she knows that all of your other things are here, near you. It would be easier to keep up with it and to make sure everyone knows it's your copy if it is with your things than if it were with her things."

"I don't want her to die. She's already old enough. Why does she have to get older?"

"How old you are doesn't depend on anything you try to do. It is just a matter of the time in days and years that you stay alive. God decides when you die. It doesn't matter how old you are."

"I sure hope He decides to not let Grandma Martha die."

"Me too Moses."

"Mom, can we write a book about old people? Not to have a project for people to learn to get older, but for other people who got old and didn't have a chance to tell their stories, yet. Some people don't have somebody, like you to let them write their stories that might help other people feel better."

"You know, if you keep coming up with these book ideas, you are going to have to write them yourself. We have three books in the process, now. I don't think I can do anymore."

"Mom, I can't write a book. I'm just a little boy."

"I think you can do some of the things. You helped Grandpa Marshall with the windmill book. Why don't you see how far you and Grandma Martha and Salome can get while I am finishing up the others?"

"If Salome helps, we will get ahead way fast. She is very smart, like you."

"She is just a little girl, too."

"I know, but she acts older."

"Yes, I agree with you, there."

"What are we going to get for Grandma Martha for her birthday? She told me that she doesn't need one more thing."

"Well, I have a secret, myself."

"You have a secret you didn't tell me, yet?"

"Yes, I do. It's for Grandma Martha's birthday. You two have been spending a lot of time talking, and I would be very sad if you accidentally told her the secret. It would spoil her surprise and keep her from having such a big smile on her birthday. So, I will tell you when it is much closer to the day. How about that? I just want you to know that we are getting her something exciting and special. Although she doesn't need anything, I know she will like our gift."

"Oh, Mom, I want to know."

"You will, very soon. It's going to be a surprise for everybody. This is very special."

"On my birthday, everyone always knows what I want. I tell them, so they don't make a mistake. So, my birthday present is not a surprise."

"No, it's not, but that's okay. We're glad that we don't have to guess and maybe get something that doesn't make you happy. Right now, I think it is better that we know exactly what you want. When you get older, maybe you can let us guess."

"Okay."

Joy sighed as she parked. The foundation office location was a good idea. On Tuesdays and Thursdays she was able to focus on the work of the various projects, she found these the most satisfying days of the week. Joseph said he had sent some emails for her to review and she was looking forward to an uneventful afternoon. She entered the reception area to check her mail cubby. Belinda, the secretary anxiously stood behind her desk. and rushed over to her.

"Miss Anderson?" she said frowning.

"Good afternoon, Belinda what's wrong? Any messages for me?"

"Yes, yesterday a Mister Kyle Bundi Kinoti came by. He asked to make an appointment with you, so I told him to come by at 2:30 today."

"Why did you tell him today?"

"You are always here on Tuesday afternoons, and he said it was important."

"What is the appointment for? Anyway, that's fine. Please let me know as soon as he arrives." Joy picked up the handful of mail from her cubby hole and headed back out the door to her office across the hall.

Belinda followed. "He'll be here any minute. I told him to be on time."

"Good! Thank you, Belinda."

"Oh. There he is, coming down the hall now," Belinda said in a forced whisper.

Joy turned and saw that Kyle was walking towards them in the hall.

"Kyle, you can come right in. I just got here, so let me switch on the air," She entered leaving the door ajar, and went to find the remote control for the air conditioner.

"Hello, Joy. Thank you. I wasn't trying to rush you. I was just trying to be on time," he said closing the door behind him.

"No problem. So, what brings you in today? Oh, excuse me. I meant to thank you so much for the work you are doing at the Kimathi Road Children's Home."

"Thank you for the opportunity. Actually, that's why I'm here today. I wanted to let you know that I won't be the lead there anymore. I'm recommending that you appoint David. He has been the second in charge and loves the kids. He's good at organizing everything and has run things over the last three months."

"Thank you for the recommendation, but what's going on? Why are you leaving?"

"Well, it's kind of a difficult story."

"What happened?"

"I have really enjoyed working with the kids, and it has gradually become more than a one weekend per month thing. Anyway, one of the kids, this little boy JJ, got sick and I went to see him at the children's hospital. He was pretty sick when I got there, but so were a lot of the other kids in the hospitals. He kept asking me to promise to bury him nicely if he died. I thought that was odd, so after my visit, I stopped by the nurses' desk to ask the nurse what was wrong with him. She told me that he was HIV positive and was beginning to have AIDS symptoms. I guess I must have looked a little shocked because she asked me to sit down in her office. She explained to me that all of the kids on that ward were HIV positive, and that some of the children at the orphanage were as well. Most of those kids had watched one of their parents die from AIDS. So, death was not an unfamiliar thing to them and they talk about it all the time. You know, I had never thought about why those kids were orphans or why they went to the hospital so often. That day, I was deeply moved and was lost for a while as I sat in the hallway. Instead of going home, I went back to the ward and read some more stories to them. I went back every day after work for the next month. I just wanted to spend time with them, to comfort them in some way. I ended up reading stories and talking to them one by one. I'd bring sweets sometimes. I don't know why, but I couldn't stop thinking about them. JJ stayed for three weeks, then he got a lot worse. When I went after work one day, his bed was empty. I was so happy because I thought he had gone home. I turned to the room thinking they would be happy that another one of the groups was better. They were all avoiding my eyes and looking down, and then it hit me. I ran to confirm with the nurse. JJ had died that morning."

"Oh, no!"

"I felt lost and powerless as I wandered back to his empty bed and sat down at the foot. Nellie—I think she was the oldest of the kids there—came over and sat next to me.

She said 'He's gone to heaven, now, and he'll never be sick again. We shouldn't be sad', then she took my hand and held it…" He took a deep breath and coughed appearing to fight off the tears, but his voice was unsteady. "Can you imagine? This little girl was so brave facing death… and was trying to comfort *me*."

"My goodness," Joy whispered back, as her eyes were starting to tear.

"Well," he said, "I remembered what I had promised JJ and did everything I could for his burial. I brought a nice little suit, socks, shoes, and a coffin. The nurse arranged for us to have a memorial service, right there in the chapel of the hospital. All the kids walked over from the ward and the kids from the orphanage attended. The nurses carried those who were too sick to walk. The pastor, who usually came to the orphanage, was there to lead the service."

"Aw."

"After the service, I went to say goodbye to the kids on the ward. I know most of them by now. Nellie came up to me and took my hand and said, 'Mister Kyle, will you buy me nice clothes to be buried in when I die? JJ looked so nice and happy.' I tell you, at this point, I broke down in tears. W h e n others came toward me. Nellie announced that I was going to buy her nice clothes when she died as I did for JJ. They bombarded me with the same simple request. Imagine, Joy, these were children, but there were no requests for toys or to go to a park or a fun place."

"That is the saddest story I have ever heard."

"And it is not just one child's story, but the story of so many. Although the kids at the orphanage were important there is an entire team dedicated to them. The kids at the hospital have nobody, as yet. I tried to do both for a while and found that it was just too much for me. I'm going to try to get a few other people to work with me in the hospital ward. I hope that there is one person a day there among them, not for their disease, but for them as people. You know what little Kiki asked me the other day?"

"What?"

"She asked how I managed to adopt all of them. She thanked me for being her dad. All I did was read her a story and play with her on the swings ... that's all. I'm going to be there and focus on them from now on. I didn't want you to think that I was flakey when you heard that I was no longer at the Kimathi Road Home."

"Wow, that's quite an undertaking, investing in kids that you know may never grow up."

"I know, but it's a good kind of challenge. I am determined to get others in there so I don't get overwhelmed. There are only so many beds on the ward, but they are usually full. Who knows? With medications improving, some of them may grow up."

"I don't know what to say... May God bless you and strengthen you in this calling. I pray that the best of all things come to you."

"Thank you. It's because of you that I discovered this opportunity." He stood, extended his hand to shake Joy's hand. "Goodbye."

"Goodbye, Kyle." Joy firmly shook his hand. She walked him to the office door where they nodded to each other. He then walked out into the hall.

Chapter  18

"Do you know where this place is, Dad?" Joy was in the passenger seat as Marshall drove down the street in a wealthy Nairobi area.

"I think so, but I thought it would be good to come with you and go over everything to be sure. It's left at the next corner, right?" Joy nodded and Marshall put on the turn signal.

"Yes, then go down two lights and turn right. It's the second building from the corner."

"Okay, great. How did you pick this place, anyway?"

"It's big enough and within walking distance from the hotel where most of the guests will be staying."

"That's very logical and thoughtful."

"Dad, I am so excited. I have confirmations from fifteen people besides our family. The one coming from the farthest distance is Mrs. Vera Bell from California. I wasn't so sure Mrs. Bell would come at first, but she is on her way. Being the brave woman that she is and having the sterling example of Grandma, she got her passport for the first time at the age of 75. At least, I have met her before in person when we took Grandma to her old church during the time you all came for Peter's wedding."

"Yeah, I remember she had married an older man, Asa Bell, who was a good friend of Grandpa Joe's. I'm glad she's coming."

"The others are mostly the orphans she helped select for Claire's Corner or met personally. I have Fode from Sierra Leon, Kofi from Ghana, Tafari from Ethiopia, Kamara from Cameroon, Mwikisa from Malawi, Welcome from South Africa, Nginda from Uganda, Dande from Zambia, Mogae from Botswana, Kalusha from Zimbabwe, Shivute from Namibia, Ntsu from Lesotho, Matu from Kenya and Budeba from Tanzania. It's a good thing they kept in contact by mail with her, or I never would have been able to get in contact with them or write and invite them."

"That is quite an impressive list."

"Do you remember Rosario from Mexico?"

"We met him the first time we went to see Claire's Corner. Is he coming?"

"No. He wanted to come, but the same day is the baptism service for his first grandchild. You know what he wrote in reply to the letter? He said that 'next year nothing else will be scheduled for that day. I have already blocked it off on my calendar'. The woman is one hundred years old and he says to invite him to the one hundred one-year birthday party celebration."

"That is pretty optimistic."

"Anyway, others are coming from town, and family from the village. Uncle John and Savanna are even coming. This is one of the few times when this many people are coming together for a celebration as opposed to a funeral."

"And she doesn't know anything about it. This is the best surprise I have ever been a part of."

"I wouldn't put it past her to think that there was something brewing, I mean it *is* her one hundredth birthday."

"You're right, but I hope she is somewhat surprised by the extent of the effort that everyone has made."

"I can assure you that she will be pleasantly surprised."

"So how do you have this arranged?"

"Well, we are going to tell her that we are having a big party later that day and are taking her out to a restaurant for lunch first. We will sit her down to a table, and we'll all order lunch. This is to let everyone get in place in the party hall in the back. There is a back entrance, and I've told everyone to come through there. I'll use some excuse to make sure everyone is ready… I know! Why don't you come in through the front door when everything is ready? Then you can excuse yourself to the men's room to wash your hands. I'll ask Grandma Martha to go to the ladies' room with me and instead of returning to our table I'll lead her to the party surprise."

"I hope we're able to keep everyone quiet," Marshall said.

"That's why we're staying at a distance. It doesn't matter if they are noisy. It'll just seem like someone is having a party. She'll not think it has anything to do with her, because we are having a big party for the family later at home like we always do."

"Okay. What do you want me to do?"

"Well, you know most of the people and other ones you'll have a good idea of from the list. You and Mom can help get them organized, seated at the right tables, and answer questions about where to put the gifts. Oh, yeah. We asked them to bring any pictures from the past with her or of her and to have a short story typed up. This is so we can make a memory book, as a gift instead of a lot of nice, but useless, things for her."

"I have my short story already. I was surprised to read the one your mom typed up."

"Why?"

"I kind of knew about the story but didn't know the details of something in particular that happened while she was staying with Grandma, just after we were married."

"It will be fun to hear a lot of things like that; things that were so important to other people and her but that the rest of us never heard about."

"Yes. It was a very good idea. You've been coming up with a lot of those lately."

"I've been listening to other people with good ideas and taking them seriously. This whole book thing started in the hospital when you suggested I try something different when I couldn't draw for a while. Grandma Martha suggested the project for the art institute. Then Moses and other people came up with ideas for other books."

"I like what you just said. You listened to their ideas and took them seriously."

"Yeah, that was something else I got from Grandma Martha at Peter's wedding. She said that 'the Bible says that the wise person, even wisdom herself, is easily entreated. The wiser you become, the more approachable you are and willing to share with others'. That just really stayed with me, along with some other things she said that same day. I want to be wise."

"The act of seeking to be wise is always the first step. It seems to me you are moving in the right direction."

"Thanks. Here we are. You are going to be so pleasantly surprised. I chose the theme of *Stars in the Orange Groves*. They have these artificial orange trees that are scented and florescent star appliqués for the ceiling."

"She is going to love this. So will a lot of the rest of us. You have to promise me a dance under the stars amid orange trees."

"That's a promise. I have to make sure that they have real oranges for the centerpieces and check on the tablecloths and napkins. The food here is absolutely wonderful. I knew if I did not make sure of that at an event for her, it would have been unsatisfying in her mind."

"You know your Grandma Martha very well."

"I hope so. Well, that is everything, Dad. Park as soon as you see a space. There, it looks like this guy is leaving."

Marshall pulled into the vacated spot and rolled up the windows, preparing to leave the car. Joy gathered her papers and opened her door.

"Wasn't that a timely blessing?" she asked as Marshall came around to her side of the car, and they headed toward the restaurant front door.

"All blessings are timely, Joy. We just don't realize it sometimes."

"That has to be right because God is not haphazard, is He?"

"No, He is not. Let me get that door for you."

※

Grandma sat looking over the group of adults seated around the restaurant table. "I still don't understand why you decided to have a luncheon for my birthday when we are all going to be together this evening."

"This is a bit quieter without the kids. It's special because this is number one hundred one century. It won't happen again for another one hundred years."

"Oh, my," Grandma said.

"I have to visit the ladies' room. You want to go, Grandma Martha?" Joy said.

"Yes. That would be best before the food comes. Please watch our things?"

"I will be in charge of your things," Natalie said winking at Joy.

"Let me help you, Grandma," Marshall said arriving back at the table. He nodded to Joy the wordless sign that things were ready as he helped Grandma Martha stand.

"I'm glad you're back. I was beginning to be concerned. We all ordered. You'd better let them know what you want."

"Okay, I will. You take your time." Joy nodded back to him, greatly relieved. She then turned her attention to the guest of honor.

"I think it's down this way," Joy said as she waited to let Grandma Martha lean on her arm.

They made their way to the women's toilet and on the way back, Joy turned to go down the hall to the party room as planned. She glanced to make sure that everyone had left the dining table where they had been moments before.

"Joy, aren't we were supposed to go the other way? I don't think this is the way we came."

"This is the way we are supposed to go. I am sure of it."

"But we didn't pass by this room with all of these people when we came from the table. What are you doing?"

"I am looking to see who is in there," Joy said as she peeked through the slightly ajar door, searching for her father. As soon as he saw her, he began trying to get everyone's attention to prepare for Grandma Martha's entrance.

"What? Why would you disturb someone's party? We'd better get back to our table Mmm, it smells like oranges, doesn't it? Come on." She pulled on Joy's arm a little, in the direction of the table.

"No, I think we should go inside," Joy said resisting the pull and continued to watch. Finally, her father gave the sign that they were ready.

"Go inside? Whatever has come over you? Why would we go inside?"

"Because they are all waiting for you," she announced. She threw the ballroom door open and pulled the hesitant Grandma Martha to stand just inside the doorway.

"Surprise! Happy Birthday!" everyone yelled.

A rapid series of expressions crossed over Grandma's face: confusion, shock, recognition, then pleasure as the children ran to engulf her in hugs. A chair was brought to the front for her to sit on.

"My, goodness! This *is* a surprise; all of you hiding out back here, in the orange groves, no less. This is amazing, orange blossoms in the air, orange trees on every side. I feel like over twenty-five years have been washed away You, little ones, are the anchors to the present, though."

"Grandma Martha, I am sure if you look around the room closely you will notice that this is not the usual family birthday party crowd. Instead of the oldest and the youngest being accounted for this time, let's account for the farthest and the shortest distance traveled in your honor."

"Okay. Who has come the farthest distance?" Grandma Martha asked.

"I am told that I did?" Mrs. Vera Bell stepped out from the crowd to walk toward her. "From one grove to another."

A gasp of disbelief, and finally joy crossed Grandma Martha's face, "Vera!!! I can't believe you came all this way," she stood, reached out and the two women hugged each other. The ever-present handkerchief, which had been hidden in the cuff of her cardigan, was put to use at the corner of each eye. "Let me look at you," she said as she held her at arm's length., then drew her back in for another hug. "You came all that way!"

"It wasn't easy, I will admit, but I am so glad that I did! What a wonderful time I've had just talking to people. I feel special to have been invited to such an august assembly."

"My goodness! Who are some of these people you have been talking to?"

"Now, Grandma Martha you haven't asked who traveled the shortest distance in your honor."

"That's right, but that must be one of you, a member of the family."

"Go ahead and ask. You may be surprised."

"Okay then, who travelled the shortest distance?"

"I am told that I did," a handsome well-dressed man stepped out into the center in front of her.

Again, a frown appeared across her face, this time without any sign of recognition.

"I actually began working in Nairobi when I was elected a few months ago, but it was in Machakos that you first met me and so graciously arranged for me to live in Claire's Corner. You and Ms. Washington appeared like shining angels at the orphanage where I was sure I would die. It was just after the last member of my family died, and I was a skinny little nine-year-old left alone. Do you recognize me, Mrs. Johnston?"

"There is something about you that is familiar, but I haven't placed it yet."

"It has been a long time, and I may not have been as consistent in my letter writing as I would have liked to have been. I am here with my wife, Sonya, and my son, Michael."

Grandma Martha seemed to continue to search her memory as she looked for clues. She watched a young lady step into the center with a very shy, skinny little boy who clung to her side partially hidden as she stood in front of the crowd.

"Say hello to Mrs. Johnston, Michael." With his father's encouragement, Michael hesitatingly stepped from behind his mother. He looked up at his mother and seeing her nod her head as well, he quickly walked up to Grandma Martha.

"Hello Mrs. Johnston," he said shaking her hand as if he had practiced.

"Hello Michael. It is very nice to meet you," she replied shaking his hand in return. He then looked up at her with a little curiosity. This triggered a knowing smile from her.

"Ah. That's right, of course, Machakos. You know, Michael, you look so much like your father did when he was a little boy." Michael turned and hurried back to his mother's side. "I guess you're just as shy," she commented as everyone laughed. She turned toward the young man who had come forward and smiled at him. "For a moment there, Sammy, it was like meeting you on the first day, all of those years ago. How good to see you. I thought your letter said you were a lawyer." She motioned for him to come closer in order to give and receive a hug.

"I am, but I decided to see if things would improve faster if I worked on passing clearer laws, so I am in politics, now. I still teach law at the university and run the law office, though. Now that I am in Nairobi, I can come and visit you and keep you up to date, personally."

"Wonderful, that would be just wonderful."

"Yes, indeed," Sammy smiled and returned to his seat.

"Now," she said turning to the crowd in the room, "I want the rest of you to know that in our family usually when we say that everyone in between is here, it means we can get started with the celebration. This time, however, I have no idea who *'everyone in between'* are, so I think that each one of you should come up and spend some time with me."

"Now Grandma I am so glad you feel that way, because we have asked each person here to bring a favorite story about you with them. They are all typed up and with pictures so that we have a book of your visitors by the end of the evening."

"That is very good."

"Some are going to read them so that we can all enjoy them together. The rest will be in the book to be enjoyed later. But don't think that we are the only ones who have to do some talking. At the end we want you to speak."

"That will be a pleasure!"

"Listen everybody. First is the dinner buffet. After that, you have a lot of choices. You can dance. You can talk and spend time with Grandma Martha, also known as Mrs. Johnston. You can spend time with each other. I will be here at the memories table in the corner to accept stories and pictures from all of those who brought them. Enjoy!"

The tape with some of Grandma's favorite songs caused some to start with the dance floor. Almost everyone headed noisily toward the buffet table. Some of the children ran around playing. Sammy, his family and Vera Bell chose to gather around the guest of honor. Joy sat behind the memories table and saw Faith walking toward her.

"Joy, you want me to help you collect the stories?"

"Thanks. I have this little system with these removable numbered stickers. You put the name of the person on the list by the number that will be placed on the story, and any photos that go with the story given by that person."

"That's pretty clever. Okay, I will sit beside you so we can handle this twice as fast, and we can join in the celebration."

"Go eat first and then when you are done, you can take over."

"Okay. I'll be back with my plate. You want anything?"

"I have my eye on some of the mixture in the last dish in the line at the table over there."

"Done! I'll be right back with both plates. It smells wonderful in here."

"Hi," Joy said to the vaguely familiar young lady who stood in front of her.

"Hello, I think this is so nice. I hope you send a copy of the final book with all of the stories to everyone. I would love to hear them, but I know I'll not be able to talk to everyone tonight. It would be nice to have the opportunity to read them, later."

"That's something I didn't think of. I just had in mind that it would be a gift for her. The idea of copies as keepsakes for the ones who came to share tonight is a very good one. I will have to see the best way that can be done."

"Okay, I get to be number one. I have a story and three pictures."

"Just write your name right here by the number one. I'll put number one stickers on the story and each of the pictures. I know you from somewhere, but not clear about where. Of course, you are Sandra from church. These pictures bring back a lot of memories. You have really grown up."

"Yes, I have all of my teeth now. I had copies of the pictures made for her today because they are so precious to me. I still have the originals at home in my album. I hope I get to take some new ones tonight. Cameras have gotten so much better at taking such clear pictures."

"Oh, my goodness, I forgot the photographer!"

"I saw someone taking pictures," she said scanning the room. "There he is. He's not using a flash so you don't notice it so much."

"Thank you," Joy sighed with relief when she spotted the photographer pointed out by Sandra. Turning back to the photos on the table, she placed the number on photos given her. "There you are, all safely filed."

"Thank you. This was a wonderful idea. I am so glad I ran into Natalie the other day and asked about Mrs. Johnston or I might have missed all of this."

"Why, thank you again. You should get something to eat now before it disappears."

"Thanks, I will."

Joy placed the pages and photos in a zip lock album page file. Just as she readied the list and stickers for the next person, Moses ran up to the table.

"Mom, are you in trouble?"

"Why do you ask that?"

"Because Grandma Martha called me and Salome up in the front and asked us if we knew about this party and all the people that were coming last week. You know, when Auntie Natalie dropped us off at her house after school while you ran errands?"

"She did?"

"Yes, she said you pulled a fast one, and she wanted to know all of those involved. I told her that you didn't tell anybody so that they would not tell her by accident. She just said, 'Is that right?' Then she looked at us real hard like she does when she's trying to look inside your mind. You know what I mean?"

"Yes, unfortunately, I know exactly what you mean."

"Then this man came up to talk to her that used to be an orphan and she told us to 'shoo away' because she would talk to us later."

"Did you eat something? I am not going to cook when we get home. You had better eat more than cake while we are here."

"I did. I just ate some chicken, and they have that rice like you make at home. Salome told me I had to have some green beans, too. I'm going to find Mike and Marsh."

"Okay, but don't go outside. There will be stories in a little while."

"Okay, Mom."

Chapter 19

Faith arrived at the story's table carrying two plates. "Here you are. There was roasted meat that they just brought out, so I put a little on your plate, too. You are managing to keep up with the stories and photos, it seems."

"Great, thank you, Faith." Just as she set the plates down, the next person appeared in front of the table. Pretty soon a crowd had accumulated at the table with their contributions.

They worked feverishly for a while until there were only two people in line and the album was quite full."

"Maybe you can look through them and choose a couple that you think would be good to have read tonight."

"Okay," Faith said as she replaced the stickers for number twenty-seven on the table. She took the bulging album and began to leaf through it.

Just as joy finished labeling number twenty-eight, Faith began laughing uncontrollably as she read one of the stories.

"Joy, this is hilarious. Hope wrote about the time Grandma Martha did babysitting for the whole group of great grandchildren, while the parents all went to a church meeting. She said Grandma Martha asked them what they wanted to play, and they decided to play this track and field video game with the power pad. After a while, everyone had their turn in the competition, except her. With the kids cheering her on, she stepped onto the pad and took her turn. They were surprised when she didn't hold back but did everything, all the running and jumping. They started cheering even more as she passed from one event to the other. Hope says that the fact that she had agreed to start was so encouraging to them because none of the other adults had bothered to play with them. When she continued with gusto, they actually got quite excited. At the last event they were all gathered around loudly cheering her to the finish line, to great applause. Listen to this part, 'I saw that no one was looking at the timer as she ran the last race. We were just so happy that she finished. We started jumping around and hugging her and gathered around her and congratulated her and the score didn't matter. What I learned was that when someone does more than you expect because they want to do it, everyone is happy. Since that day, whenever I think to give up or stop something that seems a little hard, I remember Grandma Martha being so brave to go to the end. I just continue until the end now because I want to congratulate myself in my mind to finish what I begin. I knew that Grandma Martha was tired, because she was old, but that did not stop her.' Listen to what she says at the end. 'It was only a game, but Grandma did it for us because she loves us. I think Grandma Martha knows that games are important, too, with your family and especially with little kids that play them with you because they can learn a lot.' Isn't that precious? I am sure she had some help from her dad."

"That is a good one. Yes, we should have Hope read that one. What about the others? We need at least two more." Joy said.

"Okay. How about this one from Vera Bell? It was when Grandpa Joe and Grandma Martha helped her and Asa Bell during the time he was so sick and then died?"

"What does she say? We don't want this to be a sad time."

"No. It's not at all sad. She sums up 'the graciousness of two people, who did things, because it was the right thing to do. This .was without making you feel that you're beholden to them'. She says that 'real love for God is shown in actions that help people when they need it, even if they don't ask for it and can't give anything in return. Even if you never went to church with them or knew how much they prayed or tithed, just watching how they reach out to their neighbors was evidence that they knew a loving God, A God who was ready to be as loving to you as they were'. I think that is very positive."

"That *is* very positive." Joy agreed.

"Then the one by Sammy is good, too. It says that after watching his new baby sister first, then his dad and finally his mother all die for an unknown reason, he was sure he would be next at the age of eight. His mother had been so sick the six months, before she died that he had missed school to stay home and care for her. He said he had hoped if he could be perfectly obedient that somehow, she would not die. He woke up the last morning he was at home, to find that his mother had died during, th the night and thought that he was to blame. He had stayed in the house crying, not daring to go out to tell anyone, the whole day. The social worker came by that evening, found him and, brought him to the local orphanage. He has no idea what happened to his mom after that. He was terribly distraught and thought he was going to die. He ate very little and refused to do anything, like going to class or playing with the other children. One day Ms. Washington and Ms. Johnston came by, and they talked to a lot of the children. When it was his turn, they asked him questions, but he didn't have much to say. He heard Ms. Washington whisper to Mrs. Johnston. 'I think he's the one we've been looking for.' And she responded, 'I definitely agree. He is perfect for the job.' He said he looked around the room to see who they were referring to, as they continued talking to each other. 'He's going to have to work very hard.' 'Yes, he only has a short time to get ready and there is so much to be done.' Finally, they asked him if he was willing to go to America and work hard to come back to Kenya and do a very important job for the country. He looked around the room again to make sure they were talking to him. He agreed that he could work hard, but he wanted to know if they were aware that he would probably be dying soon. He said that instead of running away they smiled and said that was okay as long as he promised to get through school and come back and work first. They told him that the doctors had told them, he should live long enough, if that was what he wanted to. 'So, the decision is yours. God sent us here. Do you think you can trust God enough to help you do a good job?' He hesitated as it was a big shift to go from waiting to die at any minute to planning to go to America and prepare to come back a do a job, any job for a long time. He says, the moment he said that he could trust God to help him, the two women in front of him seemed to shine. 'A light came and dispelled the darkness in my life and I have not thought about death as my destiny again, but have focused on living to do a good job with the help of God.' That's positive, huh?"

"Yes, that's also a very positive story. So, let's see. We have one from her generation, the following generation, and then the last or present generation. That's very good. Okay, I will let them know that we expect them to read their stories. They need to come and get them to prepare themselves."

"Okay, I'll stay here, this time. Can you announce that anyone who was waiting for the line to get shorter may now come to turn their story and photos in?"

"Sure. Let me take the plates." Joy grabbed the plates and found all three and sent them to Faith to recover their stories.

Placing the plates on the waitress's standing tray in the corner, she caught sight of her father walking toward her.

"How are things going?"

"I think you are doing a wonderful job to bring a wonderful idea to life."

"Thank you, Dad."

"Only one thing is missing."

"What's that?"

"You promised me a dance."

"No time like the present," she said smiling. She paused before she reached for his extended hand to confirm the three story readers were rehearsing their stories next to the table beside Faith.

Marshall spun her around and then began waltzing her on the dance floor where a few others were dancing to the music which had been playing in the background.

"So, Dad what is the importance of this dance?"

"When I was a teenager, I once told my grandfather that I would never find a girl who would think it a fun thing to dance in the orange groves under the stars. He answered 'you never know', and he was right. God brought me the most amazing woman to share my life with; her first day in California, she happily danced with me in the orange groves. Now all these years later, I have the pleasure of dancing, again, with her daughter. She is a beautiful, goodhearted, intelligent young lady, who even created an orange grove just to make some people feel at home. I am doubly blessed. If I didn't get it the first time, I definitely get it now."

"How wonderful God is," Joy said.

"Yes, indeed."

As the song ended, Marshall gallantly bowed to her; and she curtseyed in return.

"I have to now go find your mom for our dance together."

"Faith is waving to get my attention. I guess the story tellers are ready. I'll give time for one more dance."

Joy signaled, and they came to stand by Grandma Martha.

When they were in place, Joy made the announcement.

"After this next song, we are going to have three people come and share their stories."

As the next song played Joy watched as her parents danced as if they were the only ones in the grove.

While Faith supervised the story reading, Joy went to make sure the cake with all the candles was ready. She waited by the side door with the waitress. As soon as every had clapped for the last story read by Hope, Joy signaled to her mom and dimmed the lights.

Kathombi's beautiful alto voice led the Happy Birthday song as the cake was marched into the room.

"Now, you know that I am not going to manage to blow all of these candles out at once by myself. I accumulated them one at a time, you know, so I am asking all of those who played Track and Field with me to come and be on my candle-blowing team."

The kids all ran happily forward giggling to be at the center of attention.

"Now, we are all going to blow together when I count to three, okay?"

"Yes," they all chimed. "One, two three."

There was a loud inhaling of breath and then the room was dark for a few seconds as Joy found the light switch again.

"Great job, team," Grandma Marth congratulated them.

"Yea!" they cheered themselves.

The waitress took the cake back to the corner table and placed ice cream and cake on each plate. Others rushed to deliver a plate in front of each guest.

When the majority of the room had finished the cake and ice cream and the rest of the food had been cleared away, it seemed like even the kids were sitting quietly in expectation. Now, Joy thought was the time for the finale. "Okay, everybody. We saved the best for last. You are welcome to stay and continue the fun and celebration as long as you like, but this the last scheduled item on the agenda. We are going to ask Grandma Martha for some words to live by. She has touched us all in so many good ways along the way to this special day. You are one hundred years old, today. We feel especially blessed by God and are so grateful, because we know you are here to continue to speak health and wisdom into our lives. So, in addition to all of the other things you have taught and showed us over the years, what would you say at this moment in time is the one thing you would like us to remember most? Also, if you have some advice on how to stay so young for one hundred years, I know the ladies would like to hear that as well."

"Hear! Hear!" the ladies in the room chorused

"Grandma, you have the floor." Joy said as she smiled at her. Marshall rushed up, helped her to stand, then nodded his head in encouragement and stepped back.

"Thank you, Marshall. Joy, I must say you have had some good ideas in your life, but this is one that is **very** good. I might add that it was also a very well-kept, secret."

"Thank you, Grandma Martha. Keeping a secret from you is no small feat."

"Yes, well… I'm just going to sit instead of standing to talk," she said as she supported herself with the arm of the chair and sat back down. She fidgeted with her handkerchief for a few seconds and then folded it and tucked it in her sleeve cuff at her wrist. "Let's see. What would I like you to remember most? Well…First of all, I would like to say that over the years, I believe God has blessed me to have the privilege to have wonderful and loving people around me. This allowed me to see that He will always find a way to show His love, no matter where or in what situation we find ourselves. This is very important, even though we tend to take it for granted. When we take it for granted, it is because we don't understand the amazing value of this truth. We fail to see that it is not just something we fall back on, as a default. It is something we use to strategize with and act with. If we consider God's love as a guide, then we won't have to ever think of it as a default for those times when nothing else works. God's love is proactive. It allows you to use His wisdom to make decisions as if you had the experience or intelligence of an expert. Wisdom is using the right information, in the right situation, to make the right decision and do the right action. I have myself wondered how I managed to arrive at a thought, at a moment when it was most important. You know, being at the right place at the right time is called serendipity by some and good luck by others, but is nothing but the grace of God. Depending on His wisdom assures these occasions will happen regularly in our lives. God's wisdom is given freely by God to His children when they ask for it. Something you've received freely and with unlimited supply is something that you can feel free to give to others in the same way. You also realize that God gives the same to His other children, and they also give to you freely. It's a wonderful thing to have God's wisdom surrounding you.

"People from the outside might say 'you live in a dream world' and 'nothing bad happens to you' or even 'you are living in a fool's paradise'. We know that bad things do happen sometimes to good people, even God's children, but that He gives us the wisdom to see how it is for our good as He promised. Unpleasant and sad things happen all the time, but wisdom shows that there is a season for all things and that God is there to help us through difficult situations. We know our source and the purpose of our lives. We have to be open to hearing God's explanation of the real situation, not just what we can see with our earthly eyes. I hope and pray we all remember that God's wisdom is easily entreated. If we really want to look back over our lives with some degree of satisfaction, we will seek true wisdom and we will also be ready to yield our habits, traditions, and personal desires when truth requires us to do so. There is just no getting around the fact that this means we also have to, sometimes, be willing to sacrifice our own desires and convenience, at times, for the good of others. Now, Joy, where are you?"

"Yes, Grandma Martha, I'm right here."

"For you and the rest of the ladies, here is my secret for getting older without getting old. I think the greatest part of it is to live an open life every day so that none of the poison from bitterness, envies or unforgiveness stays in you to make you ugly. It doesn't hurt to work hard and laugh a lot. Well, I think I'm finished. That's the few words I have to say."

Joy came to stand by her and began the applause. People rose to their feet and the applause rose higher. Suddenly, Grandma Martha waved her hand, and Joy bent down to hear what she was saying. She signaled for the others to hold their applause and helped her to stand.

Grandma stood to her feet proudly straight and took a deep breath before she spoke again. "Oh yes. There is one other final thing. I want to thank all of you for coming to honor me, today. It is really very heartwarming. When I see all of the efforts that was made and so many people coming from places far and wide ... I could have never imagined as an only child without friends for sixteen years, that God would bless me with such a huge family and world of friends; but He knows the desires of our heart. I just wanted you all to know, I am so satisfied with what He has chosen as my portion in life. I am so pleased to be here with you all, today."

The room burst into cheers and applause. Marshall came beside her and whispered something in her ear and she smiled in response. She turned and whispered to Joy, who also smiled. On cue, the three of them lined up to begin the happy dance. Immediately, the other family members joined in, with the youngest ones getting in line behind Grandma or being held by their parents. Soon everyone had joined in.

"See what you started, Marshall Anderson, with your tribe?' Kathombi called as she danced behind him.

"Oh, this is just the beginning, Thom. The tribe is getting bigger, and I'm not looking back. Let's see who and what God will bring into our lives. Did you just see that?"

"What?"

"I think Little-bit, and Grandma Martha just did a very unusual step. Did she teach him or did he teach her?"

"Umm. It's hard to tell. You'll have to watch those two, closely."

Marshall reached out and grabbed her hand as they continued the happy dance.

"Sounds like a job for two, armed with prayer."

Chapter 20

JOY SET HER TRAVELING gear by the door. She sat down and made an effort to clear her desk, going through the stack of papers in front of her. She was of course distracted by the noise created by the excited students on the bus the school had rented for the trip to the Kenyan coast. The noise reminded her that they would occupy her time for the next week. Looking over the list of the American students selected to come for the next term, Joy was apprehensive but far too preoccupied to make any decisions at the moment. She placed it back in the folder of things to do in the corner of her desk.

After ten years of the exchange program between the two art institutions, there seemed to be an organized administrative side functioning well enough to settle into regularity. The students, however, managed to come up with new or unexpected extracurricular activities that required more and more of her time. It was admirable they were so innovative and energetic, but someone had to be there to keep them out of harm's way. The task to make sure they returned to California safe and sound was her responsibility. Sometimes extracting one of them from social quicksand or keeping their heads above water demanded time she had intended for herself or Salome or Moses or the foundation activities.

Today was a case in point. This week was the first week of school break and most of the students had gone away for the holidays. A small group decided they wanted to take part in a national art competition, despite the fact that they had never done this kind of competition before. Instead of getting to relax after the final push to the semester's end, they asked if she would accompany them and guide them on how to set things up.

Their request involved an entire week away from home and meant that the decision to go to the Mombasa Art Festival to help with the students' displays had not been an easy one. She'd struggled most over leaving Moses and Salome behind; but once she told the students yes, everything else seemed to fall into place. Moses was at Peter's house to spend a blissful week with the twins, Mike and Mark, and the five-year-old twin girls, Christa and Trisha.

Joy smiled at the thought of Natalie having a second set of twins. The scene from Moses' fourth birthday party came to mind when Natalie had told Salome she wanted a little girl and was waiting for God to send one. Salome had assured her that she would start praying for her. The twin girls were born about a year later. *I warned her to watch out when Salome prayed for something!* Joy chuckled to herself.

Salome was spending the week with Joseph's family, happy to have more time with Hope and the other two girls of the house, Grace, and Mercy. They had been born after Richard, who was always bewailing the fact that he was surrounded by girls but everyone knew he loved his sisters with a passion.

Joy had let her maid take the opportunity to go for a family visit. Her car was at Joseph's house, which left Grandpa Marshall with the responsibility of checking on the house security guard every now and then. The Visions of Joy Foundation was in the capable hands of a talented manager who had been impressive with her ability to get things done the way Joy wanted. The Art Institute was on holiday break, without any student responsibilities. There were no worries from any of her life's fronts, except for the students waiting in the courtyard outside, eagerly discussing plans. They were determined to win their selected competitions.

The office door opened and one of the students, Lisa, excitedly stuck her head in.

"Prof, everyone is here and the bus is ready to go. Can I help you with your things?"

"Sure, that's nice of you. I just have my duffle bag and the portfolio. If you want, you can carry one."

"Okay. Wow, this portfolio is sure nice and light. I need one like this. You can put everything in here, huh?"

"Yes, at least, all I need to do my sketching. Let's go."

Joy was the last one to get on the bus. The monitor, Theresa, handed her a clip board. Joy smiled in appreciation that they were really making an effort to be organized.

"Hi, Professor Anderson. Here is the list of the students going and their projects. The second page is a list of passengers." They were checked-off indicating all were present.

"Thank you, Theresa. Looks like we're all here, so let's get going," she told the driver and took her place in the first seat.

As she looked out of the window, she sighed and leaned back comfortably. There was a lot of excitement in the air as the students discussed display plans and life in general. When Joy awakened sometime later, she was surprised that she had fallen asleep. Looking around the bus, she noticed that most of the students were sleeping as well. They had better rest now she thought. Once they arrived, there will be a lot of work and little rest as they set up for the opening day. She repositioned herself to be more comfortable and went back to sleep.

As she expected, for the first three days there was a lot of adapting to the unexpected, arranging materials and spaces and arguing over design for the displays. The students had brought creations they were entering in three festival competition categories and each wanted the first pick of supports that put their work in the best light. Miraculously, they were ready on time for the inspection the evening of the second day with the opening ceremony to take place the next morning. Declaring her work done, Joy let the students take full charge for the rest of the festival activity. The next morning, she kept her resolve and slept in past her usual 5:30. When she finally arrived in the guest breakfast restaurant at 7:30, the others were excitedly heading out through the lobby. She waved goodbye and sat down to a leisurely and enjoyable meal. An hour later she was starting to feel very lazy and was tempted to go back upstairs to her room and sleep.

She walked to the glass door to the terrace, and whispered to her reflection, "Come on. Didn't you want to sketch some beach scenes? How often do you get a chance to lounge on the beach these days?" she chided herself as she shook her head.

She forced herself to stand and walk outside onto the terrace. The weather was so nice and the ocean views so inviting, she soon found herself trudging through the sand to the water's edge. She closed her eyes and absorbed the ambiance, the ocean breeze, the sound of waves breaking, and the ocean smells, before beginning to slowly walk along the wet sand at the wave's edge.

As the hissing from the froth of the wave's edge, she wondered, how God ever think of making waves? It was the organization within the chaos of the ocean; not because it wanted to be or made any effort to be organized. The irresistible force of the moon, from such a great distance and the invisible winds, made it so. Amazing she thought. You couldn't visualize the evidence of either of the forces, but there were undeniable results. God's pull on people's lives was kind of like that.

After this short stroll along the shore, she was fully inspired and awake. She hurried back to her room to get the large sketch pad, pencils, and a ground easel, and she was soon setting up her things on the beach, not far from the hotel restaurant terrace. She had expected a crowd of people to arrive soon. Surprisingly, the next couple of hours she was pretty much alone on the sand. Slowly the morning haze began to burn off and the ocean changed from its nighttime to daytime identity.

Happy for the calm and solitude, she finished the first sketch, which had consumed most of the morning, and began a second ocean sketch. Quite pleased with her progress, she again glanced out at the ocean. This time out of the corner of her eye, she noticed a man walking along the surf in her direction. She sighed at the distraction and refocused on her sketch. As he approached and entered her field of view the distraction increased. She paused hoping he would quickly and quietly pass by on his way. Unfortunately, he seemed to have a lot of leisure time as well. Instead of efficiently covering the distance along the shore, he repeatedly stopped to look toward something on the land with his back to the ocean. At this point, she was almost completely distracted by his movements. Her drawing was making slow progress.

Stopping her work completely, she thought it was strange activity. *Who comes all the way down to the ocean, to look back at the land? What is he doing? Maybe he's a lunatic or something. I'd better watch out for any threatening or sudden moves.*

When he got closer to her spot on the beach, he changed the trajectory angle of his path. It seemed as if he were going toward the restaurant terrace behind her. *Oh well, my question as to what he was doing didn't get answered, but at least the distraction is gone.* She resumed her sketch. A few minutes later, curiosity got the better of her and she turned to confirm his entrance into the hotel. To her dismay, he was standing not very far away behind her. He appeared to be staring intently at the sketch she was working on. She immediately turned back around and began nervously adding a few minor lines to the sketch. *This is so embarrassing. He has to have seen me turn to look for him and I don't know what he must think.* Engrossed in her nervous thoughts, she didn't realize he had started walking toward her until she heard a voice right next to her.

"It is so beautiful!" The words were spoken passionately, with an accent she couldn't quite place.

Startled, she dropped her pencil. He rushed forward to pick it up and reached out to hand it to her as he kept his eyes focused on the sketch. She was at a loss as to what to do. *He doesn't seem threatening, but how could one be sure? Who is this man anyway?* Her thoughts raced as she stared at him, poising herself to run.

When he noticed she didn't take the pencil he was presenting, he frowned and turned toward her. The expression on her face caused him to take a step backward. He quickly bowed his head in respect.

He spoke softly, "O' Senora, I am so sorry. I didn't mean to frighten you." His eye moved back to the sketch. "But I had to say something when I saw your work." He turned and smiled at her directly and for a second time offered the pencil.

"Thank you," she replied quickly accepting it this time.

He bowed his head in respect again and immediately gestured as he looked at the sketch.

"You have somehow captured the massive power of the water and yet a soft, sweeping peacefulness. You must love the ocean to be able to do this. Yes. Looking at this makes me want to look more at the ocean."

"But you're here at the beach and all you keep doing is looking back in the other direction."

The surprised look on his face at her remark, made her immediately regret it. What had provoked her to say such a rude thing to him? She regretted it even more when he slowly turned to look at her fully. His expression was at first curious but soon evolved into a broad smile. He bowed his head in respect, once more, toward her.

"I am so sorry, again. Your art has so affected me, I have acted outside of my usual behavior. May I introduce myself?" He bowed his head and waited.

"Oh!" she said, realizing he was waiting for her reply. "Yes, of course." At her words, he looked up at her again.

"I am Eduardo Delgado Silva, son of Pedro Delgado and Beatrix de Silva, a humble senior civil engineer from Mozambique, 'mixing business with pleasure', as you say. I am on vacation, but could not help noticing many of the older buildings have very little erosion of their oceanfront façade. On the other hand, many of the more recent facades have crumbled and the building has fallen into decay and irreparable foundational ruin. I have been turning to look at the buildings on the shore to see if there was a secret in the angle of the façade to the ocean or the height of the retaining walls. I have mentally noted which buildings to have a closer look at for details of wall thickness and materials ... but I bore you. Forgive me."

"No, I'm not bored at all. It makes perfect sense, now. Thank you for being kind enough to answer my impertinent question."

"If you are not bored, I will complete my explanation. The thought just came to me about the story in the Bible of the two houses built, one on the sand and the other on the rock. I told myself to make sure I check to see if the foundations' bases were different as well, with the closer look at the buildings tomorrow. I had noted that there was someone doing art but saw that I was very near when I turned to walk again. You seemed very intent on your work, so I decided to try to walk behind you to not disturb your view or distract you. I hoped to pass behind you quickly. But when I saw your drawing, I was, as you say, smitten. I have never been this close to someone with such talent in the process of creating such beauty. I was tempted to come closer. Of course, it was the very thing I was trying to avoid. I didn't want to interrupt you, but when you turned around, I think that you were taking a break and I came for a closer look. It is so beautiful. It made me see the ocean in a different way. I saw things that must have always been there, but I never saw before. It was like, when you read something the first time and find it pleasant; but then you read it again another time and it means something so clearly helpful for you. God has put all of that beauty in the ocean, which I have looked at so many times before. Somehow today, because of this drawing, I can clearly see it. Your work speaks loudly of your love for the beauty God has put there; I heard it...it got my attention. I finally see it through your interpretation. It was a revelation, a... I had to say something."

"Wow, thank you Eduardo Delgado. I'm so glad that you came by and decided to kindly avoid disturbing me by passing behind me. I'm even happier that, in the process, you saw something I had done, which caused you to give God praise. I'm Joy Anderson, daughter of Marshall Anderson and Kathombi Karima, a humble artist from Nairobi. Did I do that introduction correctly?" She extended her hand confidently this time to shake his.

"It's a pleasure to meet you. "He shook her hand. " May I help with one part of your introduction, please?"

"Yes?"

"You made one small mistake when you introduced yourself. You did not say your husband's name after your father's name."

"Oh, that was not a mistake! There is no husband's name to say after my father's name because I'm not married."

He nodded thoughtfully. "Ah, I am the one, who is mistaken, Senhorita Anderson."

"No problem; you could not have known."

"You are too kind. I wonder if it would be too much of a disturbance if I watched you finish this drawing? I promise I will not say anything; I will only watch."

"That would be fine. I'm pretty far along."

As she sat down to continue the drawing, Eduardo took a seat at a respectable distance near her on the sand. She suddenly had an idea and turned toward him to pose her offer.

"You may stay only if you let me give you the drawing as a gift, in memory of the day the ocean showed you its God-given beauty."

"Oh, no," he said wide-eyed in surprise and then firmly shook his head. "I could never accept such a valuable gift. I could not—"

"Okay, then you'll have to go, no more watching," Joy said wagging her finger. She purposefully turned her attention back to the drawing, pretending to dismiss him.

"No. Please ... Okay I will accept your generous gift, but only if you allow me to take you to dinner for the ceremony of the official gift presentation."

"Official gift presentation ceremony? Are you making this up?" She turned to see if there was any suspicious sign on his face but found only a sincere expression.

"No, it is true. With something of this value, there must be a commemoration with photos taken."

"Okay. Okay, this is getting complicated. I don't know about all of that."

"You don't have pictures from other events?"

"Yes, I do, but ..."

"Is this not an event? It is for me. When I left my hotel at the other end of this beach this morning, I never thought that God would grace my day with such a lovely surprise, such a valuable gift."

"Hmm..."

"If you like the dinner can be here, but the other day, I found a wonderful Portuguese restaurant not far from here. It would be the perfect environment."

"Okay, we can go to your perfect place and take pictures, but we have to go early and get back early and ..."

"Good, thank you. I am very happy you have accepted to do so. Now, I can accept this amazing gift. What is the 'and', which you added to the end of your sentence?"

"The 'and' is that you have to let me draw your portrait right after I finish this."

"Oh yes. That would be wonderful." He looked down at his clothes, suddenly unsure of himself. "But am I looking okay for a portrait?"

"Yes. You look wonderful."

"You think I look handsome?" he asked smiling.

"Yes. You are very handsome, but that's not the reason I want to draw you. I have a lot of portraits of people I've met. This is an amazing story and I want to remember and share it."

"Please make two, so that I can also have one to remember and share."

"Of course. I want one with you smiling. You can decide what you want for yours." She checked the time on her watch. "My goodness, at this rate we're going to be here all day."

"Oh please, I don't want you to be tired for the dinner tonight. If it is too much work, I can come tomorrow for the portrait. I will be in Mombasa for four more days."

"We'll see how it goes. I hope you can sit still for a while without moving."

"You didn't tell that to the ocean." He laughed with his entire being, leaning back like her father.

"No … but the detail is a different type," she said a bit flustered.

"I will obey you now because you are the expert at drawing. At the dinner ceremony, you will obey me because I will be the expert. Yes?"

"Okay, yes."

"*Tá bem*. Good."

"Now let me get on with the work."

Eduardo silently gestured that he was zipping his lips closed. He then motioned with his hand for her to proceed, using the exact same shoo fly gesture that Grandma Martha used. True to his word, he was quiet as she finished the ocean sketch. He wordlessly went and secured a large hotel umbrella to provide shade for her as the sun began to shine brightly down on them. He left again, wordlessly, and returned with bottles of cool water. Her bottle was half-empty by the time she finished.

"There! It's not finessed, but good enough for me to sign my name at the bottom," She signed her name with a flourish and then handed it to Eduardo who gingerly accepted it.

"I don't know what to say. It was wonderful before. Now, I feel that I can as easily step into the picture as walk down to the shore. Beautiful. I will go now and buy the cover for it. It must be protected, yes? I want it to last as long as I do."

"Wait, I forgot to seal it." She motioned for him to give the drawing back. When he did, she placed it on the cardboard backing of the pad of sketch sheets, and reaching inside the portfolio, she recovered a small can of hair spray and shook it.

"What are you doing?"

"I'm sealing it so it won't smudge." She sprayed the sheet lightly all over. "The sunshine will dry it quickly and you can take. It's only paper and pencil, but a glass covering and frame will help protect it."

"You understand that I will take it for the right measurement of the cover, but I am not accepting it before the ceremony tonight."

"That's fine. Well, I think there may be time to start one portrait sketch of you, but you will have to come back tomorrow for me to complete it and do the one for you to keep."

"I will do this gladly."

Chapter

21

With pictures of ships and ocean relics that had been on the wall for ages, the restaurant was quaint. The food, however, was extremely good. It was as Eduardo had said, 'the perfect environment'. He had told the staff of the planned ceremony. They had brought a stand for the framed and now gift-wrapped sketch and treated her with obvious deference. She was finally convinced that, at least for Eduardo's culture, it really was an important thing to do.

During dinner Joy found herself asking Eduardo a lot of questions and answering just as many. It was a pleasant, enjoyably relaxed time. Suddenly, there was a flurry of movement around them. She turned questioningly to Eduardo who answered the unspoken question.

"The photographer is here to take pictures. We will begin the ceremony."

Everyone gathered around to watch the unveiling. They were obviously impressed with the framed sketch and looked at her with even greater admiration. They crowded into the space, around Joy and Eduardo as they held the frame on either side for a photo. Everyone around their table and other diners listened as Eduardo spoke about pleasant surprises and hidden treasures. Everyone laughed at his small jokes and applauded at the end.

"You have to say something now, Joy."

"I didn't know I was supposed to say anything. I'm not prepared," she explained to the grumbling of those around them. She was finally prevailed upon to say something in return.

"I think it is amazing that so often when you decide to give something away, you don't always see you have already gotten something of greater value in return. It has been my pleasure to meet you, Eduardo, and to come to know you a little bit. I am thankful to have the opportunity to have dinner in this lovely place and to meet all of you. My life is enriched so deeply and simply because I wanted to give this sketch to someone who found it beautiful. I thank you all, again, for your hospitality and encouragement. I thank you even more for helping me to better understand the value of giving things freely."

Everyone clapped and Eduardo beamed.

The next morning when the portraits were completed, Eduardo invited her to celebrate with lunch. As they finished, the students called to say that the first elimination rounds in the art competition were to take place shortly in the afternoon. The site was halfway between the hotel and the restaurant so she invited Eduardo to rush with her to the art festival to watch. They cheered as it was announced that four of the students went on to the final round. Eduardo suggested they all go out to dinner to celebrate. He was the life of the party with his jokes and proverbs and even made the students who had not advanced feel that they had accomplished something by their noble effort. By popular acclaim, the students insisted that Eduardo come back for the final completion rounds the next morning.

When the results were posted, it happened that two first-place and two second-place ribbons were awarded to her students, Eduardo was as happy as she was and hosted a simple celebration luncheon for the group at the Portuguese restaurant. As they were leaving the restaurant, he asked her to go with him the next day. He was to do the detailed investigation he had planned for some of the buildings he viewed on the first day they met.

"You must help me since you caused me to spend time away from this purpose."

"I didn't force you to spend time with me and my students' art."

"This is true. It was a willing decision that I do not regret. You must as willingly help me. Your drawing skills will be very useful. Come help me, please? I only have one more day."

"Okay, but only the morning. My students can take the displays down by themselves, then but I want to be with them when they go sightseeing around town tomorrow afternoon."

"Then to reward your generosity, I must take you out to dinner. It is the last night. Yes?"

"Yes, it is the last night and dinner would be nice."

"*Tá bem*. I know the perfect environment for such a dinner," Eduardo said with a serious expression.

"*Tá bem*." Joy whispered to herself and just shook her head.

That evening the dinner was just as delicious and enjoyable as ever. They laughed and told stories about themselves.

"So, you learned to speak both languages at an early age because of school? I thought it was from your family. Did your mother speak English as well?

"Huh? I don't know."

"What do you mean, you don't know."

Eduardo was quietly looking down at the table. He swallowed, then spoke, "Well, my mother went away when I was just a baby. My dad is the one who raised the three of us. I had no real memory of her until I was fifteen. There were pictures all over the house; wedding pictures, even a picture of her with me on her lap in the last family photo before she left. It always seemed strange to me that she was the only one not smiling. I didn't believe my dad when he said she just forgot everything one day and went back to her childhood family home, up in a mountain village. I couldn't understand how a mother could forget her children. I thought that he must have chased her away and was just trying to hide it. He had said she loved guitar music. So, I learned to play and practiced very hard. I wanted her to be pleased with me. Then, I decided one day to go and see my mother and get the truth. My father told me it was useless to go, but you know how young men are. I was determined."

"And you found her, obviously, because you said you saw her. Was it a good experience?"

"No," he said shaking his head. "I found her in her sister's home. She was sitting in the living room, well dressed, but looking very distracted. When I arrived, her sister, Isabel, warned me that all was not well. We were standing on the front porch. She didn't explain things very much, but she did tell me not to force my mother to remember anything, or she would rush out of the room. She also told me it would be better if I left my guitar on the porch. I was confused and uncomfortable, but I had come so far and waited so long. I knew I had to try. So, I left my guitar on the porch table and followed Isabel into the house. That was when I saw my mother, sitting in the living room, all alone. I almost rushed over to her to hug her, but Isabel must have read my thoughts, and she motioned for me to remain where I was standing."

"And then what happened?"

Eduardo's expression showed that his thoughts raced back to that day in the village. He began describing a very painful story. Having motioned for him to wait beside her, Isabel spoke softly to her. She told her there was someone there to see her and then left the two of them alone in the room.

"I told her my name but there was no sign of recognition. I told her I was looking for my mother. There was no response to any of the questions about her past life. She finally wished me well in my search and turned her attention to staring at the wall. I sat asking, myself if that was it? Was there to be no further conversation? Was I being dismissed? You know, I realized that if she didn't know who she was, she could not accepts who I was?"

Joy continued to watch Eduardo as clouded expressions swept across his face, revealing the review of unpleasant memories. When he sighed deeply, Joy decided the story had lasted long enough.

"This is earth to Eduardo." Joy said playfully.

"Ah! I am so sorry. Would you like some more water or something else?" Eduardo came back to the present with a swift shake of his head.

"No, I'm fine. How are you?"

"It has been a long time since I thought about that day, I went to see my mother up in the village. I left that same day but promised to send Isabel a little money each month for food and clothes. She was my mother after all and it wasn't right that she'd be a burden to Isabel. When I got older, I sent more money, but I never went back until she died. I got caught up in my studies and then work. Then I got married. My wife kept urging me to visit again but it was too painful for me to think about. I told myself I would take my child to see her. But I never had any children before my wife died."

"How hard that must have been for you. So, what happened when she died?"

"When we heard she had died it was a hard time for us. My dad had died about two weeks before. Actually, his burial was three days before. My wife had died three months before that. We were exhausted but how many times do you get to go to your mother's funeral? It took us two days to get there. It was the first time for Monica and Ernesto to see the town. Everything was positive, meeting that side of the family. I did not bother to do it when I went the first time. Isabel's daughter, Selma, had inherited the house and the care of my mom. She couldn't thank me enough for the money I had sent every month. I decided to keep sending it to help them out."

"That is such a sweet thing to do."

"To me, it was the right thing to do. Tonight, Joy, I think it is the right thing for me to tell you that I do not want to leave here with the thought that I will never see you again. I am sad that I must leave tomorrow for Beira and leave you behind. Will you let me come to see you in Nairobi next month? I was invited to be a speaker at a workshop there. I wasn't going to go, but now I definitely will if I can see you."

"I would be delighted for you to come and see me in Nairobi, although I don't know of any perfect environment restaurants."

"It does not matter. I would like to see how you look away from the ocean."

"I can promise you that I look no better in the city. I may even look worse because I have just been relaxing and enjoying myself here the last 4 days. That being said, I would like very much to see you in Nairobi …"

"*Tá bem.* Good! Then I will give you the dates when I will be there. We can see if we can have maybe a lunch or two and dinner, no valuable gift exchanges. You have such a rare talent, Joy Anderson, this is something everyone can see, but you … yourself … your personal being is something amazingly rare and beautiful … I just want to spend time with you. Your presence is value enough."

"I think *you* are a poet." Joy declared.

"No, I am not a poet, but I do sketch a bit and …"

"What?"

"No. No, I do nothing like your sketches. My work looks like a child playing around in comparison. It is just for buildings."

"I see that I will have to investigate this a bit more with time. Okay, what was the 'and'?"

"The 'and'? Oh! I was saying that I sing and play guitar, very well, I am told."

"Yes, of course, you would have to bring music."

"I'm sorry, I do not know what you mean?"

"One day I will explain what I mean You play guitar, so you will have to play for me."

"Of course! I will have to find the right song that captures how I feel, and I will sing for you. I want to impress you."

"I assure you; I am already impressed ..." She cleared her throat. "When you come to Nairobi, I will try to impress you. I'll invite you over for dinner and show you the books we've published with sketches and poetry ..."

"When you say we, you mean you and who else?"

"Remember I mentioned my two adopted children and there's a whole wonderful family. You will love them."

"I know that I will. Now, of course, this cannot be one-sided. You must come to Beira to meet my family and see Mozambique. I know you will find many things to sketch and make your heart happy."

"Yes, I am sure I will."

"I have no books to show you, but I will try to impress you as well with my wonderful family and my completed projects."

"I am impressed already, you know."

"That's good."

"You forgot to say, "Tá bem."

"Está muito bem! That's very good."

"Oh my goodness, I was just getting used to 'Tá bem' and there's a new and improved."

"This is just the beginning; you will learn a lot of Portuguese when you visit Beira."

"Tá bem!"

"So how was Mozambique?"

"It was absolutely amazing, Beira, that is. We didn't get to see much of Maputo, that's the capital city. We flew in late at night and left early the next morning for Beira. We were out on a sightseeing schedule for the first week. There is this really old lighthouse on the beach, just a short distance from where Eduardo lived as a child in the same house his brother lives in now with his family. He told me they used to have foot races around the lighthouse without a clue as to its historic value or rarity. There were kids still doing the same thing the very day we visited. There are some ship remains and old buttresses on the shore around it, all quite picturesque. I sketched until my fingers wanted to fall off. There was this other place, further toward downtown that I just could not bring myself to sketch, not even once. I get chills just thinking about it."

"Why is that?"

"It was just so deeply saddening to me. It was a monument to all of the waste, short-sightedness, and mismanagement in Africa today."

"One place? One building, Joy?"

"Yes. It was and is still called the 'Grand Hotel'. On a huge property, a luxury hotel was built to be a resort, years and years ago. It had the fame of being the grandest hotel in all of Africa. The architecture was pretty advanced for its time. When national independence came, the Grand Hotel, along with many other industries and buildings was nationalized. This is the history that was given to me. At that time, the local people demanded to have their share of land and resources to build houses for their families. As the local tribal leaders decided how to proceed, someone pointed out that there was already existing shelter in the form of this luxury hotel. To them, it would be a solution to both problems if each family was allowed to occupy a portion of the building. A scheme to share the building was devised, and they moved in. Most of them had probably never been exposed to carpeting and indoor plumbing. Things were misused and abused. Others suffered from the lack of regular maintenance or care. The property has now eroded to the point that the building is close to collapse; the plumbing has long ago ceased to function properly. Maintenance was not done, doors and windows have not been replaced by appropriate fixtures but with disordered and bare timber pieces and, sometimes, mud. Walls are covered with mold, others badly soiled. There's no working electricity. The pool and fountains have become muddy, moldy, cracked eyesores."

"That's a shame."

"When we went to the site, I was totally unprepared. I must admit, I was soon overwhelmed. I just wanted to leave to get away from there. As we were leaving, I saw some teenagers, near where the car had been parked, sitting around, in the middle of the day, on a stack of rubble that appeared to have been once the security guard cabin at the entrance. They were listening to a broken-down transistor radio, looking bored and hopeless. They apparently had no jobs but didn't see any use in doing anything to clean up the mess around them. They had never seen the Grand Hotel as it was meant to be and had no idea how to make it better."

"How did the leaders let that happen, Joy?"

"That was my question, exactly. I mean they could have kept the hotel as a resort and used the income to provide the resource money for developing their community. They would have even had jobs for those teenagers. All they have now is a building that will fall and probably injure or kill people. People still live there, so they never built the houses they needed. Now they have no options. I wanted to know why the leaders didn't help the people to make a better or long-term decision."

"What did you find out?"

"Nobody that I talked to had an answer."

"You know, it's hard to be able to judge why people did something looking back after a long time. Maybe they didn't know that the place needed a large upkeep. It was a European culture that built it. I bet when some of the people moved in, they thought that it would stay that way. It could have been the first time they had seen anything like it. There were probably some who thought that they had the right to enjoy what outsiders had enjoyed to the exclusion of the indigenous population during colonial times. Maybe some even thought it was their duty to reclaim it for their families. Don't be so hard to judge the actions of people in the past. They often did the best they could with the knowledge they had in a very different context than we know today. We wouldn't know down JoJo's hut and build a modern house for her"

"I guess you have a point, Dad."

"You know, when I was growing up, there was some debate about the roles that Blacks used to play in movies or on radio programs in the past. These roles were, for the most part denigrating in the eyes of us young people. Some of us even started saying that these actors had been in collaboration with racists to keep black people mentally subjugated, Uncle Toms we called them. I remember clearly that an elderly gentleman stood one day and said something that I shall never forget."

"What was that?"

"He said, 'Actors play all kind of roles. The more skilled they are, the more they can convincingly play a role very different from themselves in actual life. The 'dumb' partner in a comedy duo is often the most intelligent one in actual life. He has to be able to do the 'dumb thing' always on time and in a convincing manner. Yes, there is always the choice to say *yes* or *no* to a role offered. When the only role available is one requiring them to act as an unintelligent person or someone with poor judgment, if you say *no* as an actor, you and your family will not eat or have a place to live. No one will know of your sacrifice because, first of all, who's going to tell them and secondly, someone else will be glad to take the job. Taking these roles is how they were able to survive. They lived to have the chance to make other decisions and to make the money that would give better choices to their children.' After he spoke, he just sat down. It really made us think."

"Hmm. That's an interesting point. I just hope the leaders explain that to their children, or the lesson may be lost."

"Little Sister, that is true!"

"These leaders have to be willing to live with choices their children make subsequently. I have often thought about how you used to tell us you came to Kenya to do something that would benefit the people. Then decided you would stay to have a place for your children to call home, where we would be surrounded by a culture where they would not be prejudged by the color of their skin. I was reflecting the other day on how we felt so free, we didn't see that objective as being important. We felt okay to marry people from still different cultures. My children will be exposed to French, American English and UK English, Kiswahili, Kimeru, and Portuguese. Will they feel more at ease everywhere or never feel at ease anywhere?"

"I guess we will have to wait to see. Let me ask you about the point where you said 'we all felt it okay to marry people from still different cultures and the other point about your kids being exposed to, among other things, 'Portuguese'."

"Yes."

"What happened in Mozambique that you have *forgotten* to mention? What else did you do, besides all that tourism?"

Chapter  22

"I MET EDUARDO'S FAMILY. THEY'RE wonderful. You would almost think that they were an extension of our own, so loving and caring. Moses and Salome were picking up words and phrases as soon as we arrived. I was fortunate Monica and Ernesto his family speak English."

"That's right! You went to meet the family and …"

"I spent a lot of time talking to him about what he believes and wants to accomplish. I saw how he was seen by the people he grew up with and worked with. He has built some amazingly beautiful buildings. He has a lovely home that he built when he married fifteen years ago. I feel like I have known him for a long time and I love everything about him."

"Whoa! Whoa! Just a minute. There are two things there I want answers to. Does he want to live in Mozambique in this wonderful house? Where is his wife?"

"He says he wants to leave his house because of all the old memories. His wife died of cancer there. He wants to start seeing things like the ocean in my sketch the morning we met… Dad, he asked me to marry him and he is planning to come here to ask you and Mom to give me away to him."

"I see... So, what do you think?"

"I feel so alive when I am with him. He is always looking for ways to take care of me. I know that at this point I would say yes, without any hesitation. I need to hear from you guys that he is the one you would give me away to."

"I guess it is obvious that you both have prayed about this and you think God is pleased."

"Yes. I have prayed and prayed and prayed. I feel in my heart that this crazy man is perfect for me. We agree on almost everything, at least the important things and he plays the guitar marvelously. You will absolutely love him, Dad."

"Seeing you this happy, I already do. We kind of knew there was something going on the way you just waltzed him in here. It was like he was already part of the fixtures when he was here for that week. Are we talking a big wedding soon, Little Sister?"

"No. No big wedding. We both agree that a small ceremony would be okay, and we'll use the money for projects we're working on."

"He fits very well. We have no other musicians in the family. It's time we did."

"He has a sense of humor that will keep you laughing. He said that God didn't have us meet before because He knew that I would only be interested in an orphan."

"That *is* funny."

"What is funny?" Kathombi said as she came and sat by Marshall.

"Joy just told me that Eduardo asked her to marry him and she wants to say yes. He's coming to ask us to give her away to him. He joked with her, that God waited until his parents died to let them meet because He knew she would only be interested in an orphan."

"That *is* funny. Joy, this is great news," she said as she gave Joy a big hug. "I prayed with a strong focus since you had him over here last month. Grandma Martha told me when you left after dinner, that had God told her she would live to see you married. She was beginning to think we were going for a world record. She also said you better have the baby soon, or she won't have the strength to hold him. She's been waiting for the news. Have you told her?"

"No, but I heard anyway." Grandma Martha entered, a little unsteadily with her cane.

Joy stood to her feet quickly and helped Grandma Martha to sit in her special chair.

"Thank you, dear. Now, go on with the story of this young man who finally found you."

"You know the story about how we met on the beach in Mombasa."

"He already had you curious about him before you even met him or saw his face."

"Yes, Dad, he did, but he had not even seen me either. He made a big thing out of the sketch I was doing of the ocean, ignoring me all together. I offered to give it to him, and he insisted that it be given formally with a ceremony and everything at a special dinner."

"Dinner, of course, he's no dummy."

"Marshall, be nice," Kathombi said and patted Marshall's knee.

"Yeah, maybe I was snookered just a little, but I won in the end," Joy declared.

"Looks like you both won. There are no coincidences with God," Grandma Martha said.

"Only God could have set up something so jumbled together. I wasn't supposed to be there. He came at the last moment. There was the timing of the art festival, his beach stroll, just at the time, I was out sketching instead of sleeping. It's a miracle we even met."

"God specializes in the impossible, child," Grandma Martha said.

"Yes, He does."

"He seems a little older than you. I had a concern about that. It's hard for men who have lived by themselves for so long to adapt to living with someone else. As you just told me he was married for fifteen years before his wife died of cancer."

"Ah, that explains it," Kathombi said nodding.

"They never had any children, but he is so good with Moses and Salome. He's teaching Moses to play guitar."

"Well, your mom and I have been praying, as you know, and we are sure that God would have made it so if he is the one."

"Yes, you're right. Oh, my goodness ... he finally found me. The man I will marry finally *found* me."

Two months later Eduardo found the job and made the other arrangements he had given as necessary points before he accepted to live in Nairobi and set the wedding date. A few close friends and family members were invited. All of the concerns and whispered prayers over the months had ushered them forward to the wedding day.

Standing in her simple wedding gown, Joy thought to herself that all was as it should be. She smiled up at her dad standing beside her. His hair was almost completely gray and very distinguished looking as he stood trim and fit. He will never get old, she thought as they waited for the bridal march music to signal their entrance from the foyer into the church auditorium. He turned to her and laughed.

"Remind me to tell Eduardo about the Anderson women's *sum-up stare*."

"Don't you dare start giving him inside information about my secret weapons, you hear me? He already outguns me. He is ... amazing."

Marshall laughed again. "You have been daughter, little sister, artist, teacher, poet, author, mother, foundation president. That's a lot to have done in your few thirty-seven years. Now, you will be a wife. Are you ready?"

"Yes. Finally, I can say, yes. Thank God!" she said as the music started.

"Then let's go, he's waiting for you. We've all been waiting for this and, thank God, we lived to share this joyous moment with you."

The ushers opened the doors, and Joy happily walked down the aisle beside her father, toward the smiling Eduardo standing near the altar, flanked by Ernesto, Joe, and Peter. Pastor Muku stood in the center and Hope, Faith, and Wambui stood on the other side. Joy wondered if it might have been her imagination that it seemed like everyone was smiling as she walked by all of the close friends and family members. Monica had flown in for the ceremony as well, and Moses and Salome had decided to sit by her so that she would not feel alone. They are good kids, she thought as she glanced over them. On the other side of the aisle on the first row was Grandma Martha in one of her rare appearances outside of the house, determinedly standing one space away from her mother, Kathombi. That space would be where her father would stand once he handed her off at the altar. Grandma Martha was smiling amid her tears of joy, kept in check with the ever-present handkerchief. She showed no sign of the arthritis pain that had begun to limit her movement at one hundred five years of age.

The ceremony had been planned to be simple, elegant, and meaningful. Joy wrote a poem to be read as they lit the unity candle.

Loving family all around
Orphans' laughter did abound
Colors bright and new designs
Books with sketches and new rhymes
But no music could be heard
No tune for the poet's word
My heart's strings did quiet lay
Waiting for your fingers' play
Now there's music all the while
Clearly heard each time you smile
God brought us music through you
His glory's songs did renew
His promise faithful ever
His words fall amiss never
All Things working for our good
No longer as two we stood

As one in Him united
A single flame is lighted
And one plus one equals one
Yes, one plus one equals one

Everything went as planned. Joy sighed knowing there was one last item on the program.

Pastor Muku closed his little book and smiled at the two of them. "I now pronounce you man and wife."

Everyone clapped, but Pastor Muku held up his hand for quiet "Before the groom bestows a kiss on her, he has a surprise for the bride."

A surprise indeed! Joy thought. This was not in the script! Joy turned to him a little confused. "Eduardo?"

"Yes. You remember, I made you a promise once, and I will keep it today. I told you I would find a song that expressed how I felt and sing it for you but I never found a song that was a perfect environment. I looked everywhere without success."

Joy slowly shook her head. She had a puzzled look. *What was he up to?*

He continued a little nervously. "So, I decided to write a new one for you."

The crowd began to murmur excitedly as Moses recovered the guitar from under the pew and brought it forward to Eduardo. Despite his formal suit coat, Eduardo managed to quickly position the guitar strap and began to strum softly. He turned to face Joy and sang.

Standing here in front of you, I'm amazed again at what our God can do;
How he brought us both through time and space to this same and very place.
I love you. I love you and I hunger so for your love in return.

How could our two paths have crossed? We were born in worlds
so very far apart.
Such a lovely miracle, I've found the partner of my heart.
I love you. I love you and I pray God makes our love grow ever true.

*Come join hands with me my love, and let us see what our
good Lord will bring
Trusting side by side we'll stand, songs of loving bliss we'll sing
I love you. I love you and I pray God makes our love grow ever true.
I love you. I love you and I pray God makes our love grow ever true.*

By the time he had finished the song, the lump in her throat had swelled to the point it was impossible for her to speak. She looked at this man that God had brought into her life and was so grateful. He handed the guitar back to Moses and smiled at her.

"Well," he turned to the people sitting in the church, "she didn't run away. That's a good sign." They all laughed. "But she didn't say she liked it either. In fact, she didn't say anything, yet."

He turned back to her and reached out his hands. "Did you like the song I wrote?"

"I love your song. I love you," she whispered as she reached out to take his hand.

"You may now kiss the bride," Pastor Muku declared.

∞

"You want to name him, Isaac?"

"Yes. His name should be Isaac because I have been waiting so long for him to be born."

"Are you sure it's not because I am so old when I'm pregnant?"

"I know you are joking, Joy! You are not old."

"You should tell that to the doctor who wants me to come in for ultrasounds every time I turn around. She said it's because I am over thirty-five and have an increased risk of complications, whatever that means. I guess I should be thankful because otherwise we would not have known the baby was a boy, and a healthy baby boy at that."

"The baby is Isaac Pedro Delgado Anderson."

"He won't know where he's from, poor thing."

"Why do you say that?"

"He will have names from three different continents."

"Yes." Eduardo laughed. "He will be a man of destiny who will speak of what big things God can grow from small unexpected beginnings."

"I love you, Eduardo Delgado. Okay, Isaac, it is. He's supposed to be born almost a year to the day we were married, you know?"

"I will be jealous if he is born on the same day because you will always think of him instead of me."

"I'll always think of you no matter what. He would never have been born without you."

"*Tá bem.* Even when they are not poems, your words are beautiful. October will be a wonderful month for the rest of my life."

"Amen."

Chapter

23

"M<small>OM, PLEASE SAY</small> I can go. This is really important," Salome said hurriedly getting into the car and proffering some paper to Joy.

"What is it, Salome?" Joy accepted the papers but placed them on the seat beside her as she scanned the entrance for Moses.

"It's a program that my teacher's doing for the summer. This big group of scientists is coming from America for a science camp. There are only twenty-five places, so I have to fill out the application and get it in fast. It doesn't cost anything, Mom. You just have to make sure I get there on time in the morning for the four weeks. Mom, I will walk all the way home if you can't come and get me. I just want to go."

"Let me read this and ask Grandma Kathombi about it. Why is it so important, honey?"

"I want to be a scientist and all different kinds of scientists are going to be there. I can ask them all kinds of questions and see what the differences are and what kind of things they do. It's like doing eight research projects all at once."

"I see. Let me call Grandma Kathombi when we get home, and we'll talk about it a little later. What is holding up your brother?"

"He's trying to get Sesa to come over this weekend. The twins are going to Mombasa?"

"Oh, that's right. Peter is the best man for one of his friends."

"Yeah, and Moses thinks he's going to be too lonely without them. He tried to get Aunt Natalie to invite him along. She said there wouldn't be room because the car seats for Christa and Trisha take up all the space on the back seat. You know what, Mom? He even told her he could ride in the luggage space, but she said that it was going to be full of the things the family would need and their clothes for the wedding."

"That is very sad."

"So now, he wants Sesa to come over. I don't want him to come over. He's very bad and gets in trouble at school. I hope he's grounded again by his dad so that he can't come."

"That is even more sad."

"Yeah, Moses is becoming a sad case. Where's Isaac?"

"He went out with your father for most of the morning and didn't get to take his nap until late. He was still asleep when I left. I didn't have the heart to wake him. Lucie is watching him. Moses finally trotted over to the car and got in without a word. He sulked for most of the ride home. Finally, he asked in desperation. "Mom, can I go over to Sesa's house tomorrow?"

"Who is Sesa?"

"He's a friend of mine from school."

"Would I know his parents from church or school activities?"

"No. They don't go to our church and he's kind of new at school."

"Where did he go to school before?"

"I don't know. I think they moved from another place."

"Well, I would like to know a little more about Sesa and his family before I let you spend the day at his house."

"Why? We're just going to hang out?"

"That's why. Some young men have gotten into serious trouble just hanging out. Why don't you call Bennie or Lawrence? They're your friends, and I know their parents' standards."

He gave no response and remained quiet the rest of the way home.

Moses and Salome went off to their rooms, and Joy went to the den to read through the papers Salome had given her about the science camp. A few minutes later, Moses appeared at the hallway door with his arms crossed.

"Mom, can you please change your mind about me going over to Sesa's house?"

"No, Moses. You may not go over to Sesa's house; I don't know him or his parents. Why don't you ask him to come to spend time here?"

"I did, but he said his dad won't let him."

"Why?"

"I don't know … he's on punishment or something."

"Maybe I can meet his parents first, and we can talk about the environment you will be in if you go over to their house, but at this moment the answer has to be no. Do you have the family telephone number?"

"Why are you always making me do what you want?! You never want me to have friends that I choose. You always want to have your way. You must hate me and I hate you!"

Joy tried to remain calm as she watched Moses stand a few feet away in a sea of anger. She took a deep breath and spoke in a low and what she hoped was a calm voice. "I am sorry to hear that, but it does not change the fact that I love you very much. I always have and always will. I don't understand why you are acting like this …"

"Maybe that's just the way I am!" he yelled and stormed away to his room.

Joy slumped back against the sofa cushion in exasperation. Who was this crazy kid who had inhabited the body of her dear son? No, all this talk about teenagers getting out of control was not going to have a chance to add a story in this house. She walked determinedly down the hall to Moses' room. She paused and then knocked on the door. There was no answer. She knocked again and there was still no answer. She opened the door.

"Mom this is my room. You can't come in without permission," he barked as she entered. He didn't take his eyes off of the ceiling as he laid on his back full length his bed, with his hands laced behind his head. He may have appeared to be at total ease, but she knew by the set of his bottom lip and the tightening of his jaw that he was not. The fact that he stared straight forward and did not look at her as she entered the room was added proof that he was uncomfortable.

"Little bit …"

"Would you please call me by my name? My name is Moses." His voice was hostile. It was not discontented or selfish as it had sometimes been in the past when he didn't get his way. This was a new side of Moses that she had never seen. No, she corrected herself. This was not Moses, but her son under the influence of something foreign. She quickly decided that she would not let herself be influenced by the same thing. She would focus on being the loving and principled mother of her son, Moses Anderson Delgado. She breathed a prayer, took a deep breath and calmly spoke again.

"Moses, I understand that this is your room. *I* am the one who gave it to you to use, to keep your things, and have a little privacy. You see, *I* could do that because this house belongs to Eduardo and me. This being *my* house, I own all of the rooms and can decide who may use any of them and when. I **did** knock, before I came in, showing my respect for your privacy. Unfortunately, you did not respond in an equally respectful way. So, as is *my* right, I came in to see if everything was in order in *my* house. I came to say two things. The first is that I have known you since the day you were born. I have cared for you and watched you grow. I have seen how you act and have spoken with you on many occasions about what you believe, what you hope to do, and what you like and dislike. I

know you, and I can assure you that you are ***not*** the way that you just acted. I don't know who is, but I know it is ***not*** you.

"The second thing is that I want you to know as well, God did not make me your ***mother*** to be your ***friend*** or to do what it is that ***you*** want to do. I am here to teach you about God and to make sure that you have the right direction as much as I possibly can. I have done many uncomfortable, difficult, and demanding things for ***your*** benefit over the years. All of this I have done gladly because I love you very much. The one thing I ***refuse*** to do is to blindly follow ***your*** lead as to what you should do so that ***you*** are pleased. I do ***not*** want to one day stand before God and have to explain to Him why ***I*** did something I ***knew*** was wrong because ***you*** wanted me to. I am ***not*** going to put myself in that situation. I love you very much, but I will ***not*** do something ***wrong*** just to make you happy.

"So, you can understand or not. You can want to obey or not, ***that's*** up to you. What is ***not*** up to you is this. As long as you are living in ***this*** house, you ***will*** obey the rules and treat people with the respect due them. Listen ***carefully***, my son. In the future, you will ***not*** leave my presence stomping off in obvious anger, and you ***will*** answer the door, respectfully when you hear someone knocking. All of these are things you know and did not demonstrate today but ***will*** in the future. ***Do*** you understand?"

"Yes, I understand," he replied begrudgingly, still staring at the ceiling.

"Thank you," she said and softly closed the door behind her. Walking back down the hall, she checked on the sleeping Isaac in the next room and smiled at Salome doing homework in her room across the hall before walking back through the living room to the den.

She sat down again on the sofa and gave a sigh of relief. She had stood her ground. Eduardo would be home later and would probably have something else to say, but for now, she wanted there to be nothing blocking or changing the relationship she had taken 14 years to build with Moses. The questions resurfaced which had plagued Joy often over the years. Why had Moses' mother been alone when she came walking into the refugee camp the day he was born? Was she running from an abusive husband? Was she the victim of merciless roaming bands of soldiers raping and pillaging the countryside? Did she have an inherited mental or physical disease that she could have passed on to Moses?

With a deep sigh she bowed her head and whispered a prayer. "Dear God. Why did you bring this child to me? It was for a specific reason that only you know. He's brought such joy to me and my family, especially my father and the twins. You have helped me every step of the way. Now, what am I supposed to do when after all of the hard things you have guided me to help him through, he suddenly accuses me of not loving him? I have fought for his well-being and happiness... for his very life, since the day he was born.

How could he think that I don't love him or want the best for him? I feel as frantic as the first day I saw him left to slip into a quiet death, knowing there is something I had to do to save him. Today, unfortunately, there seems to be nothing I can do, no mental or spiritual milk I can buy to help his true self stay alive. Only you have that formula. Please help me to see what more I should do, now, after fourteen years of doing my best? I am ... I don't know what to say ... maybe, at the end of myself."

"Mom?"

Joy jumped, startled at the sound of another voice in the empty room. The voice was definitely the voice of the gentle Moses she knew. She quickly wiped the tears from her cheeks and turned around to see him face to face. He was standing, hesitatingly, at the doorway. This was what he did when he was unsure of himself.

"Yes, Moses. Come sit down." She patted the sofa beside her.

In response, he slowly walked across the room to the sofa and sat on the edge of the seat cushion beside her.

He cleared his throat and took a deep breath before he spoke, "Mom, I'm sorry about what I said. I don't want to be the reason God would ask you questions. I see you trying so hard to do the right thing. I don't want to be the reason you messed up. ... And, Mom,

I know you love me. I don't know why I said that. I was just mad or something. I take it back, okay?"

"Come here." She reached out to hug him. "I love you very much and always will."

"I love you too and always will, too."

"I know you do, Moses, no matter what you say sometimes."

He smiled uncomfortably as he looked at his hands fidgeting in front of him.

"So, tell me what is so attractive about Sesa that you feel you *must* hang around him. He apparently is *not* a good influence on you if he causes you to act the way you just did."

"I don't know. He's not afraid to stand alone. And he is alone most of the time. He only has a brother that is much older than him and doesn't live at home anymore. He's always getting in trouble at home and in school. I feel maybe I can help him or something."

"I see. You know, sometimes, when you go out into the water to try to rescue someone, you find that they are so afraid of drowning, they don't think clearly. They can start thrashing around so desperately they can't see you're reaching out to help them. If you can't get their attention, they can injure you enough that instead of rescuing them, you drown yourself. You understand that you can't rescue everyone. If you aren't careful, someone may ruin your reputation, scare you, discourage you from trying or something worse in the process. You may have to just leave them and swim back to safety to get help. At least one of you will live and maybe bring help to save the other. Don't change the correct way you act or think because you're trying to help them. How can you prove you are able to help them if you're doing the same thing they are?"

"I know, but sometimes the things he does are cool and they work."

"Maybe they seem to work because he can manipulate people; but someone eventually sees through it and he's in trouble, right? Isn't he in trouble much of the time in both of the main places he spends time? Let him know what you stand for and what you will not do, and see if he will change to be healthier for himself. Now, does that sound like a reasonable plan?"

"Yes, Ma'am."

"Moses!" Isaac, fresh from his nap, trotted across the room to Moses and climbed up to sit on his lap. He looked intently at Moses' face, then at his mother. Turning back to Moses, he said, " Moses, don't be sad. I love you, Moses." He reached up and gave Moses a big hug around the neck and then laid his head on Moses' chest and sighed.

Moses looked at his mom and shook his head smiling as he hugged Isaac back. "Come on, Isaac, you want to play hide and seek?"

"Yeah!" Isaac happily jumped down and ran out of the room.

"He's so dumb, Mom. He always picks the same place to hide. It's like he forgets that's where I always find him. It's like I will forget this time and won't find him."

"Maybe he's not so dumb. It's just that your goals are different. You want a challenge, while he just wants your time and attention. He's happy when you find him. Someone, your own age would be disappointed."

"I guess so."

"Enjoy it while you can. He will grow up all too quickly, just like you did."

"You know what? It doesn't seem so quick when you're the one growing." Moses stood and stretched, before he called, "Isaac, here I come."

Chapter

Joy stood in the street in front of her house, anxiously searching for Eduardo. Neighbors were arranging a bucket brigade as she watch the flames shooting up from the roof. She saw Eduardo, in the process of rushing toward the front door.

"Eduardo!" Joy called, "thank God you're okay. She was relieved until she looked around him. "Where's Isaac?"

"I thought he was with you," Eduardo said looking around the yard. "I was in the work studio just across from the bedroom terrace when I heard the explosion. I ran and opened the studio door and saw smoke pouring out of the hole in the wall of the back of the house. Part of the door had been blown off. The smoke was so thick I could not get in the house, but I could see flames from near our bathroom. I ran around to the side garage door, and the garage had no smoke, so I ran to the hall door. There was much smoke in the hall, so I ran to the kitchen to make sure you were okay, but there was no one there. I used your cell phone lying on the counter to call the fire brigade. I kept calling your name and searched around but didn't see you or anybody in the den or living room. When I got no answer and I saw that the smoke was getting thick, I went back to the garage outside. I thought I would find you here. When I came around the side just now and didn't see you, I decided to head back in through the front door."

"When I heard the explosion, he was the first thing I thought about. I ran down the hall to his room, but he was nowhere to be seen. I called his name, but when there was no answer I just thought that he must have wandered past me to see you in the bedroom and that you had grabbed him on your way out. I didn't see you and called for you too, but the smoke was so strong my eyes were burning. I was coughing so much I couldn't see anything or even breathe, so I ran out expecting to see you here with Isaac."

The sound of distant sirens filled the air as neighbors began gathering on the sidewalk near the front yard. Desperately trying to screen out all of the distractions from the main focus for the moment, Eduardo and Joy held on to each other. They fixed their attention on each other's faces as if by doing so they could force themselves to think more clearly.

"Where could he be, Eduardo? He was not in his room. Moses and Salome aren't home yet. I didn't even check their rooms."

"The smoke is not so bad on that side I could go in and check their rooms to see."

"But he never goes in their rooms if they're not there."

"Maybe he went out in the backyard. I'll go check there." He turned to run around the back of the house when the sound of sirens pierced the air and two fire trucks pulled up briskly in front of the house, and the first fireman ran up with questions.

"Is everyone out of the house?"

"No, I think my three-year-old baby is in the house somewhere. Can you go and find him?"

"We each thought he was out here with the other one," Joy explained.

"We looked everywhere, but didn't see him," Eduardo said.

"I'll send someone in right now to look for him," the fireman said. "Can you show me the direction where you last saw him?"

"Sure," Eduardo said, "It's on this side of the house."

They watched as the second fireman received instructions from his commander, and with a mask on headed toward the front door. The small crowd of neighbors pressed in around the two of them.

Joy tearfully blurted out to Eduardo. "Isaac said that he was practicing for when Moses came home to play hide and seek. Moses should be here any minute. I got busy preparing dinner and thought Isaac was occupying himself."

"Don't worry we'll find him," Eduardo reassured her.

⁓∞⁓

"Mom!" Moses called

"Mommy?" Isaac called gleefully and wriggled in Moses' arms in an effort to get down and go to her.

"Wait, Isaac. Let me take you."

Joy stopped talking and quickly turned in the direction of the boys' calls. She stared at them in disbelief as they walked toward her. She and Eduardo stood up and rushed toward them .

Moses with Isaac in his arms, was engulfed in a giant hug formed from the combined arm spans of their parents. After a few minutes of quiet hugs, Joy got her voice back.

"Where were you? Where did you find Isaac? Wait a minute. I need to sit down." She looked around for a place to sit as Eduardo took Isaac. Joy draped her arm through Moses' and leaned on him as they headed back toward the chair provided by a neighbor. A fireman came up to Eduardo to ask for him to let Isaac be examined since he had been in the house during the fire. He signaled Joy that he was going with the firemen. She nodded.

Sitting in the corner of the front lawn, she sighed deeply. "So! Tell me what happened."

"I was walking up the street from school, when I realized that the fire engines were at our house. I ran up and heard you talking to Dad. When you said that you couldn't find Isaac and that he had said he was going to practice for Hide-and-Seek with me. I knew he had to be where he always hides. Remember? I told you, he never changes, no matter how many times I find him. I always thought it was so dumb, but today I was so glad to find him right there as usual. I was so scared he wasn't okay at first because he was lying there and not moving. I was just praying as hard as I could that he would be okay. You know, he is always following me around and bothering me, but when I thought that he ... that something bad might happen to him, I got so scared and sad at the same time. I just prayed. I crawled into the duct from the side of the house. Soon I could see Isaac lying at the end. He was just where I had expected him to be, but he was not moving. I called but he didn't answer. I called again and tried to squeeze toward him. I was scared thinking about what if Isaac was dead? That would be terrible. He is always so happy and tells me every day that he loves me. I started crying and I asked God, to please help baby Isaac to be okay. When I arrived right next to him, I was afraid to touch him. I asked God please, again then I saw Isaac was breathing. His chest moved. I started yelling at him to wake up! I was so happy when he opened his eyes. You know what he said, Mom?" Moses's lip trembled.

"What?"

"He said 'You found me again, Moses', such a dumb little kid." Moses shook his head. "I just had to convince him to play a game to crawl out so that he wouldn't be afraid."

"I see. Oh, thank God!" She hugged him again. "Well, I want to tell you how proud I am of you, but ...I would definitely like to know next time what you're up to, please."

"Okay."

"Thank you, Moses, for saving your brother."

"Aw, Mom, it wasn't hard or anything. You know, Mom. I think I know part of what God wants me to do. I just like saw or something, when I was crawling out behind Isaac."

"You did? What did you see?"

"It was that people who have children who die don't have any special place for them to be taken care of. I mean if a kid's parents die, they go to an orphanage where someone does the things that a parent would do. If you're an adult and your kid dies, where do you go to have someone do for you the things your kid would do? Who's going to run around bothering you, or coming to sit on your lap so that you can tickle them, or give you a big hug just because you're there? Even if the kid wasn't so little, who's going to sit and talk to you, or ask for advice and things? There needs to be someplace the parents can go, not to live there, but to feel that they can still do some of the same things to help a kid to grow up. They can, at least, know someone cares and needs them. I don't know what can be done for people like Grandma Martha when Grandpa Marshall's mom died, but there has to be something. I don't know. Isaac is not even my kid, but I would feel really bad if he died or something," Moses said.

"Wow. That is huge Moses. I think this is fantastic. You can talk to Grandma Martha and whoever else you can get ideas from. You know what? You could start by making a book with stories of parents who have lost their children and what kinds of positive things they did and what they wish others had done to help them survive. Eduardo and I would be glad to do some illustrations if you want, or Uncle Peter could take photos. Your poetry is getting pretty good you know? You could even put some very good ones in the book as well. I'll help you as much as I can. This does feel like a pretty big thing," Joy said.

"Yeah, I'll work on it, and like you always say, 'See what God will bring'."

"Yes, I forgot. I was talking to your Grandpa Marshall. He is on his way over right now to take us to spend the night at his house. We'll get a good night's sleep and talk about things again in the morning."

"Okay, but I have a project group meeting in the morning. Maybe we can talk in the afternoon. You guys will probably be pretty busy in the morning anyway," Moses sighed.

"You're probably right, but don't let that make you hesitate. You know I have always—"

"Moses! They let me be a fireman with the mask and everything." Isaac was excited and happy as Eduardo carried him back toward them.

"They said he looks very fine." Eduardo declared smiling.

Eduardo's smile faded. "Joy, What's wrong? You don't look so fine. Let them check you, and you too, Moses. Joy, why not call your dad and tell him that we will drive our car to his house. Tomorrow we will need our cars to run all of the errands, anyway. We shouldn't have to bother him. Right, Moses?"

"Yeah, I think he has meetings all day tomorrow. You know it's almost time to pick Salome up from the science thing. Boy, is she going to be mad? I hope her project is okay."

"I almost forgot about Salome. Eduardo, I'll ask Dad to head over to the school to get her. He's on that side of town and can take her directly to his house."

"Good idea. The fireman said this part of the house is safe to go into for a few minutes now that the fire is out and the smoke has cleared. We can get a few things from the house and then go there, too."

Joy nodded and dialed the cell phone as Eduardo escorted her to be checked. "Dad, the boys are fine. I'll have to tell you about our hero, Moses. Listen, we forgot about Salome at the science camp thing. Could you swing by and get her, then meet us at your house?"

"That is great news. I'll head over to get Salome. Are you driving your cars here?"

"Yeah, we'll need the cars in the morning," Joy explained. "Thanks, Dad."

Her guard came hesitantly around from the far side of the guardhouse.

"Oh, Humphrey, I forgot. Can you call one of the other guards to come and work with you tonight? We are not going to be able to lock the house completely because windows and doors are missing."

He nodded his head and took out his cell phone to make a call.

"I want to go see if my stuff is okay and to see if Salome's things are okay so that I can tell her," Moses said.

"Okay, see if there is something clean for you to wear tomorrow and bring it. Don't stay long. We'll wait here until you come back. I don't think it is good for all of us to be running around inside at the same time and no one making sure everyone is okay."

"I'll be right back." He ran into the house and shortly returned carrying a load.

"Moses, you need to get checked now. Joy, tell me what you want me to bring out for you. I do not want you to go inside there now. You look really tired." He handed the sleeping Isaac to her.

"I feel completely exhausted, but they said I'm fine," Joy assured him.

They agreed on the things that would be needed before tomorrow, if possible. Eduardo came back also in a very short time. "I found everything."

"Great! I think Salome can borrow some things from Hope just for the night. Let's go, I'm really tired."

Moses and Eduardo started loading the things in the car. Most of the things fit in Joy's car trunk and back seat.

"Take my car since Isaac's seat is in it. I will meet you at Dad's house," Eduardo said.

Dinner was eaten mostly in silence as exhaustion began to engulf them, and they shuffled off to their interim beds.

The next morning Moses and Salome left early with Grandpa Marshall. Walking into the Kitchen, Joy found a sheet of paper with Moses' handwriting, lying on her purse on the counter.

Pried Away
By Moses Anderson Delgado

It's not supposed to be this way; I should have gone before
I'm supposed to welcome you, when you reach heaven's door
Completely at a loss now; sailing with no rudder,
The rule is broken and I'm adrift without a tiller.
Unused and far before preparation was complete,
Death's hand came and removed you, your smile, even your seat,
Leaving me with pictures and memories bitter sweet
I'm the one who held your hand to safely cross the street,
Gave the key to joy and strength, and wisdom meant to guide
All the years I would be gone, no longer by your side
Educating, disciplining, to help make you strong
Arming you with all the things you'd need for your life long
My hands safely held and my secure arms carried you,
Strong enough to protect and guide your way ever true
I know that I'll see you there; my heart thrills at the thought
Standing right beside you, praising God for all He's wrought
Now I sit with dreams undone, because you did not stay
My grasp too weak to hold on, as death pried you away

"Eduardo, you have to read this poem that Moses wrote last night." As Eduardo entered the room, she handed the paper to him.

"He had time to write something new last night?" He took the paper and read. Sighing he looked up at Joy. "This is amazing. This kid is so very special. I only wish that he was going to be around longer for Isaac to know him better. I keep telling myself that your family provides such a nurturing environment for all of the children. It is as if they cannot go the wrong way. I had a wonderful family but always felt the lack of my mom. Like something, a part of me, was always missing," Eduardo said.

"That is so sad,"

I finally felt whole when a few years after I moved away, I married a wonderful woman, who was one of my university classmates."

"I see," Joy said with pursed lips.

"I'm not saying she was wonderful to make you jealous but to let you know that my standards are high."

"Let me know how are you going to climb your way out of this hole you've dug?"

"I shall escape by telling the truth."

"And what's that?"

"You not only surpassed any standard I have ever had but made me aware of some others I should have had in mind if I intended to find someone as marvelous as you."

"Well, you did get out of that hole rather well."

"Oh, yes?"

"You even gained a few feet of elevation in the process," Joy smiled.

"As long as I am telling the truth, I have to be honest about one other thing."

"What's that? You are not going to quit while you are ahead?"

"When my wife Anna never became pregnant, I was secretly relieved. I did not want to have to be watching for the same De Silva thing to happen in one of my children."

"Now that you married such an old woman and you have a son, you may still have to worry about it or something worse."

"No. Now you listen, Joy. When I asked you to marry me, I had already done some deep reflecting to let God help me get rid of all of those little secret worries weighing me down. I decided that God always knows what He is doing. I have to trust Him. We will have as many children as God decides to give us and it will not matter whether they are girls or boys. They are gifts from God and I will treat them and think about them just as that. I'm not running and living under the De Silva or any other curse. I choose joy not fear. That I found you is a *miracle*. I will expect only miraculous things as a result."

"Why Mr. Delgado, that is a very fine speech you just gave. In fact, it was perfect as far as timing, because I was going to tell you that I have been so tired lately, because—"

"Oh, yes? Is it true?" Eduardo questioned excitedly, without letting her say anything else.

Joy nodded her head as he hugged her.

"Another Isaac … No, I hope it's a little girl with sparkling eyes and endless energy and talent like you." Eduardo leaned back in his chair and laughed. "*Elcolhida alegria,* our "Chosen Joy".

"Mr. Delgado, you are gaining altitude by leaps and bounds," Joy said as she sat down.

"The 'leaps' I understand, but what is 'bounds'?" Eduardo asked.

"Well, if a 'leap' is a high jump, then a 'bound' is a big or long powerful jump."

"Yes! I want to "bound" all the rest of my life with you."

"We have got so much to do and so much from God to do it with, I'd say we'll be joyfully bounding away for a very long time."

"Let's go tell Grandma Martha."

"You told me she knows these things. She probably already knows."

He hugged her again and then started doing the happy dance. He pulled her gently up from the chair. "Come on, you have to join me dance. This is your family's tradition, yes?"

"Have you forgotten that we just had our housed burned yesterday?"

"But we are all fine and better than fine."

"Yea!" Isaac had come into the kitchen and started dancing joyfully.

"You see he doesn't even know about his sister and he is dancing happily. He's not worried about the house, because this is the perfect environment."

"Está Muito bem!"

www.ingramcontent.com/pod-product-compliance
Lightning Source LLC
LaVergne TN
LVHW041754060526
838201LV00046B/1003